Counting the People in 1980:

AN APPRAISAL OF CENSUS PLANS

Panel on Decennial Census Plans
Committee on National Statistics
Assembly of Behavioral and Social Sciences
National Research Council

NATIONAL ACADEMY OF SCIENCES
Washington, D.C. 1978

NOTICE

The project that is the subject of this report was approved by the Governing Board of the National Research Council, whose members are drawn from the Councils of the National Academy of Sciences, the National Academy of Engineering, and the Institute of Medicine. The members of the committee responsible for the report were chosen for their special competences and with regard for appropriate balance.

This report has been reviewed by a group other than the authors according to procedures approved by a Report Review Committee consisting of members of the National Academy of Sciences, the National Academy of Engineering, and the Institute of Medicine.

International Standard Book Number 0-309-02797-7

Library of Congress Catalog Card Number 78-70863

Available from

Office of Publications
National Academy of Sciences
2101 Constitution Avenue, N.W.
Washington, D.C. 20418

Printed in the United States of America

PANEL ON DECENNIAL CENSUS PLANS

NATHAN KEYFITZ (Chairman), Department of Sociology and Demography, Harvard University
PATRICIA C. BECKER, Department for Planning, City of Detroit
CHARLES F. CANNELL, Institute for Social Research, University of Michigan
WAYNE A. DANIELSON, School of Communication, University of Texas
WALTER E. DUFFETT, The Conference Board in Canada (retired)
LEOBARDO F. ESTRADA, School of Architecture and Urban Planning, University of California
LESTER R. FRANKEL, Audits & Surveys, Inc., New York
CHARLES B. KEELY, Center for Policy Studies of the Population Council, New York
HYLAN LEWIS, Department of Sociology, Graduate Center, City University of New York
DWAINE MARVICK, Department of Political Science, University of California
JAMES N. MORGAN, Institute for Social Research, University of Michigan
PRISCILLA C. REINING, Office of International Science, American Association for the Advancement of Science, Washington, D.C.
T. JAMES TRUSSELL, Office of Population Research, Princeton University
EDDIE N. WILLIAMS, Joint Center for Political Studies, Washington, D.C.

LENORE E. BIXBY, Staff Officer
HAROLD GOLDSTEIN, Staff Officer
JESSICA A. KAPLAN, Research Assistant

COMMITTEE ON NATIONAL STATISTICS

Conrad Taeuber (Chairman), Associate Director, Center for Population Research, Georgetown University
Morris H. DeGroot (Associate Chairman), Department of Statistics, Carnegie-Mellon University
David R. Brillinger, Department of Statistics, University of California, Berkeley
Stephen E. Fienberg, Department of Applied Statistics, University of Minnesota
Clifford G. Hildreth, Center for Economic Research, University of Minnesota
J. Stuart Hunter, School of Engineering and Applied Science, Princeton University
Nathan Keyfitz, Center for Population Studies, Harvard University
Howard Levene, Department of Mathematical Statistics, Columbia University
Nancy R. Mann, Department of Operations Research, George Washington University
Paul Meier, Department of Statistics, University of Chicago
Geoffrey H. Moore, Vice President for Research, National Bureau of Economic Research, Inc., New York
Ingram Olkin, Department of Statistics, Stanford University
Edward R. Tufte, Department of Political Science, Yale University

CONTENTS

PREFACE

The census count of the population has never been complete, and public concern about incompeteness is increasing. The census is relied on more heavily than ever for matters in which incompleteness is not easily tolerated--specifically, the distribution of revenue sharing and other federal funds. At the same time, improved statistical techniques permit the Census Bureau to estimate incompleteness with greater accuracy than in the past. Thus, concern about the census springs, ironically, on one hand, from the highly professional work of the Census Bureau and, on the other hand, from the extraordinary confidence in the Census Bureau that is implicit in the way Congress mandates the distribution of large amounts of federal funds.

The growth of grant programs with population-based formulas, including federal revenue sharing, and the principle of "one-man, one-vote" have put fresh emphasis on the accuracy of the counts for states and for the smallest political entities.

The Census Bureau has attempted to improve its procedures and to strengthen its relations with minority groups in an effort to reduce underenumeration. Despite these improvements, however, at present no way of sharply reducing or entirely eliminating the undercount is known. Concern about the undercount issue has led to a number of legislative proposals. Although the objectives of the proposed legislation address the relevant issues, serious defects in some specific proposals have been pointed out by diverse groups--the Census Bureau, professional statisticians, demographers and other social scientists, and organizations of federal data users representing a wide spectrum of interests.

This brief summary describes the background for the request of the Secretary of Commerce to the Committee on National Statistics of the National Research Council (NRC) to undertaken an independent evaluation of the technical and procedural designs for the 1980 census. In 1969, the National Academy of Sciences had established the Advisory Committee on Problems of Census Enumeration to conduct a study for the Census Bureau on ways to improve the completeness and accuracy of information collected in the decennial censuses and in intercensal household surveys conducted by the Bureau and other government agencies. The report of that committee, America's Uncounted People, was published in 1972. A review of its recommendations and how they have been implemented is included in this report.

In response to the Secretary's request, under the supervision of the Committee on National Statistics, a 14-member Panel on Decennial Census Plans was established in December 1977. The Panel was composed of individuals knowledgeable about statistics, communications, demography, sociology, economics, and anthropology and experienced in the conduct of large-scale surveys as well as in city planning. (Biographical sketches of all Panel members appear in Appendix E.)

The Panel was given four charges:

1. To examine decennial census improvement plans. In addition to considering proposed field procedures, to review strategies for increasing community participation, the anticipated impact of selected questions on response rates, and other matters related to public cooperation with the census.

2. To review proposed procedures for handling contested counts.

3. To investigate the feasibility of adjusting census counts, and subsequent population estimates, for underenumeration, and assess the implications of such procedures.

4. To consider plans to evaluate the 1980 census and recommend steps to improve planning for subsequent censuses.

In order that Panel recommendations might influence the 1980 census, the evaluation was to be completed in six months.

The Panel interpreted its terms of reference fairly strictly. Some tangential matters do have the same effect as the undercount--for instance, the accuracy of reporting of income in the census, which affects the distribution of federal funds among geographic areas. Our time was limited and we did not try to deal with these other matters.

The full Panel held three meetings--in January, February, and April, 1978. In addition, several groups of Panel members met separately to work on particular issues. All Panel members participated in the writing of the report, either by individually drafting a section or by preparing a draft in cooperation with others. The staff also wrote parts of the report and made a cohesive whole out of these disparate sections. Thus, this report represents the Panel's consensus, with creative input and active participation by all.

Contact was established with two congressional subcommitteees overseeing the census: the House Subcommittee on Census and Population and the Senate Subcommittee on Energy, Nuclear Proliferation, and Federal Services. Staff from these subcommittees provided the Panel with copies of recent congressional hearings that were useful in summarizing public opinion, the viewpoints of community groups, and the positions of state and local governments about different aspects of the undercount problem.

Two Panel members, who are also members of the Census Bureau's advisory committees for the 1980 census on the black and on the Spanish-origin populations, respectively, have been able to convey to the Panel the concerns of those groups. The chairman and chairman-elect of the Asian and Pacific Americans advisory committee met with the staff to present the views and concerns of that group.

In the time available, the Panel could not make a thorough study of all the difficult issues involved in the taking of a census. It is our hope, however, that this review by an outside group with expertise in a variety of fields related to the conduct of a census has been able to bring an independent viewpoint to the examination of selected issues. We have tried to focus on realistic options for dealing with the undercount. We hope the questions raised and recommendations suggested will be helpful to the Department of Commerce and the Census Bureau as they proceed with plans for the important task of conducting the 1980 census.

The Panel has studied the actions that the Census Bureau proposes to take, and, in the report that follows, we commend some, criticize some, and add specific recommendations of our own. Some of these last might be incorporated in the remaining dress rehearsals, some in the 1980 census, some not until the censuses of 1985 and 1990.

The Panel has been aided by the cooperation of the staff of the Census Bureau. Key personnel spoke to the entire Panel at the first meeting, detailing results of the pretest censuses and outlining plans for the upcoming census. Panel members and staff visited the Census Bureau and studied the extensive documentation that was made available to us.

The Panel recognizes and appreciates the time and effort given by Manuel D. Plotkin, director, and the staff of the Census Bureau to ensure that Panel members were kept fully informed. In particular, we wish to thank Sherry Courtland, assistant chief, program and policy development office, our liaison with the Census Bureau, and David L. Kaplan, assistant director for demographic censuses: they willingly answered our questions (or directed us to those who could) and freely shared their expertise.

The Panel's work and this report bear the marks of the Committee on National Statistics at many points. Committee members read and reread our drafts and offered much useful advice: Margaret E. Martin, executive director of the Committee when our work began, provided invaluable guidance to the Panel; Edwin D. Goldfield, present executive director, was generous with advice; and the Committee's entire support staff helped in many ways throughout the preparation of the report. This report also benefited from comments by several members of the Assembly of Behavioral and Social Sciences and several outside experts, who gave generously of their time to serve as reviewers, and from the editorial skill of Eugenia Grohman, executive associate/editor, Assembly of Behavioral and Social Sciences.

Finally, the Panel staff--Lenore E. Bixby, Harold Goldstein, and Jessica A. Kaplan--had the responsibility of coordinating project activities and the difficult task of synthesizing numerous sections into one report. If our finished report has merit, it is largely due to their technical competence and editorial skill.

Nathan Keyfitz, Chairman
Panel on Decennial Census Plans

1. THE PROBLEM OF THE UNDERCOUNT

Introduction

It is virtually impossible to count every single inhabitant of the United States--at any cost. Some undercount of the population occurs in all censuses, even in small countries with relatively homogeneous populations such as Sweden and Norway. The U.S. Bureau of the Census (referred to hereafter as Census Bureau) has conducted extensive research to evaluate enumeration completeness in the censuses of 1950, 1960, and 1970. A common finding of these studies is that there has been differential completeness by sex, age, and particularly race. Blacks as a group, and especially black males of working age, have been underenumerated far more often than have whites.

Because underenumeration differs by geographic area, by race, in some cases by ethnic origin, and perhaps systematically with the incidence of poverty and educational deficiencies, an undercount rate for the nation of 2.5 percent (as estimated by the Census Bureau for the 1970 census) has serious ramifications. Increasing concern about underenumeration reflects the growing awareness of the political, economic, and social consequences of the underenumeration.

Political representation is at issue, not only at the federal level, but also at state and local levels. The census count is used in determining seats for the U.S. House of Representatives as well as for various state and local legislative bodies.

The undercount also affects distribution of federal and state funds for social service programs. Funds for education, health, transportation, housing, community services, and manpower programs, as well as federal funds for the general revenue sharing program (enacted in 1972), are allocated by statutory grant-in-aid formulas in which population is an important element. Local officials, mainly from cities with heavy concentrations of people with characteristics thought to be associated with a higher probability of underenumeration, maintain that their share of federal and state funds is less than it should be. They claim that the intercensal estimates used in allocating funds start from decennial census counts that are incomplete. This point was emphasized before a subcommittee of the U.S House of Representatives in testimony on the Camden (New Jersey) pretest for the 1980 census: "...An undercount does [not] merely suggest that black Americans are being shortchanged, but the greater consequence is that all persons, black and white, poor and middle class, who live in cities like Camden ... are being shortchanged" (U.S. Congress 1977c, p. 171).

In addition to their interest in an equitable distribution of funds, local governments are concerned about the absolute numbers in the population count. They are concerned in part because, under present law, cities are eligible for certain programs only when their populations exceed a given number--such as 100,000 or 500,000--so that

Table 1. Preferred Estimates of the Amount and Percent of Net Underenumeration of the Population, by Sex and Race: 1950 to 1970

(Numbers in thousands. Composite of analytic estimates, corresponding to set D estimates (adjusted). Figures relate to the resident population. Base of percents is corresponding estimate of corrected population)

Sex and race	1970[1]		1960		1950[2]	
	Amount	Percent	Amount	Percent	Amount	Percent
All classes	5,301	2.5	5,063	2.7	5,132	3.3
Male	3,353	3.3	2,990	3.3	2,934	3.8
Female	1,947	1.8	2,073	2.2	2,198	2.8
White, total	3,446	1.9	3,249	2.0	3,400	2.5
Male	2,175	2.4	1,918	2.4	1,933	2.8
Female	1,271	1.4	1,330	1.6	1,466	2.1
Negro and other races, total	1,855	6.9	1,814	8.1	1,733	9.7
Male	1,179	8.9	1,071	9.7	1,001	11.2
Female	676	4.9	743	6.6	732	8.2
Negro, total	1,873	7.7	1,630	8.0	(NA)	(NA)
Male	1,180	9.9	977	9.7	(NA)	(NA)
Female	693	5.5	653	6.3	(NA)	(NA)

NA Not available.
[1]Based on census figures which have been adjusted for race misclassification in the complete count.
[2]Figures relate to 50 States and the District of Columbia.

NOTE: Set D estimates is the preferred set, a composite of the data, methods, and assumptions used in three other sets.

SOURCE: U.S. Bureau of the Census. *Estimates of Coverage of Population by Sex, Race, and Age: Demographic Analysis.* 1970 Census of Population and Housing, Evaluation and Research Program, PHC(E)-4. Washington, D.C.: U.S. Department of Commerce, 1974. Table 3.

a small numerical difference becomes a difference in kind when a city's population nears the threshold (U.S. Congress 1977b).

Officials also decry the inadequacy of data required to design the type of social planning and physical development an area can undertake (U.S. Congress 1977b). In this instance, errors in the reported social and economic characteristics are involved as well as missing individuals and their information. There may be, for example, substantial errors in mortality and morbidity rates for black males because the denominators used in calculating the rates are too small.

Another impetus to the increasing concern about the undercount is the growing self-consciousness and desire for recognition on the part of cultural, racial, and ethnic groups and their desire to share equitably in programs for social and economic improvement.

Finally, it is obvious that an adequate and accurate data base is needed to measure progress under various social programs and also to measure the effects of policies and programs to remedy past discrimination.

For all these reasons, the undercount is a critical issue and one that generates substantial political and social pressure on the Census Bureau. This chapter discusses underenumeration in detail, with sections on the size and distribution of the undercount, hypotheses about why individuals are missed, implications for political representation and funds allocation, specific concerns of minority groups, and recent congressional action.

Size and Distribution of the Undercount

Coverage of the total population in 1970 and net census errors, reflecting errors in reporting age, sex, and race as well as incompleteness of coverage, have been estimated at the Census Bureau by Jacob S. Siegel, using analytical techniques similar to those used by Ansley Coale, Melvin Zelnik, and N. W. Rives, Jr. (U.S. Bureau of the Census [hereafter cited as Census] 1974b). The general method is to develop an estimate of the population independent of the census, using birth and death records for previous years, immigration and emigration data, Medicare data, and previous censuses. The accuracy of the estimate depends on the consistency of the statistics used. (The method is further described in Chapter 5). While the data have deficiencies--notably the immigration and emigration data--the estimates are probably the best that can now be made. Siegel's composite of three alternative sets of estimates calculated with different data, procedures, and assumptions are referred to as preferred estimates. They show a modest improvement from 1950: while the undercount was estimated at 5.1 million in both 1950 and 1960 and 5.3 million in 1970, the rate dropped from 3.3 percent in 1950, to 2.7 percent in 1960, to 2.5 percent in 1970.

According to this set of estimates, almost two-thirds of those missed by the 1970 census were white. The rate of undercount, however, was four times as high for blacks as for whites, 7.7 and 1.9 percent, respectively (see Table 1). For each sex, the undercount rate was also about four times as high for blacks as for whites; it varied from 9.9 percent for black men to 1.4 percent for white women.

Although persons of races other than black and white do not appear from the data in Table 1 to have been undercounted, this inference is not valid since data and techniques of estimation do not permit reliable coverage estimates for Asian and Pacific Americans or for any specific race other than black or white. (The undercount estimates in

Table 2. Preferred Estimates of the Percent of Net Undercount of the Population, by Sex, Race, and Broad Age Groups: 1970 and 1960

(Composite of analytic methods, corresponding to set D estimates (adjusted in 1970). Base of percentages is the corrected population. Minus sign (-) indicates a net overcount. Estimates for 1970 are based on census figures which have been adjusted for race misclassification in the complete count, affecting some 327,000 persons, mostly of Spanish ancestry, and for a gross overstatement of centenarians amounting to about 103,000 persons)

Year and age	All classes	All races		White			Negro		
		Male	Female	Total	Male	Female	Total	Male	Female
1970									
All ages	2.5	3.3	1.8	1.9	[1]2.5	1.4	7.7	9.9	5.5
Under 5 years	3.5	3.6	3.3	2.1	2.3	2.0	10.1	10.1	9.8
5 to 9 years	3.0	3.2	2.9	2.3	2.4	2.2	7.3	7.7	6.9
10 to 14 years	1.3	1.4	1.2	1.0	1.1	0.9	3.2	3.5	2.8
15 to 19 years	1.2	1.5	0.8	0.9	1.3	0.5	3.7	4.3	3.2
20 to 24 years	2.3	3.3	1.4	1.8	2.5	1.1	8.5	12.1	5.2
25 to 34 years	4.3	5.7	2.8	3.4	4.3	2.4	12.5	18.5	6.7
35 to 44 years	3.1	5.3	0.9	2.0	3.6	0.5	10.7	17.7	4.0
45 to 54 years	2.1	3.6	0.6	1.4	2.7	0.1	8.7	12.4	5.3
55 to 64 years	2.6	2.9	2.4	1.1	2.2	1.9	8.0	9.2	7.0
65 years and over	1.8	0.9	2.4	1.8	1.2	2.2	1.2	-3.1	4.2
1960									
All ages	2.7	3.3	2.2	2.0	2.4	1.6	8.0	9.7	6.3
Under 5 years	2.2	2.6	1.8	1.5	1.9	1.1	5.8	6.6	5.1
5 to 9 years	2.3	2.8	1.9	1.9	2.4	1.5	4.7	5.1	4.2
10 to 14 years	2.4	2.9	1.8	2.0	2.5	1.5	4.4	5.0	3.9
15 to 19 years	4.2	5.0	3.5	3.2	3.8	2.4	10.9	12.3	9.6
20 to 24 years	4.7	6.1	3.4	3.4	4.3	2.4	13.9	18.4	9.5
25 to 34 years	3.6	5.5	1.7	2.3	3.6	1.0	12.5	18.5	6.5
35 to 44 years	1.7	3.3	0.3	1.0	2.2	-0.2	7.6	11.5	3.8
45 to 54 years	3.3	3.4	3.1	2.5	2.5	2.1	9.9	11.0	9.0
55 to 64 years	2.0	1.2	2.8	1.1	0.5	1.7	10.1	8.5	11.6
65 years and over	1.9	-	3.5	2.2	-	3.5	-1.0	-5.8	2.8

– Represents zero.

[1] Required figure, as given in tables 2 and 3 of original source, is 2.4 percent.

NOTE: Set D estimates is the preferred set, a composite of the data, methods, and assumptions used in three other sets.

SOURCE: U.S. Bureau of the Census. *Estimates of Coverage of Population by Sex, Race, and Age: Demographic Analysis.* 1970 Census of Population and Housing, Evaluation and Research Program, PHC(E)-4. Washington, D.C.: U.S. Department of Commerce, 1974. Table 6.

Table 1 for "Negros and other races" were, in several instances, built up from data for native blacks.) An attempt to apply demographic techniques to estimate the enumeration completeness of American Indians and Alaskan natives in 24 reservation states in 1970 indicated the likelihood of an undercount of these groups (Johnson 1973). Representatives of Asian and Pacific Americans believe that their population was undercounted in 1970 because of the relatively large number who had immigrated shortly before 1970 from non-English-speaking backgrounds and non-Western cultures--people who may not have understood census forms and procedures. These representatives also call attention to recent high rates of immigration of Filipinos and to the influx of Indochina refugees since 1975 (U.S. Congress 1977c).

By age, undercounts varied widely, from less than 1 percent for white females aged 10-19 and 35-54 to 12 percent for black males aged 20-24 and 45-54 and 18 percent for black males aged 25-44 (see Table 2). Black girls and boys aged under 5 were missed at a 10-percent rate; black girls and boys aged 5-9 were missed at a 7-percent and an 8-percent rate, respectively. The undercount rate peaked for all men at ages 25-44, but at about 4 percent for white men and 18 percent for black men. For black women, the undercount rate ranged from 4 to 7 percent for each age group beginning at 20-24 years (Table 2). The negative undercount rates (i.e., overcounts) shown in Table 2 for some groups (especially in 1960) may reflect misreporting of age in the census, but they also serve as a useful reminder of the possibility that some overcounting can occur: for example, if an individual is enumerated both at a family residence and at some other place and if the duplication is not caught by checking procedures.

The estimates of net census undercount differ in reliability because of differences in the quality of the basic data available for evaluation and in the adequacy of the assumptions and methods used to prepare them. The result is that estimates of net census error are more reliable for the white than the black population and for those under 35 years of age in 1970 (under 25 in 1960) than for those 35 and older. Even with these qualifications, however, it is evident that men and women aged 20-50, together with children under age 10, made up close to three-fourths of those not enumerated. This finding, along with the evidence that nearly three-fourths of the blacks missed in the 1970 census were in enumerated housing units, should be useful in assessing proposals to reduce underenumeration in 1980 (Census 1975).

With respect to ethnic groups in the population, no solidly based estimates of the undercount in the 1970 census can be made; there are no series of birth and death records nor of population counts in previous censuses based on reasonably consistent definitions of ethnic groups. It seems likely that the Spanish-origin population is disproportionately undercounted, on the basis of partial evidence, including: population surveys in individual cities; the large number of undocumented aliens in the United States (many of them of Spanish origin) who are reluctant to be identified in an official count; and the fact that many Spanish-origin people have the same low economic status as many blacks and live in the same kinds of poor and "difficult-to-enumerate" neighborhoods (U.S. Congress 1977a, U.S. Commission on Civil Rights 1974). Such factors may have resulted in relatively large undercounts of some other ethnic groups as well.

Little is known about the exact geographic distribution of the undercount except that the rate is highest in the South (Census 1975). The various methods tried by the Census Bureau to estimate the undercounts by states yield widely differing results (Census 1977a).

If state estimates of net underenumeration are based on the "basic synthetic method" (with the estimated national undercount rate by age, sex, and race applied to the counted population in that group in each state), all but 3 of the 16 states in the South had undercounts above average. On the other hand, all the New England states, 6 of the 7 states in the Census Bureau's West North Central division, and all 13 of the states in the Mountain and Pacific divisions had undercounts lower than the national average of 2.5 percent. Excluding Hawaii (with 1.3 percent) and the District of Columbia (with 6.4 percent), the range was from 1.9 percent for 10 states up to 3.7 and 3.8 percent for South Carolina and Mississippi, respectively (Appendix A, Table 1).

As a second example, if state estimates are based on a set of composite estimates in which demographic estimates are adjusted by selected results of a Census Bureau current population survey match study, there were larger-than-average undercounts in 1970 in most of the states in the South Atlantic and East South Central divisions, (although the highest rates were 7.8 percent for New Mexico and 6.9 percent for Alaska); lower-than-average undercount rates were most common for states in the East and West North Central divisions (Appendix A, Table 3).

On the question of whether the undercount is higher in larger cities, Siegel says (Census 1975, p. 9):

> In sum, the available studies do not permit us to make a categorical statement that the people who were missed in the census were disproportionately concentrated in large cities, as is often assumed. Although the most serious problems of conducting the enumeration in the 1970 census seem to have occurred in the iner city and the field operations were most protracted there, these are also the areas where the most intensive and sustained efforts were applied and where experienced census staff members were often employed in supervisory capacities. Moreover, the use of the address register, a verified list of addresses, in the built-up areas of the country, served to bring about nearly complete enumeration of housing units in metropolitan areas. In view of the higher undercoverage rate of the black population, however, it is reasonable to surmise that cities having heavy concentrations of blacks have higher undercoverage rates than areas with much smaller concentrations of blacks.

The difference in the racial composition of persons missed and persons enumerated in the census suggests that the overall income and educational level was probably lower for persons missed than for persons enumerated. Several studies based on matching census data with independent surveys confirm this income and educational difference.

Major Factors Contributing to the Undercount

Plans for improvement in coverage can best be evaluated in the light of the reasons underenumeration occurs. Although it is possible to list a variety of hypotheses, the Panel is disturbed by the fact that little quantitative information is available on which causes of undercounting are most important.

Post-enumeration surveys provide valuable information on the economic and social characteristics of the population, but the same kinds of people tend to be missed in post-enumeration surveys as were missed in the census. The post-enumeration surveys of the 1950 and 1960 censuses showed that about half of the missed persons lived in households that were missed entirely and half of them either lived in households that were enumerated incompletely or did not live in households at all. According to the 1960 survey, an estimated 70 percent of the whites missed in the enumeration and 30 percent of the non-whites missed were in missed households. Steps taken to improve the coverage of the 1970 census were most effective in improving the coverage of households (especially the vacancy check), and the Census Bureau believes that more than half of those missed in 1970 were persons living in households that were enumerated incompletely or persons not living in households at all.

Some additional clues on possible causes of underenumeration may be gleaned from the race, sex, and age composition of the undercount. As noted above, undercount rates were highest for black males aged 25-44 (18 percent), but were above average for black men in the entire span from 20 to 65 years of age. The undercount was also serious for black girls and boys under 5 years of age (10 percent) and 5-9 years of age (7 percent). Although coverage was much better for white men than black men, almost one-quarter of the total undercount was among white men aged 20-49; they accounted for about one-sixth of the population, as corrected. Among the hypotheses on causes of undercount, those that apply particularly to men of working age and to young children appear to be likely to have the greatest quantitative weight.

Reasons for Missed Households

There are many situations in which inhabited dwelling units may be difficult to find for enumeration, either from directories or from Postal Service checks or by canvass or precanvass. In rural areas, there are obvious opportunities to miss dwelling units. In urban areas, hard-to-find dwelling units include those in alleys, basement and attic apartments or rooms in what appear to be single-family dwellings, or dwelling units in multi-family structures that have been subdivided. One problem in reaching these units is the absence of mailboxes, which may have been destroyed or were never installed, so that the Postal Service does not know of the existence of the separate units. If the residents of such units get mail, it may be "in care of" someone who has a mailbox or through general delivery or in a post-office box.

Residents of unusual dwelling places, such as campers, trailers, boats, tents, or wigwams or hogans on Indian reservations are hard to find, especially if their dwellings are mobile.

Lofts, apartments, or rooms in industrial or commercial buildings may not be recognized by the Postal Service as residential units; even if mail is received there, they may appear to be business addresses. This may be particularly true of business places where people live, such as stores or small workshops.

One of the largest recognized problems is that of residences that appear to be vacant but in which people are living. Some of these are abandoned or condemned properties, whose residents do not wish to make their presence known. In others, the residents may be away from home frequently or for long periods of time, so that enumerators find no visible sign of occupancy after several visits and close them out as "vacant."

Reasons for Missed People

One class of people difficult to find are those without a fixed residence at all--those who sleep in railway or bus stations, all-night movie houses, on top of warm-air gratings, under bridges, etc. Some workers sleep regularly on the floor, under a counter, or in other catch-as-catch-can spots at their places of work (restaurants, shops, etc.), which are not recognizable as dwelling places.

A second group of missed people, probably accounting for a significant part of the underenumeration, are those living in households with family units or other persons who are omitted inadvertently from the listing of persons living at the address. These might include boarders, roomers, distant relatives, domestic employees, or hired hands.

Persons temporarily staying in enumerated households may not be listed because they have a usual home elsewhere, but may not be enumerated at the usual home address either. Other temporary residents may have no regular home elsewhere, as, for example, a child who stays with an aunt for a while and then with a grandmother, or an older person who lives a portion of each year with one of several adult children; in these cases, no one may list the temporary resident.

Most difficult to find are those deliberately omitted by the respondent for a household for a variety of reasons, such as: undocumented aliens; fugitives from justice; men behind in child support or alimony payments; debtors, garnishees, criminals; persons engaged in illicit activities; men whose presence in a household may affect eligibility for welfare; persons in excess of the number allowed in an apartment in public housing; persons with an ambiguous or unconventional relationship to other members of the household (boy friends, girl friends, etc.); illegitimate children; and many others.

A general reason for incomplete enumeration of all members of a household may be the problem of language: if the respondent does not understand English well and if the enumerator does not speak the respondent's language, the respondent may not understand the instructions about whom to include.

The Census Bureau is, of course, aware of these difficult-to-enumerate situations and has tried to build into the conduct of the census special procedures for dealing with them. Some cannot be handled by any procedures, as in the case of individuals who deliberately hide. But for others, the problem is often that the procedures are vulnerable to human error and to lack of skill, thoroughness, or persistence on the part of the enumerators or other census staff. For example, the Census Bureau estimates that 62,000 additional housing units would have been found in 1970 but for errors by its staff: the questionnaire asked how many housing units were in the building where the respondent lived, to check the completeness of the Bureau's records of housing units, but Bureau staff failed to note or follow up on discrepancies in many cases; this resulted in the omission of the 62,000 units (Census 1974a).

Implications for Political Representation and Allocation of Federal Funds

Political Representation

Underenumeration may affect the apportionment of representatives to the U.S. House of Representatives. Under the "equal proportions" method, a small shift in a state's population--even a shift of one--could in theory result in a change in the state's representation. Within a state, differential undercoverage could have an effect on the delineation of congressional districts, state legislative districts, or city council districts. The possibility of undercoverage having an effect on district boundaries depends on the average size of the districts, the coverage rates by race, the proportional distribution of the population by race, and the number of contiguous districts with high undercoverage rates.

Siegel speculates that there may be other political effects of underenumeration, e.g., the attention paid by elected officials to various groups of voters tends to be related to their perceived size. Another issue is whether voting districts are drawn in a manner that minimizes or maximizes the voting influence of various groups (Census 1975).

Allocation of Funds

The concern expressed by many city officials--particularly those from cities with large minority populations--stems from the use of population figures not adjusted for underenumeration in federal formula grants-in-aid. In fiscal 1975, funds obligated for the 75 formula-grant programs that used data on population or per capita income totaled $33.7 billion and accounted for about 22 percent of state and local expenditures (Ellett 1976, U.S. Congress 1975). The total has been growing (U.S. Office of Management and Budget 1977).

General revenue sharing, administered by the Department of the Treasury, is the largest of the 75 formula-grant programs and provides the largest single source of local government population-based grant income; it totaled $6.2 billion in 1975. Another 8 revenue sharing bloc grants accounted for $5.7 billion, and 6 matching grants accounted for $13.3 billion. The remaining 60 programs, for which $8.5 billion was obligated, were categorical grants (i.e., grants for narrowly defined purposes) as opposed to the broadly defined purposes such as health, manpower, or fiscal assistance, of the bloc and revenue sharing grants.

Although the Treasury Department's general revenue sharing is the largest single program, the Department of Health, Education, and Welfare administers the most population-based grant money: $15.6 billion or 46 percent of the total. Most of the remaining funds are administered by the Departments of Labor, Housing and Urban Development, Transportation, and Agriculture.

By definition, the distribution of money under these programs would change if there were a change in the population count. The change would tend to be smaller when a program's funds are fixed than when a program has open-ended funding.

The effect of the undercount on each state's share of a fixed total of funds distributed according to population is shown in the table below. While we have no accurate count of population by state with which to compare the official count as of 1970, it may be approximated purely for purposes of illustration by using various methods with which the Census Bureau has experimented. One is the basic synthetic method, by which the estimated national undercount ratio for each age-sex-race group is applied to the counted population in that group for the state (Census 1975). The second is a composite estimate in which several methods are combined for estimating population by state, including a demographic method using birth, death, and migration patterns for each state and the results of matching the 1970 census data with an independent source, the current population survey (Census 1977a).

The following table shows the percentage change in each state's share of $1 billion (distributed according to population) that would result from adjustment of the published 1970 census results by the two different estimates of the "true" distribution of population (derived from Tables 2 and 4 of Appendix A).

Change in Share of Funds	Number of States as Affected by	
	Synthetic Method	Composite-2 Method
Increase of 2 percent or more	1*	9*
Increase of 1 to 1.9 percent	3	7
Increase of 0.5 to 0.9 percent	5	5
Increase or decrease of less than 0.5 percent	20	6
Decrease of 0.5 to 0.9 percent	21	9
Decrease of 1 to 1.9 percent	1	11
Decrease of 2 percent or more	-	4

*Includes the District of Columbia

By the synthetic method, 20 states would gain or lose less than .5 of 1 percent, and 46 states would gain or lose less than 1 percent. The District of Columbia would gain 4.1 percent, or $152,000 of $1 billion, while Hawaii at the other extreme would lose 1.3 percent, or $48,000 of every $1 billion. As is implied by the figure for the District of Columbia, large cities with a high proportion of black population would gain somewhat more than would most states, which generally have smaller proportions of blacks. The largest increase in dollars would go to Georgia, $207,000 per $1 billion or 0.9 percent. California would lose the largest amount, $237,000 per $1 billion but only 0.2 percent (Appendix A, Table 2). The amount of money gained and lost is obviously related not only to the size of the estimated net undercount but also to the size of the population.

By the composite-2 method, the adjustments would be larger and some would be in a different direction. In only 20 states would the change be less than 1 percent. New Mexico would gain 5.7 percent; Alaska, 4.6; West Virginia, 4.5; and South Carolina, Florida, Georgia, Arkansas, Hawaii, and the District of Columbia would also gain 2 percent or more. Largest losers would be Wisconsin, Utah, and Minnesota, 3 percent each, and Connecticut, 2 percent. If $1 billion were distributed by population adjusted by the composite-2 method, three states would gain more than $500,000 (Florida, $915,000; Texas, $760,000; and Georgia, $646,000), and three would lose more than $500,000 (Wisconsin, $658,000; Minnesota, $555,000; and Ohio, $537,000). California, which would lose $237,000 if population were adjusted by the synthetic method, would gain $295,000 by the composite-2 method (Appendix A, Table 4).

The information by state for the two methods of estimation is drawn together in Figure 1, which illustrates the diversity in results from different procedures. The diagram also highlights why some state and local officials express dissatisfaction with the original census count, while others would prefer the original count.

In the general revenue sharing program, per capita income is also an important component of the allocation formula. Siegel indicates that adjusting this component has a greater effect on the allocation of funds than adjusting the distribution of population (Census 1975, pp. 19-22). Underreporting of income is known to be at a higher overall rate than the overall estimate of the population undercount, 2.5 percent (U.S. Social Security Administration, Budd et al. 1973, Yuskavage et al. 1978, Census 1977b), and there is evidence that the people missed in the census have a lower average income than the general population. Therefore, population undercounts cause errors in the estimates of per capita income. However, the bulk of the error in the per capita income estimates is believed to arise not from population undercoverage but from the underreporting of income by people enumerated in the census.

The population count is also important for allocation formulas used in health, educational, and social service programs, in which the absolute number and proportion of target populations are directly related to funding. Under the Comprehensive Employment and Training Act, for example, funding is distributed according to each locality's share of national unemployment, the estimates of which are affected by the differential geographic undercount, as well as by local unemployment rates, which are probably minimally affected (Johnston and Wetzel 1969).

These factors point to the importance of enumeration and the proper classification of the people counted for optimum program planning. Information on the characteristics of the uncounted is essential to estimate accurately the effects of the undercount on the measured characteristics of the population. While the accuracy with which the census collects information on characteristics is not the major concern of this Panel, its members wish to note the importance of the measures the Census Bureau will take to ensure as accurate responses as feasible to the questions on income, employment, and other characteristics.

Concerns of Local Governments

Reaction of local governments to the undercount has included challenges to the count and to the procedures for taking the census. In the *Procedural History: 1970 Census of Population and Housing*, the Census Bureau (1976, p. 1-14) reports:

> By November 1970, the Bureau had received almost 1,900 complaints from various communities that not all residents had been counted. Many of the undercount complaints were satisfied by an explanation of census procedures or an arithmetic check of the figures. In about 500 communities, a verification of corporate boundaries was required to make certain that the Census Bureau and the community were in agreement on the exact areas covered by the enumeration results. In some cases, a "Were You Counted?" campaign was

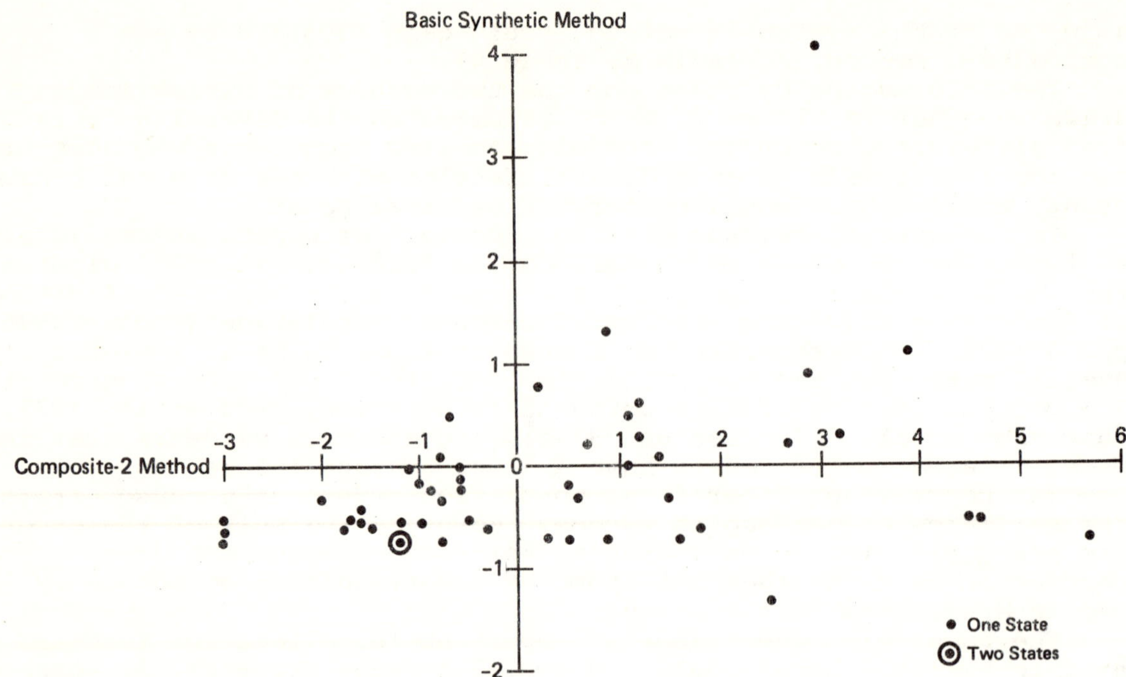

FIGURE 1 Percent changes in population-based fund allocations to states when 1970 census counts are corrected for net underenumeration by basic synthetic method and by composite-2 method (See Appendix A, Tables 2 and 4).

instituted to obtain lists of persons who beieved they had been missed in the census, so that the lists could be compared with census records. When there was an indication of a poor enumeration, the regional offices conducted field checks. This was done in 187 places. As a result of all these activities, the counts for about 600 communities were revised prior to the publication of final figures. On the average, additions to the census constituted five persons for every 10,000 originally enumerated in these communities.

Before the start of the 1970 census enumeration, in early 1970, according to the same report (p. 1-13):

> ...two class-action suits were filed in San Francisco, and one each in New York City and Washington. All sought preliminary injunctions against taking the census under the mail-out/mail-back procedures planned for 1970. The suits alleged that minority groups, notably those with English-language barriers, would be handicapped in answering the questions, that the mail procedures were inadequate for finding and enumerating all persons in these communities and that the communities would be adversely affected as a result of undercounts. Three of the suits asked that the court require door-to-door canvassing, and one requested that the sample questionnaire be used on a 100-percent basis for all members of minority groups. The plaintiffs' motions for injunctions were denied in all of these cases.

No adjustments in the population data for states and local areas have been made to compensate for the differential effect of the 1970 undercount. The Census Bureau has taken the position that it has not yet been able to develop an accurate and acceptable method to make population adjustments for the purpose of assuring more equitable revenue sharing allocations. In a case brought against the Office of Revenue Sharing, Department of the Treasury, by the cities of Newark (New Jersey) and Baltimore, the court recently upheld the Office of Revenue Sharing, whose defense had been that there is no recognized procedure for distributing the undercount below the state level (City of Newark vs. W. Michael Blumenthal 1978).

Major Concerns of Minority Groups

Because the 1970 census enumeration undercounted blacks and probably other minorities more heavily than it undercounted whites, minorities and the communities in which they live believe that they are disadvantaged in federal and other programs where population is an important factor in fund distribution. Concerns voiced on this and related issues led the Census Bureau to establish, in the mid-1970s, advisory committees on the black population, on the Spanish-origin population, and on the Asian and Pacific Americans population to give advice on how the 1980 census could be improved in coverage and usefulness to meet the concerns of these groups. Each advisory committee meets at least twice a year, and individual members meet periodically with Census Bureau officials. Several joint meetings have also been held.

In pursuing their mandate to help the Census Bureau avoid or reduce the undercount in their respective communities in 1980, these four advisory committees have focused their attention on four broad issues: content of the census questionnaire; employment of minority people by the Census Bureau; attaining the cooperation of minority people; and adjustments for any undercount that occurs. These issues are summarized here to throw additional light on the problem of the undercount and on how different perceptions of the reasons for the undercount may lead to a variety of suggestions for remedial action; Census Bureau responses to the recommendations made by the advisory committees are briefly noted.

Questionnaire Content

Most of the concerns expressed by the advisory committees on this issue have dealt with the manner in which their respective communities will be identified in the census questionnaire. They consider it crucial to list specific racial and ethnic groups in such a way that people who are part of such groups can be correctly identified in the count. Many of the committees' recommendations had already been anticipated and implemented by the Census Bureau. Others were resolved to the mutual satisfaction of the committees and the Census Bureau. Some were rejected and the reasons given.

The advisory committees emphasized a desire for more detail on race-ethnicity (e.g., identification of African and Caribbean blacks separately) and identification of people of mixed origins, such as part-Hawaiians. Filipinos, for example, say their numbers have been growing rapidly but that they have been partially "lost in the category shuffle between Spanish surnames, Asians and others" (U.S. Congress 1977b). In addition, all three committees recommended asking place of birth of parents.

The Spanish-origin and black advisory committees also noted their preference for self-identification on race and ethnicity rather than enumerator observation. The Census Bureau pointed out that this issue arises only where the form is not mailed back; and although enumerators will be instructed to ask, some will probably make entries on race by observation.

Other aspects of questionnaire content on which there were recommendations from the advisory committees included certain housing questions, the need for questions to obtain hourly wage data, identification of migrant workers, and occupation five years earlier.

Employment

A major concern of the members of all three advisory committees has been the small number of minority employees in senior and policy-making positions at the Census Bureau headquarters. Underlying this concern is their belief that an effective census depends on the quality, sensitivity, and representativeness of the personnel engaged in preparing and conducting the census. In the opinion of the committees, the absence of minorities in senior positions confronts the Bureau with two problems that cannot be overcome solely by the appointment of advisory committees. One problem is that the Census Bureau's plans, policies, and programs often lack a minority input and perspective on a day-to-day basis. The second problem is that the Census Bureau has a low profile, at best, and often a negative image in minority communities because few minority people are perceived to be associated with the Bureau in Washington or in the field and that this negative image may affect the completeness of the census enumeration in minority communities.

Since the appointment of the minority advisory committees, several senior-level minority employees have been appointed to key positions, and one of the Bureau's 12 regional offices is now headed by a minority employee, but none serves on the policy-making executive staff. The advisory committees recognize that the Census Bureau's ability to change this situation is affected by its present staffing patterns and by Civil Service Commission regulations. They note that while minority employment in senior positions has not changed appreciably, the Census Bureau has made extensive plans to recruit and employ minority community relations specialists and enumerators, including some with foreign language competence. The Census Bureau pointed out that it had obtained an exemption from using civil service registers when hiring community service representatives (although applicants must still meet the qualifications), but permanent, full-time employees cannot be exempt. A permanent appointment or promotion depends on the existence of a vacancy.

Cooperation

Minority groups feel that the Census Bureau is not taking full advantage of the advice of its advisory committees on opportunities for reaching minority communities. (The views were expressed at congressional hearings, see below.) A recent situation was pointed out as illustrative: advertising material prepared for the Richmond dress rehearsal was perceived by the black advisory committee as demeaning. Some saw the material as having a racist overtone or, at best, a lack of sensitivity and as likely to discourage rather than encourage participation.

The advisory committees made several specific recommendations on a public information program. The black advisory committee suggested expanding programs to identify grassroots leaders in neighborhoods where the undercount is expected to be highest and developing methods for training indigenous persons in such neighborhoods; it questioned use of participant-observer techniques for research in inner-city areas by graduate students. It also suggested that the Census Bureau establish working relationships with the National Black Caucus-Local Elected Officials to encourage black participation; that the media expertise of groups in the National Coalition on Black Voter Participation (which was successful in Operation Big Vote in 1976) be used; and that funds be allocated to hire people to contact organizations and data users in the black community.

The Asian and Pacific Americans advisory committee recommended that the Census Bureau establish display booths explaining reasons for the census well before enumeration and seek the help of community organizations in publicizing the operation of the census and the hiring of enumerators. It also urged improving training methods for enumerators, specifically, by the use of role-playing.

A major concern of both the Spanish-origin and Asian and Pacific Americans advisory committees is that census questionnaires and instructions, as well as publicity materials, be translated and made available in the predominantly non-English language(s) of places where a large segment of the population is non-English speaking.

Adjusting for the Undercount

Perhaps the greatest concern of the minority advisory committees has been the inequity in distribution of federal funds among states and local areas that results from the differential undercount. They acknowledge that up to now no scientific method has been developed to adjust state and local population counts for the undercount, but their view is that even crude methods would enhance the equity of the figures used in distribution.

The actual methods to be used are not specified, although some minority groups point to calculations published by both the National Urban League (Hill 1975) and the Joint Center for Political Studies (Strauss and Harkins 1974), which use a synthetic method (discussed more fully in Chapter 5). From the viewpoint of some minority groups, however, that method might not be fully acceptable since it uses data on national undercount ratios by race, but not by ethnic group: it would have the effect of increasing the share of states and cities with large black populations at the expense of states, such as those in the Southwest, with few black but many Spanish-origin people.

The minority group advisory committees believe they have had some effect upon the Census Bureau's plans for the 1980 census. There have been differences of view from time to time as to the limits of the advisory function, but overall the experience has had more successes than failures. The Census Bureau has had to learn to deal with community leaders who have a sense of responsibility toward their own constituents, and the advisory committee members have learned about technical, operational, and other practical constraints that limit action on some proposed recommendations.

Recent Congressional Action

The House Subcommittee on Census and Population, which has oversight over the Census Bureau, held hearings in both 1977 and 1978 on plans for the 1980 census. Some were held in Washington and some in areas where census pretests had been conducted. The views of minority groups, municipal officials, and other users of census data were presented. (The major concerns of minority groups are described above.)

Subcommittee Chairman William Lehman (Florida) has introduced three bills intended to reduce the undercount in 1980 and to provide procedures for correcting any undercoverage that may be found after these additional efforts. The first bill was introduced in mid-1977; a substantially revised version was substituted in October 1977 and reported out of subcommittee. A second substitute (HR 10386) containing additional revisions was introduced in December 1977, co-sponsored by Chairman Lehman and three other members; it has been adopted by the subcommittee and referred to the full Committee on Post Office and Civil Service.

By December, the Census Bureau had made some changes in its plans for the 1980 census that were directly responsive to features of the earlier bills. The question on total income was deleted from the short form, and, as a follow-up, the sampling plan was modified so that places of less than 5,000 in population would receive the long form at a 50-perent rate (instead of a 20-percent rate, as previously planned) to provide income data reliable enough to use in fund allocation formulas.

At a hearing before the subcommittee on March 21, 1978, the chief economist for the Department of Commerce, Courtenay Slater, reported on the department's plans to establish both an independent advisory committee to advise the department on a wide range of issues relating to the Census Bureau and a formal appeals procedure (Slater 1978). The latter would provide a mechanism for state and local governments who wish to challenge the Census Bureau's intercensal estimates of population and of per capita income. Under an already existing informal appeals procedure, the Census Bureau recently sent to all 39,000 units of local government, for advance review and comment, the population data elements that will in future affect their general revenue sharing allocations. The advisory committee, composed of citizens, experts, and data users, would have as its function an examination of Census Bureau policies, procedures, and quality standards, and preparation of an annual report on these subjects. (In July 1978, the U.S. Office of Management and Budget concurred in the establishment of such a committee.)

In January 1977, Congressman Charles B. Rangel (New York) introduced a bill (HR 2490) that would require that surveys be conducted to determine the number of individuals not counted by the most recent census in each state and county and in each municipality with a population of 50,000 or more. It would also require federal agencies using census data for federal assistance formulas to take into account data from such surveys. No hearings have been held on this bill.

Conclusion

The Panel deplores the small amount of solid information available on the characteristics of missed persons to use in developing plans and proposals for new approaches to reducing underenumeration. We are deeply concerned by the evidence that differential undercounts may create inequities for communities with large minority populations.

REFERENCES

Budd, E., D. Radner, and J. Hinrichs (1973) "Size Distribution of Family Personal Income: Methodology and Estimates for 1964," Bureau of Economic Analysis Staff Paper, No. 21, BEA-SP 73-021. Washington, D.C.: U.S. Department of Commerce.

City of Newark, New Jersey, v. W. Michael Blumenthal (1978) Civil Action No. 74-548 U.S. District Court for the District of Columbia, January 17.

Ellett, Charles A. (1976) "A Study of Data Requirements of Population-Based Formula Grants," _Statistical Reporter_, November.

Hill, Robert B. (1975) "Estimating the 1970 Census Undercount for States and Local Areas," _The Urban League Review_, January, pp. 36-45.

Johnson, Emery A. (1973) Letter to Senator James Abourezk from Dr. Johnson, Director, Indian Health Service, Health Services and Mental Health Administration, Department of Health, Education, and Welfare, June 4.

Johnston, Denis F. and James R. Wetzel (1969) "Effect of the Census Undercount on Labor Force Estimates," _Monthly Labor Review_, March, pp. 3-13.

Slater, Courtenay M. (1978) Statement before the Subcommittee on Census and Population of the House Committee on Post Office and Civil Service, March 21.

Strauss, Robert B. and Peter B. Harkins (1974) _The 1970 Census Undercount and Revenue Sharing: Effect on Allocations in New Jersey and Virginia_. Washington, D.C.: Joint Center for Political Studies.

U.S. Bureau of the Census (1974a) _Effect of Special Procedures to Improve Coverage in the 1970 Census_, 1970 Census of Population and Housing, Evaluation and Research Program, PHC(E)-6. Washington, D.C.: U.S. Government Printing Office.

U.S. Bureau of the Census (1974b) _Estimates of Coverage of Population by Sex, Race, and Age: Demographic Analysis_, 1970 Census of Population and Housing, Evaluation and Research Program, PHC(E)-4. Washington, D.C.: U.S. Government Printing Office.

U.S. Bureau of the Census (1975) _Coverage of Population in the 1970 Census and Some Implications for Public Programs_, Current Population Reports, Special Studies, Series P-23, No. 56. Washington, D.C.: U.S. Government Printing Office.

U.S. Bureau of the Census (1976) _Procedural History: 1970 Census of Population and Housing_, PHC(R)-1. Washington, D.C.: U.S. Government Printing Office.

U.S. Bureau of the Census (1977a) _Developmental Estimates of the Coverage of the Population in States in the 1970 Census: Demographic Analysis_, Current Population Reports, Special Studies, Series P-23-23, No. 65. Washington, D.C.: U.S. Government Printing Office.

U.S. Bureau of the Census (1977b) _Money Income in 1975 of Families and Persons in the United States_, Current Population Reports, Consumer Income, Series P-60, No. 105. Washington, D.C.: U.S. Government Printing Office.

U.S. Commission on Civil Rights (1974) _Counting the Forgotten: The 1970 Census Count of Persons of Spanish Speaking Background in the United States_. Washington, D.C: U.S. Government Printing Office.

U.S. Congress, House (1975) Federal Formula Grant-in-Aid Programs that Use Population as a Factor in Allocating Funds, compiled by the Congressional Research Service for the use of the Subcommittee on Census and Population of the Committee on Post Office and Civil Service, Committee Print No. 94-6 (October 24) Washington, D.C.: U.S. Government Printing Office.

U.S. Congress, House (1977a) The Census Reform Act, Hearings before the Subcommittee on Census and Population of the Committee on Post Office and Civil Service, 95th Congress, 1st session, Serial No. 95-46, September 12 & 23, 1977. Washington, D.C.: U.S. Government Printing Office.

U.S. Congress, House (1977b) The 1980 Census, Hearings before the Subcommittee on Census and Population of the Committee on Post Office and Civil Service, 95th Congress, 1st session, Serial No. 95-41, June 9, 10, & 24, 1977. Washington, D.C.: U.S. Government Printing Office.

U.S. Congress, House (1977c) Pretest Census in Oakland, California and Camden, New Jersey, Hearings before the Subcommittee on Census and Population of the Committee on Post Office and Civil Service, 95th Congress, 1st session, Serial No. 95-42, March 25 & May 16, 1977. Washington, D.C.: U.S. Government Printing Office.

U.S. Office of Management and Budget (1977) Special Analyses, Budget of the United States Government, Fiscal Year 1977. Washington, D.C.: U.S. Government Printing Office.

U.S. Social Security Administration, Studies from Interagency Data Linkages (especially Report No. 4).

Yuskavage, Robert, David Hirschberg, and Frederick J. Scheuren (1978) "The Impact on Personal and Family Income of Adjusting the Current Population Survey for Undercoverage," Proceedings of the Social Statistics Section, American Statistical Association, Part I, pp. 70-80. Washington, D.C.: American Statistical Association.

2. FOLLOW-UP TO *AMERICA'S UNCOUNTED PEOPLE*

In the spring of 1969, the Advisory Committee on Problems of Census Enumeration was established by the National Academy of Sciences at the request of the Census Bureau. The committee was to advise on ways to improve the completeness and accuracy of information collected in the decennial censuses of population and in intercensal household surveys conducted by the Census Bureau or by other government agencies. The work of the committee centered on 5 separate but interrelated tasks:

1. Considering how the social costs associated with underenumeration might best be estimated, along with the social benefits that might accrue from remedying coverage deficiencies.
2. Reviewing the state of knowledge about social conditions and attitudes that bear on the ability of government agencies to collect complete and accurate information from all elements of the population.
3. Providing advice on research and experimental efforts leading to a better understanding of the reasons for incomplete coverage in the census of population and in current surveys.
4. Recommending measures and procedures that appear likely to reduce or mitigate current deficiencies in coverage.
5. Designing a continuing research program directed toward the measurement and reduction of underenumeration in current surveys and subsequent censuses of population.

The advisory committee's report (National Research Council [hereafter cited as NRC] 1972) dealt with 3 of the 4 main questions before this Panel. Therefore, we thought it appropriate to examine that committee's 7 specific recommendations and determine the extent to which they have been adopted or are in the process of being adopted by the Census Bureau. Our review was facilitated by a document already prepared by the Census Bureau: in response to a request from William Lehman, chairman of the House Subcommittee on Census and Population, the Census Bureau detailed its follow-up to each advisory committee recommendation (Census 1977b). This chapter briefly outlines the 7 advisory committee recommendations, discusses the Census Bureau's relevant activities, and presents the Panel's comments on those activities. (A more complete discussion of the recommendations on research on communication and the Census Bureau's response appears in Chapter 3.)

1972 Recommendation 1

In considering the question of how much underenumeration is curable, the advisory committee pointed out that this depended on how much underenumeration is tolerable. To answer, it is necessary to know how census data are used. The committee therefore recommended: "There should be a cumulative, up-to-date register of all statutory uses that are made of census data for the purpose of allocating government funds and developing basic social services, and the Census Bureau should take the lead in establishing such a list" (NRC 1972, p. 17).

Census Bureau Activities

In 1975, the Congressional Research Service of the Library of Congress compiled a report (U.S. Congress 1975), Federal Formula Grant-In-Aid Programs that Use Population as a Factor in Allocating Funds, that identified the major uses of census data for those purposes. The Census Bureau did not attempt to repeat such a report. An update of that report was prepared recently by the Library of Congress (U.S. Congress 1978), The Use of Population Data in Federal Assistance Programs.

Panel Comment

While the Census Bureau has not complied literally with the recomendation, the Bureau has paid considerable attention to keeping up with the various uses of census data. There are thousands of uses for these data, associated not only with federal agencies, but also with state and local governments. Non-governmental users include coalitions sponsored by minority groups, trade unions, trade associations, foundations, universities, and businesses. While the Census Bureau does not know who all of the users are, it has maintained a file of interested users. These are the approximately 10,000 individuals and organizations who receive its quarterly newsletter, 1980 Census Update.

The Census Bureau also recently prepared a document summarizing the data uses of each question on the dress rehearsal census form (U.S. Bureau of the Census 1978). The document presents, for each question, a statement on the most significant federal program uses, lists of applicable federal laws and federal agency users of the data, and a final brief statement of other uses. A useful further step would be to analyze how the quality of the data affects the consequences of its use.

1972 Recommendation 2

"In addition to establishing and maintaining a register, the Census Bureau and other interested departments and agencies (including those that are not prime statistics producers) should provide support for case studies of the manner in which census data are used in the statutory allocation of federal, state, and local revenues and of the changes in those allocations that would result from adjusting the data to account for various hypothesized rates of underenumeration" (NRC 1972, p. 124).

Census Bureau Activities

The Bureau responded with a report, Coverage of Population in the 1970 Census and Some Implications for Public Programs (Census 1975), which reviewed the methodology and the extent of population undercoverage in the 1970 census and examined the implications of geographic variations in undercoverage for various public programs, particularly political representation and disbursement of public funds. Two years later, the Census Bureau issued a study using the same type of analysis but with improved estimating technqiues (Census 1977a). In addition, the office of federal statistical policy and standards of the Department of Commerce has also prepared a report on the uses of census data in funds allocation (U.S. Department of Commerce 1978). This report examines the operation of 5 of the 10 largest grant-in-aid formulas and assesses the effect of the particular definitions and data sets specified.

The Census Bureau has also prepared, either by its own staff or in cooperation with others, several documents on various effects of the undercount. In 1969 and 1970, it worked with the Bureau of Labor Statistics of the U.S. Department of Labor to study the undercount's effect on the characteristics of the United States labor force (Wetzel and Johnston 1969, Klein 1970). Two papers presented at the 1977 annual meeting of the American Statistical Association dealt with the effect of the 1970 undercount on current economic indicators, one dealing with employment (Brooks and Bailar 1978) and the other with personal and family income (Yuskavage et al. 1978).

Panel Comment

It is apparent that the Census Bureau has responded seriously to this recommendation. The Census Bureau has conducted its own studies on the effect of the undercount on the revenue allocation on a geographic basis and has examined other effects. In addition, it has cooperated with other federal agencies involved in similar studies.

1972 Recommendation 3

In planning future research on underenumeration and other social data-gathering problems, the advisory committee recommended that the Census Bureau place more emphasis on "developing new conceptual frameworks for the exploration of phenomena not usually perceived as relevant to the organized process of collecting census and survey information." Operationally, moreover, the Census Bureau should actively seek to broaden the base of social science knowledge and training to which it currently has access" (NRC 1972, pp. 124-125).

Census Bureau Activities

When the advisory committee's interim report was made (prior to the 1970 census), the Census Bureau began a series of studies and a program of research along the lines outlined above. Some have been ethnographic studies with participant-observers focusing on certain subgroups in the population; one of these was conducted prior to the 1970 census and three are currently going on. These studies should provide insight into some of the problems inherent in enumerating the poor and certain ethnic groups.

Panel Comment

While the Census Bureau has conducted a great deal of research on methodological and quantitative procedures, the Panel believes that the Bureau could profitably give more attention to the motivational and attitudinal aspects of the undereumeration problem. The Census Bureau has started work in this area: for example, the exploratory study on privacy and confidentiality as factors in survey response being completed by the National Research Council (1979) and the classroom experiments with alternative census-like questionnaires conducted in 1971, 1972, and 1977. Another noteworthy illustration of this type of research is the Oakland intensive individual interview study, in which information was obtained on the within-household dynamics surrounding the decision to fill out the census form and who actually filled out the form. The Census Bureau also experimented with telephone contact to motivate response in the Richmond dress rehearsal census.

The Panel supports the Census Bureau's continued and expanded efforts to undertake innovative and imaginative research on the dynamics of the response problem. We think that this topic is well worth intensive and meticulous research.

1972 Recommendation 4

The Census Bureau should expand its "present conception of enumeration-related research. . .in ways that place greater stress on the relationship between census-taking problems, such as underenumeration, and the social contexts in which censuses and surveys are conducted" (NRC 1972, p. 125)

Census Bureau Activities

The Census Bureau has undertaken many projects in response to this recommendation, including:

1. Ethnographic research--participant-observer studies--by post-graduate students in selected neighborhoods (noted above). These researchers report on the life styles of the people in the study area to assess the effectiveness of enumeration methods and to discover possible causes and correlates of undercounts and other types of reporting errors in censuses and surveys. Studies are currently under way in three areas.

2. Changes in demographic classifiers for censuses and surveys. The term "head of household," which some regard as a sexist term, is being dropped from the questionnaire. The Census Bureau is experimenting with alternative methods of associating members of a common living quarters so that it can continue to produce data on families and households. The classification system of "racial" and ethnic groups is being expanded in order to provide more detail than previously. (See Chapter 3 for detailed discussion and evaluation of these changes in racial and ethnic questions.)

3. An investigation of the characteristics of households that refuse to cooperate in the current population survey. This study will yield data on the social and demographic characteristics of this subgroup and thus should provide insights into the possible reasons for non-cooperation in other surveys and censuses.

4. Sponsorship of a pilot survey to examine how the promise of confidentiality may affect the willingness of households to participate in a census or survey (noted above). Promises to respondents about the length of time their answers would be kept confidential was varied to test householders' concern about this issue and to see how varying promises of confidentiality may affect census and survey response rates. Preliminary results became available in March 1977; the final report is being completed (NRC 1979).

5. Further tests of special methods, such as casual interviews and record checks, for areas where the standard procedures are the least effective. Record matching will become part of the actual 1980 census operation.

6. A new selection aid test, with demonstrated relevance to on-the-job performance, to screen applicants for employment as census enumerators and as district office workers. Special efforts are being made to assure that this test will not discriminate on the basis of race, ethnicity, or sex.

In addition, the Census Bureau is proposing a number of experimental projects, to be conducted as part of the 1980 census evaluation program, that come under the scope of this recommendation. These projects (discussed more fully in Chapter 6) include, among others, experiments with a two-stage enumeration process, alternative "list-leave" procedures, and different community service program approaches. Another approach that might be incorporated in the coverage evaluation program in the 1980 census is the network survey. Members of a household are asked about others whose coverage in the census can then be checked. For example, parents are asked about adult children living or staying at other addresses. To the extent that parents report the existence of persons who would not be reported at the address at which they are staying, there is an opportunity to pick up missed persons; however, it is necessary to guard against double-counting.

Panel Comment

The Panel notes that the Census Bureau has undertaken various projects to improve enumeration within the social environment in which the census is taken. With the exception of ethnographic research, however, these projects are mostly designed within the same framework of census operation that has been used for the past several decades. Particularly noteworthy, therefore, are the few experiments on a broad scale with innovative or radically different procedures, such as the network survey that is being considered.

1972 Recommendation 5

This recommendation notes that "a number of ideas suggested by the conceptualization of census taking as a socially organized activity can be translated into research directly aimed at improving standard enumeration procedures. Others will require longer-term exploratory studies to develop additional evidence about the kinds of people who do not get counted, and how, and why" (NRC 1972, p. 127). The advisory committee recommended that the Census Bureau undertake research projects of both kinds, and it recommended several specific activities, including research on questionnnaire wording and format, the use of local record sources, and research on communication.

Census Bureau Activities

In response to the recommendation for additional experimental studies of questionnaire wordings and formats, the Census Bureau in 1976 conducted a national content test involving two separate national samples of approximately 14,000 households each. Each sample received questionnaires with alternative versions of questions on such subjects as ethnic origin, current language spoken, and disability. A subsample of the sample respondents later underwent a detailed reinterview. The findings of this undertaking have been analyzed to study response patterns, levels of nonresponse, and respondent understanding of particular versions of a given question. For the pretests and dress rehearsals conducted prior to the 1980 census, the Census Bureau has made available, on request, Spanish-language questionnaires to assess the value of translating the form into other languages and to measure the level of use of the translated version.

Procedures to compare local record sources and census records and to conduct casual interviews, among others, were used in pretests for the 1980 census and will be used in the census to improve coverage. (The specific recommendations on research on communication and the Census Bureau's response are discussed fully in Chapter 3.)

The feasibility of hiring letter carriers as follow-up enumerators was investigated by the Census Bureau and the Postal Service; both agencies agreed that it would be neither efficient nor feasible to employ postal carriers in this capacity.

Panel Comment

Some of the Census Bureau's follow-up to recommendations in this area will result in changes in the 1980 census enumeration, e.g., use of Spanish-language questionnaires and record matching. However, the Census Bureau has confined its research to the kind of study it has traditionally done well: that is, studies to test explicit hypotheses, using a rigid design excellently executed and developing precise quantitative estimates of behavior. The Panel would like to see the Census Bureau initiate attitudinal or motivational research projects that are exploratory in nature and flexible in design, to develop insights and hypotheses that can later be tested more carefully.

1972 Recommendation 6

"Increased support should be given to analytical studies of small-area underenumeration (as well as other sources of census error) with the objectives of (a) discovering which demographic, economic, and other characteristics of an area are associated with enumeration error and (b) devising methods for adjusting small-area census counts" (NRC 1972, p. 129).

Census Bureau Activities

Assessment of the accuracy of the census count for small areas has long been a concern of the Census Bureau's evaluation programs. As early as 1950, the census evaluation program provided some information on regional variations in coverage completeness and on the demographic, social, and economic variations in underenumeration. Later censuses added to this knowledge.

The Census Bureau currently plans to prepare coverage estimates for states, major cities, and major metropolitan areas as part of its census evaluation program for the 1980 census, and it is increasing the resources available in order to achieve this goal. Specific plans for the evaluation of the 1980 census are now being developed (see Chapter 6). Those plans include an expanded post-enumeration survey and a match with Social Security and other records to provide direct estimates for states, large cities, and larger metropolitan areas, as well as information on the demographic, social, and economic variations in coverage. Also planned is an exploration of the use of regression analysis at the person or block level on the basis of a sample of small areas to make possible indirect estimates of undercoverage for small places, because record matches and a post-enumeration survey covering all such areas would be prohibitively expensive. A small-scale test of such a procedure was carried out in Oakland, California, in connection with the census pretest. An exploratory project to estimate coverage of state populations by demographic methods has also been completed, and a report on it has been issued (Census 1977); the Census Bureau plans to refine these methods for 1980. The results may be used in conjunction with the direct estimates of coverage of state populations. Modifications in the scope and methods of the evaluation program will be made as suggested by further experience and analysis.

Panel Comment

The Panel considers this program important both for adjustment of local population statistics for undercount and for better understanding of the causes of undercounts. It hopes that sufficient funds will be allocated for a large post-enumeration survey and matching projects, so that local area underenumeation analyses can be as productive as possible.

1972 Recommendation 7

". . .Much stronger efforts should be made to join the kinds of social science competence found on the [Census Bureau] staff and in the external research communities of some of the principal social data users with the kinds of scientific expertise that has been well developed by the principal data producers" (NRC 1972, p. 129).

Census Bureau Activities

With the great growth in social sciences over the past few years, the Census Bureau has become more closely allied with the social science community than in the past. This interaction has taken many forms. The Census Bureau often sponsors conferences that bring together leaders in the statistical research community and other fields to focus on particular problems. In late 1977, the Census Bureau jointly sponsored conferences with the American Statistical Association (ASA) as part of the National Science Foundation/Census Bureau project, "A Research Program to Improve the Social Science Data Base." The purpose of these conferences was "to identify broadly needed research in statistical approaches to the social sciences; particularly how such research needs involve the development and use of materials of the U.S. Bureau of the Census. Special attention was paid to research which could appropriately be pursued in the second and third years of the larger ASA/Census project's fellowship program, which is designed to give senior social scientists and graduate students an opportunity to share ideas about the experiences with real world problems of a large data-collection agency" (American Statistical Association 1978, p. 1).

Further research interchange is fostered through the American Statistical Association, the American Association for Public Opinion Research, the Population Association of America, the American Sociological Association, the American Marketing Association, the American Economic Association and other professional groups.

The Census Bureau also acts as the data collection agent for many major federal agency programs. While the sponsoring agency has primary responsibility for the conceptualization of the data to be obtained, the Census Bureau has primary responsibility for defining the survey procedures and measurement techniques by which the data will be obtained; however, each agency makes a contribution in the area of the other's primary responsibility. In this way, an interactive approach is developed.

Panel Comment

It is quite apparent that the Census Bureau has done much to facilitate interaction between itself and the social science community. (Further suggestions on this subject will be found in Chapter 6.)

Conclusion

The Panel believes that the Census Bureau has done much to follow up on practically all the recommendations of the Advisory Committee on Problems of Census Enumeration. It has experimented with new procedures, initiated various research projects, and developed ties with many professional and social science groups.

The Panel does find a major and serious shortcoming in the Census Bureau's research approach toward underenumeration: the Census Bureau has concentrated its efforts on doing better the things it has always done, without much emphasis on motivational or attitudinal aspects of the nonresponse problem. The Census Bureau has used different types of statistical approaches, involving demographic analyses, large-scale surveys, and matching studies, to identify undercounted subgroups of the population; it has conducted statistical tests of the efficacy of alternative methods for delivering and retrieving the questionnaire and on various forms of question wording; it has taken some important steps to improve its ability to measure coverage and to estimate the undercount. These are all to the good. But the Census Bureau has not done enough research on the underlying problems of nonresponse and response error.

An example illustrates the Panel's concern. Studies of the 1960 census indicate that approximately half of the undercount resulted from missing households and half from missing individuals within enumerated households. In 1970 progress was made on the first type of error, with the result that less than half the undercount was attributable to missed households. And in 1980 we believe that the Census Bureau will eliminate many of the problems of missing households through the carefully developed registers, local review, vacancy check, and other procedures it has established. However, locating missing individuals is a quite different problem than finding households. It involves information about an individual's motivation and attitude toward the entire enumeration process. Further research on this topic needs to be undertaken. The research program should be detailed and flexible enough to provide information about the causes of and possible solutions to the nonresponse problem. The Census Bureau has started such projects and we suggest that these efforts be expanded.

The advisory committee commented in 1972 on the reluctance of Census Bureau personnel to move substantially and imaginatively into the dynamics of the response problem. In 1978, we find that the Census Bureau still has not tackled the "soft side" of the undercount problem. The Census Bureau might wish to consider sponsoring a university-based contract on this topic, but whatever plans are made for this research, it remains a pressing problem of priorities that will shape the quality of future census work.

REFERENCES

American Statistical Association (1978) AMSTAT NEWS, No. 41, January.

Brooks, Camila A. and Barbara A. Bailar (1978) "An Error Profile: Employment as Measured by the Current Population Survey," in Proceedings of the Social Statistics Section, American Statistical Association, Part 1, pp. 26-34. Washington, D.C.: American Statistical Association.

Klein, Deborah (1970) "Status of Men Missed in the Census," Monthly Labor Review, March.

National Research Council (1972) America's Uncounted People, Report of the Advisory Committee on Problems of Census Enumeration. Washington, D.C.: National Academy of Sciences.

National Research Council (1979) Privacy and Confidentiality as Factors in Survey Response, Panel on Privacy and Confidentiality as Factors in Survey Response, Committee on National Statistics. Washington, D.C.: National Academy of Sciences.

U.S. Bureau of the Census (1975) Coverage of Population in the 1970 Census and Some Implications for Public Policy, Current Population Reports, Series P-23, No. 56. Washington, D.C.: U.S. Government Printing Office.

U.S. Bureau of the Census (1977a) Developmental Estimates of the Coverage of the Population of States in the 1970 Census: Demographic Analysis, Current Population Reports, Series P-23, No. 65. Washington, D.C.: U.S. Government Printing Office.

U.S. Bureau of the Census (1977b) "Responses to Recommendations by the National Academy of Sciences." Unpublished.

U.S. Bureau of the Census (1978) "Summary Descriptions of Data Use for Subjects" and "Questions Planned for Inclusion in the 1980 Census," memo from David L. Kaplan, Assistant Director for Demographic Censuses, April 20.

U.S. Congress, House (1975) Federal Formula Grant-in-Aid Programs that Use Population as a Factor in Allocating Funds, compiled by the Congressional Research Service for the use of the Subcommittee on Census and Population of the Committee on Post Office and Civil Service. Committee Print No. 94-6. Washington, D.C.: U.S. Goverment Printing Office.

U.S. Congress, House (1978) The Use of Population Data in Federal Assistance Programs, Subcommittee on Census and Population, Printed for the use of the Committee on Post Office and Civil Service, Committee Print No. 95-16. Washington, D.C.: U.S. Government Printing Office.

U.S. Department of Commerce (1978) "Report on Statistics for Allocation of Funds," Office of Federal Statistical Policy and Standards, Statistical Working Paper 1. Washington, D.C.: U.S. Government Printing Office.

Wetzel, James and Denis Johnston (1969) "Effect of the Undercount in the Census on Unemployment," Monthly Labor Review, March.

Yuskavage, Robert, David Hirschberg, and Frederick J. Scheuren (1978) "The Impact on Personal and Family Income of Adjusting the Current Population Survey for Undercoverage," in Proceedings of the Social Statistics Section, American Statistical Association, Part 1, pp. 70-80. Washington, D.C.: American Statistical Association.

3. PLANS FOR THE 1980 CENSUS

It seems clear that certain distinctive (and perhaps transitory) problems will face the Census Bureau in conducting the 1980 census. Instead of being able to concentrate its efforts to get better results, the Census Bureau may need to expend much energy just to keep up past levels of quality and completeness. Three factors account for the expected problems.

First, there has been a rising demand for the Census Bureau's product--not only from those who want more knowledge of the scope and location of societal problems, community needs, or economic markets, but also from those who want their share of public funds and governmental services. This means that interested individuals and groups as well as state and local governments will evaluate critically, and often in politically controversial ways, the Census Bureau's performance in 1980. The Census Bureau must not jeopardize its record of careful and professional judgments on how best to carry out the complex task of gathering data and providing statistics.

Second, there has been almost a quantum jump in the cost of conducting the census, reflecting its growing complexity. The 1980 census will cost close to $1 billion--compared to $221.6 million for the 1970 census (Census 1976b)--and doubtless future censuses will cost more. Cost-effective decisions will be required at every possible point: what questions to ask, what kinds of searches for missing people to undertake, what enumeration procedures to adopt, and what data base for count adjustments, if any, to compile. The task requires pretests and dress rehearsals, quality controls, corrections for errors and omissions. At every step, it calls for careful efforts to measure the effects of the procedures used on yield (both in locating people and getting full answers from them) and on quality.

Third, there are changes in the American way of life--changes in life style, in labor force composition, and in public attitudes toward governmental surveys--that make the task of census enumeration more difficult in 1980 than at any time in the last century. Each of these changes seriously affects both the quality and coverage of census results.

Overall, people are harder to find. Some, such as illegal aliens and certain separated spouses, deliberately seek to avoid being counted. The latest estimate of the number of undocumented aliens, based on data not connected with law enforcement, is about 4 million (Lancaster and Scheuren 1977). Although undocumented aliens can be assured that answering census questions will place them in no jeopardy because their responses are confidential, it seems likely that most will overwhelmingly fear discovery and possible deportation and hence will often be census evaders. Families with only one adult parent may be eligible for aid to dependent children, day care services, or housing accommodations if the missing spouse is not found at that address. Self-interest here also plausibly creates census evaders.

In addition to census evaders, new life styles have complicated the census taker's work: mobile homes are everywhere, recreational vehicles become permanent residences, people live in commune-like arrangements, shared custody arrangements for dependents of divorced parents are more popular, and there are more people who live alone, of all ages, to be reached and counted.

At the same time, the labor force has changed. In past decades, the Census Bureau could fill thousands of short-duration jobs of enumerators and field coordinating personnel quite easily, especially with relatively well-educated housewives who worked conscientiously and took civic pride in working for the census for a few weeks before again leaving the labor market. Temporary workers with such characteristics are not expected to be available in large numbers for the 1980 census; one reason is that the proportion of families in which both husband and wife hold permanent jobs has grown substantially.

The increasing proportion of married women who work also reduces the proportion of households that can be enumerated during working hours, requiring more callbacks and evening work, raising costs, and creating special problems in high-crime areas.

In racially and ethnically homogeneous locales, the premium that is placed on hiring persons of the same race and ethnic backgrounds further complicates the staffing problem; it underscores the complex issues of race, ethnicity, class, and sex, as well as equity involved in the recruitment and selection of enumerators.

Moreover, many people believe that Americans are less willing now than in the past to cooperate freely with officialdom, more reluctant to accept as benign the efforts of the Census Bureau to gather detailed and personal information. If this is true--and we have found little evidence to support this observation either way--it will be difficult to get the cooperation, interest, and good will necessary for a task that can be time-consuming and exasperating. The task may be especially hard if no help is provided to the "responsible adult" in a household who tries to fill out a long and complex questionnaire about several household members.

In summary, the 1980 census will be taken at a time when the political climate and various socioeconomic trends are expected to make the task especially difficult.

In the following six sections of this chapter, the Panel considers: first, the methods by which the Census Bureau plans to improve the completeness of the count in 1980 with some new procedures as well as with some procedures used on a limited scale in 1970 and now planned for wider use; second, the selection, training, and supervision of the temporary staff on which great responsibility rests for the completeness of the count; third, the public information and community relations programs, which can be important in motivating people to cooperate; fourth, the questionnaire itself as it affects cooperation and thus completeness of the count; fifth, issues of how a proper count will be obtained for each racial and ethnic group; and sixth, factors related to changing residence and household composition patterns and their effect on the completeness of the count.

PROCEDURES TO IMPROVE COMPLETENESS OF COVERAGE

Planned Procedures

The general plan for the 1980 census is to use a mail-out/mail-back method for about 90 percent of the population (instead of 60 percent as in 1970). This method will be used for the predominantly urbanized areas, mostly where commercial address lists can be obtained. The rest of the country will be enumerated by personal visit. Households in the mailing areas that fail to send back their questionnaires will be visited by enumerators.

In places of 5,000 or more population, five-sixths of the households will be enumerated by a short questionnaire, which has 7 questions on the characteristics of each person and 9 questions on the living quarters, and one-sixth by a long form, which has 34 questions both on personal characteristics and on the living quarters. In places of less than 5,000 population, one-half of the households will receive the long form, to provide a more adequate sample.

The details of the procedures are described in sequence below and in tabular form beginning on page 34, which shows, by comparison with the comparable procedures in the 1970 census, the changes being made to improve the completeness of coverage. (These procedures are currently planned; they are subject to change if sufficient funds are not available.)

An address register will be developed for all mail-out/mail-back areas, using commercial mailing lists matched to such other listings (such as those from the 1970 census and lists of public housing) and checked by mail carriers and by a precanvass. If commercial mailing lists are not available for a given area, a list will be developed by prelisting (i.e., a canvass) and checked by mail carriers. A final check on the number of addresses on each block will be made by local government officials.

Questionnaires will be mailed out, with a final check by mail carriers on coverage on the course of delivery. Questionnaires returned by mail will be checked against the address register, and addresses from which questionnaires are not returned will be followed up.

Respondents' reports of the number of living quarters in their buildings will be checked against the registers to see if previously unknown living quarters can be identified.

Mailed-in questionnaires will be reviewed for completeness of information--i.e., that all questions are answered for each person listed. Automatic callbacks will be made in every household listing 7 persons to ensure that no one was omitted (since there is space for only 7 people). Callbacks (by telephone, if possible) will be made to fill in missing questions.

In non-mail-out areas, traditional house-to-house enumeration will be carried out, with a post-enumeration check by the Postal Service for completeness of address coverage.

Independent lists of persons (such as drivers' license records, alien registration, membership lists of community organizations, or individuals interviewed in "casual counts" in hard-to-enumerate areas) will be checked against household enumerations to find persons missed, and apparent discrepancies will be checked with the household.

For households from which no report is received after repeated attempts, information will be sought from neighbors on how many people live there, if any. Reported vacancies will be rechecked by a second enumerator. Addresses will be "closed out" only by a supervisor.

Local government officials will be given the preliminary count by block or other small geographic area for checking, and discrepancies called to the Census Bureau's attention will be checked by re-enumeration.

These enumeration steps will be accompanied by publicity and community relations programs, walk-in assistance centers, and other efforts, detailed on the following eight pages.

Evaluation of Planned Procedures

The Panel believes that the establishment of as complete a register of dwelling units as possible in the more urbanized areas in which the mail-out will be conducted is a major step forward, since it provides a systematic control over enumerator error in identifying these units. This is especially true because one step in the development of the list is the precanvass by enumerators and another step is the use of the questionnaire to identify other units in the same building. The best features of traditional enumeration are combined with the resources of mailing list companies and the Postal Service.

In 1970, more than half the persons missed are believed to have been in housing units that were enumerated. The methods planned for 1980 are likely to result in even more complete coverage of housing units than in 1970, since address registers will be established for more areas and pre-enumeration housing unit counts will be checked in many localities by local governments. It is therefore likely that the greatest remaining potential for coverage improvement will be in reducing the number of persons missed within enumerated households and of persons not in households. Coverage improvement methods directed to this end are potentially most productive. These include checks against nonhousehold records, methods to ensure full listing of household members by respondents, the vacancy check, and public information and community support programs.

The Panel also considers that the plan to make the vacancy check a regular step in the enumerative procedure is an improvement. In 1970, a check of a sample of dwellings reported as vacant was done after the enumeration was completed, and 11 percent of the dwelling units earlier reported as vacant were found to be occupied. (The percentage varied by region and size of area.) The number of inhabitants was imputed on an ad hoc, individual matching procedure that the Census Bureau calls a "hot deck" method. (The Bureau defines a "hot deck" as a set of values that is constantly altered as questionnaires are processed, and the data for the latest people or housing unit are substituted for the values already in the deck. Allocation for missing entries is made from the latest value stored in the computer that fits the description of the person or housing unit for which the information is needed. In effect, neighbors are assumed to have the same characteristics.) This method resulted in the addition of about 1,069,000 persons, or about 0.5 percent of the population. However, location of these persons had to be estimated, i.e., people were imputed to a given percentage of the vacancies in each area--the same percentage found for the region and size class in the national vacancy check. In 1980, every dwelling unit reported as vacant will be revisited and the inhabited households not previously enumerated will be identified individually. Therefore, the people will be allocated to the proper location, even if their characteristics may have to be imputed if efforts to enumerate them fail.

SPECIAL PROCEDURES TO IMPROVE CENSUS COVERAGE

Pre-Census Procedures. The fact that the 1980 census is more dependent on the mail-out method than the 1970 census (90 percent versus 60 percent) explains the added emphasis on obtaining as complete a master address list as possible. The following coverage improvement programs are mostly pre-census procedures intended to provide a complete listing of residential units (address register).

1970	1980
Address Register	
A commerical mailing list for the U.S. was purchased by the Census Bureau after having bidders provide addresses on 48-hour notice for selected census tracts. Addresses were then checked in the field by census workers, and the list with the best coverage was selected.	Commerical mailing lists will be evaluated and purchased by the Census Bureau, but rather than purchase one list as in 1970, the Census Bureau may purchase multiple lists to allow for the possibility that different commerical mailing concerns are most accurate in different parts of the country. Commerical mailing lists may be augmented by such sources as the final address register of housing units for 1970 or independent (non-census) housing lists, such as lists of public housing.
Precanvass Operation	
This operation was carried out in selected enumeration districts (EDs) in 17 metropolitan areas. Prior to mail-out, areas with concentrations of small apartment dwellings were canvassed to verify the number of separate living quarters contained in each structure. Missed units that were located were added to address register. (According to the Census Bureau, the precanvass added 108,000 units containing 234,000 persons, and only a limited area was covered.)	This operation will be extended in 1980 to the entire mail-out area covered by commerical lists. Missing or newly built residential units will be added to address register.

Prelist Operation

This operation was used in mail census areas not covered by a commerical list. A "knock when necessary" procedure was used to obtain mailing addresses.	This operation will be used in mail census areas not covered by a commerical list. A "knock on every door with no callbacks" procedure will be used along with more structured listing instructions and a formal quality control operation.

Post Office Check

A three-stage process was followed: (1) Approximately 9 months before the census: separate card prepared for each address; mail carriers checked for completion and accuracy on their regular routes; mail carriers corrected addresses and prepared cards for missing addresses (advance post office check). (2) Three weeks before the census: all mailing pieces delivered to mail carriers, who sorted as if questionnaires were to be delivered. Mail carriers prepared cards for addresses with no questionnaire (casing check). (3) During actual delivery of questionnaires, mail carriers prepared cards for addresses with no questionnaire (time of delivery check).	The same three-stage process will be followed.
All three checks were used in areas covered by commerical lists. For all other mail-out areas, only second and third checks were used.	The advance post office check is also planned for prelist areas. Thus, all three checks will be used in the entire mail-out area.

Respondent's Report of Living Quarters at His or Her Address

Each respondent was asked to report the number of living quarters at his or her address (building). If the number was greater than the census list number and the census list number was 9 or less, an enumerator was sent to determine if all units were included. (According to the Census Bureau, for an estimated 62,000 addresses, discrepancy between respondent report and census register	The same procedure will be followed. Additional controls are being developed to ensure that enumerators have a complete list of addresses where discrepancies appeared, and enumerators' reports will be checked by crew leaders.

1970	1980
was not discovered until after editing was completed.)	

Conventional (Non-Mail-Out) Areas

1970	1980
The listing and enumeration occured simultaneously. The address register was prepared during the enumeration.	The same procedure will be followed.
As a post-census procedure, selected conventional areas went through a post-enumeration post office check (PEPOC).	All conventional areas will go through a post-enumeration post office check (PEPOC) as part of the regular census procedure.

Time-of-Census Procedures. Some of the coverage improvement procedures occur while the census is under way, such as respondents' report of living quarters at their address. The following coverage improvement programs are intended to provide checks against misclassification of housing units and of within-household undercoverage.

Vacancy Check

1970	1980
A post-enumeration sample survey of non-seasonal vacant housing was revisited. Interviews with occupants or neighbors were used to determine occupancy status during the census-taking period and the number of occupants if occupied. Of all "vacant" units, 11.4 percent were found to be continuously occupied by the same household during the entire census period (1 month for conventional areas, 3 months in mail-out areas) and thus misclassified.	This program will be part of the ongoing census enumeration procedure. Every housing vacancy reported by an enumerator will be rechecked by a second enumerator who will verify that vacancy in writing. Errors will be corrected before the census office closes.
The results were used to adjust census counts.	
A sample of nonseasonal vacant housing units were converted into occupied units by imputation: 1,069,000 persons were added to the census in this	

manner. (According to the Census Bureau, misclassification was most likely to occur in mail-out areas).

Office Edit of Housing Definition

This procedure was used to identify cases in which the housing unit definition may have been incorrectly applied (i.e., a reported unit did not have separate cooking facilities or separate entrance).

The same procedure will be followed.

Check of Movers

This procedure was used to check enumeration of people who moved during census-taking period in the same EDs that were precanvassed. Post offices supplied the Census Bureau with change-of-address cards received between March 1 and May 2. Address registers and questionnaires were then searched. Enumerators followed up on people who moved who had not been enumerated. (According to the Census Bureau, because of some problems in the clerical phase, 11 percent of movers should have been followed up but were not.)

This procedure may be extended to all areas where geocoded (geographically coded) files are available. The Census Bureau is considering dropping post-census check of movers because the vacancy check would identify post-census movers. A check of persons moving before the census date will be carried out.

Household Member List

The name of each person living in the household or staying or visiting there and without another home was requested on the inside of the questionnaire, followed by questions on each person's characteristics. Room was provided for 7 names on the long form and for 8 names on the short form, with a check item to show whether more persons lived there; callbacks were made when this item was answered "yes" or left blank.

Question 1 on the cover of the questionnaire will ask each household to list the names of all persons who were staying or visiting there and had no other home. An office edit will check that the household member list coincides with persons listed inside the form. Discrepancies will be assigned for follow-up. Automatic callbacks will be made for all questionnaires listing 7 persons (the maximum number for which space is provided for reporting characteristics) to ensure that no one was omitted due to space limitations.

1970	1980

Persons with Usual Residence Elsewhere

1970	1980
This procedure was not used.	All "Whole Household Usual Home Elsewhere" addresses will be checked to see if they were enumerated at their usual place of residence.

Non-Census Lists of Persons

1970	1980
This procedure was not used.	Lists of persons independent of the census household enumeration will be used to check on within-household underenumeration. Among the sources of lists being considered are driver's license lists, the Immigration and Naturalization Service's registration of aliens, membership lists of ethnic organizations, etc. Any lists used must be geocoded, then matched with census enumeration forms before the district office closes. If a person on a non-household list is found not to have been enumerated at the address on the list, the household is contacted to determine if the person was there on the census date; if so, an attempt will be made to obtain identifying information.

Close-Out Procedure

1970	1980
In cases where there appeared to be people living in a dwelling unit but they were out of town, away from home, or refused to cooperate and nothing could be learned from the neighbors about the household, the supervisor (not the enumerator) was permitted to close out the case and information was imputed.	The procedure remains the same, but each case will be pursued for a longer period of time to get some information where possible on the number of persons in the unit so that the computer will have something on which to base the imputation.

Local Review Program

1970	1980
This program did not exist.	(1) In early 1980, local officials will be given mail list address counts for small geographic areas together with a detailed census map for review of the counts. Identified discrepancies will be checked out and corrected. (2) After enumeration is completed, the above process

	will be repeated, using the preliminary population and housing unit counts. Discrepancies will be resolved before local census offices close.

Post-Census Procedures. The following coverage improvement programs take place after the enumeration is completed. The results of these programs are used for computer imputation.

1970	1980
Post-Enumeration Post Office Check (PEPOC)	
This procedure was used to improve coverage in the conventional (non-mail-out) census areas of the South. Mail carriers checked address registers against the addresses on their delivery routes. Mail carriers reported to the Census Bureau all addresses that did not match. A sample of all such addresses were checked with census enumeration records. A sample of nonmatched addresses were visited, and any persons living there were enumerated. By imputation, the results were used to adjust the census count by the number of missed addresses and a factor reflecting those actually enumerated. (According to the Census Bureau, this procedure added 174,000 units and 484,000 persons to the census.)	This procedure will be extended to every office where the census is taken by conventional methods. It will be part of the regular census operation, and units identified as "missed" by post offices will be enumerated before the district office closes.
Supplemental Forms Operation ("Were You Counted?" Campaign)	
This procedure used special forms to locate un-enumerated persons, including overseas travelers. The forms were not processed, however, unless the total number of persons on supplemental forms represented 1 percent or more of the initially enumerated population or 50 or more from one ED. Census records were checked to see if a person was already included. If not, computer imputation was used to add counts to each ED.	The "Were You Counted?" Campaign is planned for 1980, but there will not be a cutoff point.

1970	1980
Missed Persons Campaign	
The Census Bureau provided "Please make sure I am counted in Census" cards to community groups and organizations for distribution in casual settings. Completed cards were to be returned to census offices and checked with census enumerations. (According to the Census Bureau, 324 cards were completed and returned.)	This procedure will not be used. In its place there will be the casual count of individuals in places and sites where hard-to-enumerate persons might be found (e.g., skid row, pool halls, fairgrounds, etc.).

Public Information and Community Education. Some of the coverage improvement programs are intended to create a better climate of public opinion by increasing understanding of the importance of the census and its confidentiality provisions or by improving the performance of enumerators through better training and supervision.

1970	1980
Special Public Information Efforts	
(1) There was a national publicity effort with the assistance of the Advertising Council.	The same program is planned for 1980 but with an extended scope.
(2) Special measures were followed in the 20 largest cities: appeals from prominent blacks and persons of Spanish heritage; flyers in schools; billboards; sound trucks; news copy sent to ethnic newspapers and radio stations.	Plans for the 1980 census remain tentative to date.
Correct Count Committee	
This procedure was not used.	A local committee of elected public officials, citizen-leaders, etc., will be established to mobilize local networks for the benefit of a better census.
Minority Education Program	
There was a community education program in some of the largest cities. Black and Spanish-speaking	There will be a more extensive minority statistics program with three components:

specialists were hired to: (1) promote the census to local community groups; (2) distribute census literature; (3) encourage cooperation from hard-to-enumerate groups. Major black organizations sent census publicity materials to their affiliates and urged cooperation.	(1) advisory committees--black, Spanish-origin, and Asian and Pacific Americans; (2) national services program--contact with national minority organizations; (3) community services program--up to 200 representatives will maintain contact with local community leaders and organizations.
Special Enumeration Efforts in Large Cities	
In the 20 largest cities, there was management of field offices by Census Bureau professional staff; fewer workers per supervisor; higher pay rates; smaller enumerator and office workloads.	Special efforts will not be limited to the 20 largest cities.
Team Enumeration	
This program was used informally for clean-up work.	Plans are to use team enumeration more, especially for follow-up visits to difficult-to-enumerate inner city areas at the discretion of the district office.
Walk-In Assistance Centers	
There were centers in the 20 largest cities. People could call or visit for help in filling out forms. Some bilingual staff were employed. (According to the Census Bureau, there were more telephone calls to district offices than calls or visits to walk-in centers.)	Centers will be established in major cities for use in recruitment, testing, training, and help in filling our forms. (District office telephone inquiry service will also be continued.)
Foreign Language Aids	
Instruction sheets in Spanish were mailed out with regular questionnaires in some places and were available in other selected parts of the U.S. Enumerators were furnished with the translation. Similar aids were available in Chinese (but not mailed out).	All English-language forms will have a notice in Spanish that a Spanish-language questionnaire is available by calling in or marking a circle and mailing back the English-language form.

Another procedure that will be moved from the status of a post-enumeration statistical check to an integral part of the enumeration is at least some of the matching to nonhousehold sources of information (e.g., drivers' licenses or records of the Immigration and Naturalization Service). Enumerators will go back to households in which it appears from the matching that a person was missed, try to verify his or her residence there, and complete the enumeration. Results of using this method in test censuses show that it is effective in finding people. As with the vacancy check, this method augments the count in the proper location, rather than providing only a statistical measure of error in the census. It also provides rich information about the characteristics of individuals who were missed, on the basis of which methods might be developed to reduce the problem in future censuses or make adjustments for it. This analytical use will require that these cases be marked as having been located only by file-matching.

Still another procedure that will be used during the enumeration period, rather than after the census as in 1970, is the post office check in conventional (non-mail-out) areas. Once again, this will allow for coverage improvement before district offices close rather than relying solely on imputation.

The Panel notes that inevitably there will be cases in which the barest minimum of information about the existence of people in a location will be available. Situations will arise in which the Census Bureau is unable to interview members of a household and has to depend on information from neighbors, or in which a questionnaire page containing necessary information was damaged, not clearly marked, or improperly microfilmed or read by FOSDIC (film optical sensing device for input to computer). In such cases, characteristics are imputed by the computer program. The rule in 1970 was that a person was considered to have been enumerated if the questionnaire contained items for at least two basic characteristics. This rule is obviously arbitrary. On one hand, a single entry hardly seems enough to assure that it was more than a smudge, nor is it much basis for allocating other characteristics. On the other hand, three entries would provide more assurance than two, but might be too rigorous a standard. (Information reported for a lodger or a domestic servant, or information reported by a neighbor, may often be minimal. On the other hand, two marked circles could result when a respondent or enumerator had started to record information for an individual, remembered that the person should be enumerated elsewhere--for example, a student away at college or a relative stationed at a military base--and failed to erase the marks. An overcount could thus result.) The Panel notes the conflict between quality of data in the census and completeness of coverage; we do not recommend any change in the rule.

The Panel is concerned that reliance on postal delivery means there will be no personal contact with a large proportion of households, and respondents who need help in understanding what is wanted may not get it. The result may be that some members of the household are missed in the listing of persons in the household (question 1). It also may result in fewer requests for a Spanish-language questionnaire than are really warranted because of the limited ability of some households to respond according to the instructions printed on the English-language questionnaire. The low rate of requests for Spanish-language questionnaires noted in the pretests may reflect factors such as diffidence or unwillingness to bother the authorities. If an enumerator came around to drop off the census questionnaire, identification of linguistic abilities could in many cases be determined, and the appropriate form (either English-language or Spanish-language) could be left with the respondent.

In sum, a review of the changes in coverage improvement procedures for 1980 (compared to 1970) indicates some rather positive efforts. Integrating several 1970 post-enumeration procedures into the 1980 census operation should decrease, although it will not entirely eliminate, the need for imputation.

Improvement of the community education and public information programs and increased contacts with minority organizations should encourage mail response in 1980, although the contribution of these programs to that end will be difficult to evaluate.

Most of the efforts listed as improvements in coverage are logical extensions of programs used in the 1970 census. Only 3 major new procedures are planned: the household roster (question 1); the matching to nonhousehold sources lists; and local review. The first is a method that will be used in the office check to ensure that all persons listed on question 1 are included in the questionnaire. All discrepancies will be checked further.

It was noted above that the greatest potential for further coverage improvement lies in measures to reduce the numbers of persons missed within enumerated households, including the program of matching with nonhousehold sources. Although lacking information on specific procedural details, the Panel is concerned about this potentially important program. The availability of lists for all areas of the country, the effect of geographic mobility on the timeliness and accuracy of the lists, as well as the enormous, time-consuming effort required for manual record matching will necessarily require a large investment on the part of the Census Bureau. One issue to which the Census Bureau should be sensitive is what perceptions respondents have of how the Census Bureau obtained their name and address. In addition, a cost-effectiveness study should be conducted of this program to ensure that it will not interfere with or drain away from required enumeration procedures.

The special enumeration efforts (essentially, more staff and better supervisors) in the difficult-to-enumerate areas--used in the 20 largest metropolitan areas in 1970--will be extended to all metropolitan areas in 1980. This is a commendable improvement, and the Panel hopes that the quality of enumeration made possible by this concentration of effort will not be diluted by spreading it too widely.

All these extra efforts to improve the enumeration will be costly. The draft budget for the 1980 census includes approximately $154 million for new and intensified procedures specifically designed to improve coverage. Among the elements that are estimated at over $10 million each are improved address listing procedure in rural areas; the use of name lists from independent records to check for omissions from the census questionnaires; providing local officials with population and housing counts and keeping the temporary district offices open after the enumeration is completed to receive and review challenges by the local officials; a recheck of all housing units reported as vacant or nonexistent by the initial enumerators; a systematic check of the master address list in city areas by census employees; and a community services program with about 200 specially selected employees to help elicit the support and active cooperation of minority communities at the grassroots level. Some other elements include a special program for Indian reservations, the use of a Spanish-language questionnaire, and an expanded public information campaign with particular emphasis on minorities. In addition, a substantial part of an additional $114 million, designated for improvements in field management, relates to aspects of the data collection operation that focus on better coverage. The 1980 census should be more complete than it would be without these measures, whose aggregate cost is probably over $200 million, but the degree of success cannot be forecast.

Recommendations

1. Experiments with an enumerator dropping off the questionnaire, describing the census process, answering inquiries, listing household members, helping where it may be necessary, and then leaving the form to be completed and mailed in should be conducted in difficult-to-enumerate areas, either before or during the 1980 census. Tests should be made to see if this procedure results in a higher mail return rate, a more complete listing of persons living in the household (as judged by matching records and post-enumeration surveys), and more requests for a Spanish-language questionnaire.

2. With the cost of the 1980 census projected to be close to $1 billion, the Census Bureau will want to consider the cost-effectiveness of various procedures to improve enumeration. To aid in this consideration, the Census Bureau should compile data, as in some test censuses and as in 1970, on the cost and the effect of each procedure in increasing coverage.

3. The Census Bureau should study the pros and cons of more extensive matching than is now planned for use during the enumeration process and undertake experiments in a few places to provide guidance for 1985 and later. The difficult issue of privacy that is involved has to be balanced against the opportunity to improve the count.

Note by the Chairman

A reviewer well acquainted with the results of procedures and tests in earlier censuses expressed concern that while the report contains a number of references to the escalating cost of a census and the need to use cost-effective methods for coverage improvements, "the Panel has generally not taken into account information on this subject available from the 1970 or earlier studies, including various special studies and pretests. With the exception of a few paragraphs on cost, there seems to be a tacit acceptance of the fact that any procedure that may yield even minor improvements in coverage should be added to the Census.

"[I am] concerned that some of the methods planned for 1980 will have a quite low payoff, considering their cost.... These include especially: (a) The matching of name lists from independent records against Census returns... (b) Keeping the temporary district offices open after enumeration is completed to react to reviews of counts provided by local communities... (c) Taking large-scale post-enumeration surveys...to obtain independent lists to check against the Census returns....

"[I am] not suggesting that the Panel should recommend the elimination of these procedures. However,...the implications should be brought out and emphasized more strongly.

"...while some of the procedures look as if they'll have a rather minor effect on the population counts, they may appear useful for public relations. [I] do not question expenditures for this purpose.

"The [report] properly points out that the attempts to improve coverage are within certain constraints, and seems to assume that the constraints cannot be bridged. [I] think it would be worth expanding on this issue. ...[I am] not convinced that the sacrifices the U.S. population would be called on to make, if some of the constraints were removed, are all that great.

"...it is likely that we are close to the limit of coverages improvements that are possible by addition and change in Census procedures and by better recruitment methods. If it is important to society to have a better Census, then society will have to accept some of the burden, in addition to paying for the Census.

"...[I] believe the evidence from prior studies is quite strong that improved coverage beyond that achieved in 1970 must come from improved public desire to be covered and to cooperate (especially among some of the groups in which undercoverage has been a special problem), rather than improved Census procedures. In this regard the Panel's emphasis on public relations is well placed."

The Panel as a whole did not have an opportunity to consider these views. On behalf of the members I point out that they put a high value on improvements in coverage; that some estimates of cost and effectiveness were provided by the Census Bureau, but as of this date these are limited; and that keeping temporary district offices open longer has the additional purpose of improving public relations. I am sure that the members would agree with the reviewer that a significant component of any improvement in coverage must come from greater public cooperation.

Nathan Keyfitz

CENSUS STAFFING PROBLEMS AND ISSUES

The staffing problems and issues of the 1980 census arise largely out of a special characteristic of the decennial population census in the United States: this enterprise, so important to national welfare and to the economic and political interests of every individual and category in the population, will depend on the efforts of approximately one-quarter million temporary employees who have virtually no prospect of continuing employment in the Census Bureau. How can it be assured that they will do the meticulous and painstaking tracking down of every last household and person that is required to get a complete enumeration? That their ways of relating to respondents will engender trust and complete and accurate response?

The most difficult staffing problem of the 1980 census has to do with obtaining competent workers in today's labor market who will be able and willing to take temporary but full-time jobs to interview in the poorer and physically deteriorating sections of the cities and among racial and ethnic minorities. Two characteristics of today's labor market are directly relevant to the recruitment and the deployment of enumerators. One is that more women, especially the married women upon whom the Census Bureau depended for many of its enumerators in prior censuses, now have jobs; the other is that the unemployment rate among minorities in the urban centers continues to be disproportionately high. That there should be concern about recruitment and selection of the most effective enumerators at the same time that the unemployment rate is high among segments of the minority populations underscores the complexity of this unique staffing problem and suggests some of the equity and political, as well as technical, considerations that affect it.

The approach to staffing problems, the priorities given them, and the means chosen to deal with them tend to reflect a combination of technical concerns, organizational restraints, and fiscal limits, as well as factors external to the Census Bureau. Among other things, the problems of selecting and using temporary staff are affected to an unknown degree by the tendency (as perceived by some social scientists familiar with the Bureau's activities) for temporary employees to perceive regular Census Bureau employees--a rather specialized group of managers, technicians, and scientists--as insiders, immediately responsive to themselves and to their organizational imperatives, while regular employees perceive temporary non-scientific and non-technical personnel in instrumental terms as outsiders.

Many of the issues surrounding recruitment and selection of temporary staff for the decennial census are seen by the Census Bureau as relating primarily to its ability to conduct the census effectively. At the same time, these issues, like the goal of a more complete enumeration, may be seen as reflecting larger political and economic realities and their racial, ethnic, and class dimensions. Seen in this light, enumerator issues bear on sharing in economic rewards and in political power, i.e., temporary jobs in the short run but much more in jobs, income, and political participation in the not-so-long run. Attitudes on census employment policies reflect the premises with which one starts.

Before discussing specific procedures and some issues related to enumeration and other temporary work, it is important to stress several important facts: the Panel found the managers and professionals of the Census Bureau to be fully aware of the range of problems and issues that are involved in the staffing of a decennial census and also of many topics about which research is needed (for example, in the dynamics of the interaction between the interviewer and the respondent). The Panel believes that the Census Bureau has had significant success in dealing with a variety of technical and managerial problems.

Recruitment

According to current plans, recruitment for the 1980 census will involve several mechanisms: (1) a political referral system, details of which are currently being worked out; (2) appeals for applicants as part of an informational and public relations program that in some instances will be tailored for a particular geographic area or category of the population; (3) the use of 180 to 200 community service specialists who will work through various organizations, such as those serving blacks, Hispanics, American Indians, and Asian and Pacific Americans; and (4) the use of state employment services and other hiring channels.

Recruitment of staff is an important, if not always explicit and direct, component of the Census Bureau's continuing information and public relations programs. Although direct recruiting activities begin to accelerate during the first part of the census year, recruiting is continuous in the sense that the public image the Census Bureau seeks to create and to maintain is a key factor in attracting personnel. The Census Bureau is also aware that the experiences of temporary workers during one census may be factors that affect their willingness, and the willingness of others, to work in the next census. The Census Bureau sees its efforts to develop recruiting practices and selection criteria in keeping with federal equal employment opportunity (EEO) guidelines as matters of law, good and efficient practice, ethics, and good public relations.

Recruitment appeals were parts of the public information programs the Census Bureau carried out in conjunction with the 1980 pretest censuses in Travis County (Austin), Texas; Camden, New Jersey; and Oakland, California. In the Travis campaign there was heavy reliance on brochures and other printed handouts, traditional newspaper, radio, and television materials, and mobile assistance vans. A Spanish-language television station in San Antonio, with many viewers in the Austin area, used the press release material and public service announcements. In Travis County and Oakland, a flyer program was carried out in the elementary schools for grades four through six.

In 1980, as in 1970, the Census Bureau will seek the assistance of the representatives of national and local organizations to help in the recruitment of minorities. In 1970, the 21 community educators who were employed and assigned to 11 headquarters cities served as recruiters and public liaison officers. The Census Bureau's evaluation of the 1970 efforts at improving coverage concluded that the effects of the community education part of the program are not measurable, but are probably helpful (Census 1974a, p. 18):

> ...the Bureau is considering plans to expand the community education program beyond its 1970 scope by staffing more community educators, hiring them earlier in the decennial period, and giving them more extensive training. In addition, a pilot program is currently underway to retain a nucleus of the community education program during the intercensal period as a part of continuing community education program.

For 1980, a minority statistics program has been established: to inform minority people about the usefulness, to them, of statistics provided by the Census Bureau; to assist them in the use of such statistics; and to obtain their recommendations and support towards improving coverage and quality of data for the 1980 census. The three components of that program are: (1) the three census advisory committees on the black population, on the Spanish-origin population, and on the Asian and Pacific Americans population; (2) the national services program--for work with minority organizations that are national in scope; and (3) the community services program--for work with minority individuals and groups at the local level.

The central office staff of the community service program has the responsibility for developing technical guidelines for a program that will be staffed by 180 to 200 community service specialists who will work under regional office supervision with organizations and other communications networks serving minorities. Through these organizations and networks, the specialists will work to establish credibility for the Census Bureau, reduce hostility and apathy, and increase cooperation.

In 1970, the community educators and the local and national groups served many functions for the census, substantive as well as symbolic and public relations. The Census Bureau's evaluations of their efforts tend to be restrained and mixed for a number of reasons, many of which are recognized by the Census Bureau staff, including insufficient staffing and lack of follow-up and unreasonable or unrealistic expectations of what organizations and presumed leaders could accomplish.

The reports of the Census Bureau and of the 1970 community educators themselves conclude that one of their more effective functions was to recruit enumerators for the district offices in the areas they were assigned. More thought needs to be given to the implications for recruitment of the fact that this was judged to be one of the most effective ways in which local representatives were used in 1970. Perhaps since they are so effective in recruitment, this aspect of their work should be given more emphasis.

Selection

The key to hiring competent census employees is adequate screening and selection. The process of selecting enumerators and other temporary staff will involve three formal mechanisms: an application form, a written test, and an interview. Since 1975, and following the Supreme Court rulings on EEO guidelines on employee selection procedures, a validation team of the Census Bureau has been developing and testing procedures, primarily the written test. The validation team reports, however, that substantial consideration is being given to the interview and other selection procedures.

The application form is in the process of being redesigned, based on job analysis findings. It will be used to get some of the most important kinds of information about candidates for temporary jobs as enumerators, clerks, and district office managers. Information requested on this form may include physical condition, ability to work under certain kinds of conditions, familiarity with one's neighborhood, and willingness to work with some people who are hostile and uncooperative (questions that may be more informative to the applicant than the answers will be to the Census Bureau).

Extensive job analysis, test writing, and field tests were carried out in order to develop a shortened version of the field selection aid test for use during the census dress rehearsal in the spring of 1978. The qualifications analysis phase of the job analysis sought to determine (Lacey et al. 177, p. 5):

> ....the most important or key knowledge, skills, abilities and personal characteristics (KSAP's), to distinguish between those required upon entry into the job and those required at full performance level, to differentiate between those KSAP's which are applicable in qualifying persons for a position and those which are used in ranking them, and to determine which KSAP's one could practically expect applicants from the probable labor source to possess.

The Census Bureau plans to rely heavily on the combination of a short, simple, structured interview and the application form to obtain information about the personal qualities and abilities of candidates who might be called upon to work in the more difficult and sensitive areas. An early draft of the guide for the interview covered the following: a description of the precanvass, pretest, or follow-up enumerator job; a question about the applicant's willingness to ask personal questions in the follow-up; determination of a candidate's interest in and availability for census work; assessment of a candidate's ability to understand and to be understood in English;

inquiry regarding a candidate's access to a car in areas where a car is necessary; and where applicable, an assessment of a candidate's ability to communicate in a language other than English. The interviewers are also to report any indication of a candidate's inability to deal with the public in a friendly and pleasant way. The main factor in the decision of the Census Bureau to rely heavily on a short interview, rather than an extensive, probing one, for hiring appears essentially a practical one: most of those conducting the interviews will have had little training (Lacey et al. 1977).

The aim of the validation effort of the Census Bureau is to design and implement a set of selection procedures, all of which have content validity and at least one of which--the written test--has predictive validity. At the time the statement on validation was prepared by Lacey and others, statistical analysis of the critical and specific questions having to do with the characteristics that are related to doing an effective job in difficult areas and among different categories of the population had not been completed. A criterion-related study is now under way. One aim is to develop a test that will take no more than one hour.

Validation efforts are directed to the validity of the selective criteria for different subgroups of applicants--men, women, blacks, Spanish Americans, Asian and Pacific Americans, American Indians, and all others--as called for under federal executive agency guidelines on employee selection. In the Oakland pretest, efforts were made to evaluate the predictive validity of the test, and the statistical validation done in Oakland is being repeated during the 1978 dress rehearsals in Richmond, Virginia, and in lower Manhattan, New York. There are plans to draw a sample in 1980, to represent all census employees, whose performance records would be compared to their test scores. Although the continuing validation efforts will produce data on the proposed tests as selection devices, there remain questions on whether these efforts in their present form will or can succeed in identifying in satisfactory ways effective enumerators for the most difficult jobs, those involving tough or challenging situations and representing the most intractable problems of census enumeration. These skills involve personality qualities not easily measured.

The Census Bureau staff is acutely aware that the evaluation of enumerator performance in relation to enumerator characteristics is complex and difficult, and in particular that one danger is that all of the important variables have not been isolated. Depending on the indicators used, it is possible to arrive at different results. Most of the studies of interviewer performance that have been done were of the continuing survey programs and are not relevant to performance in a population census lasting only a few weeks. But among the relevant findings are these two: rates of failure to get interviews are functions of the characteristics of individual interviewers rather than of the area in which the interviews are conducted; and peak earnings for interviewers do not come until most of the enumeration job is completed.

Training

The training procedures planned for temporary staff for the 1980 census are basically continuations of practices in past censuses. There will be heavy reliance on some sort of job simulation in a classroom setting, using a verbatim training guide. As part of the census pretest, the Census Bureau has tested some new techniques, including group/classroom training, the use of audio-visual aids, and role playing.

Members of the minority advisory committees and observers of pretests have been particularly critical of the training of enumerators. An observer of the Camden pretest reported (Azores 1977):

> ....it was my impression that the training received by the enumerators and office workers did not prepare them adequately for performance of their duties. The lack of qualified training was reflection not so much on the ability of the local trainers as on the quality of the training manuals and the instruction and supervision (or in some cases, the lack of them) received from headquarters.

A 1970 enumerator variance study provided a mixed picture with reference to enumerators' evaluation of training. Among other results: slightly more than 1 in 5 thought their training was confusing; almost 1 in 3 said the training materials should be made more understandable; 1 in 8 said more qualified persons should conduct the training; and 1 in 3 said that problems arose during enumeration that were not covered in the written instructions or training sessions; however, 3 in 5 said that the handbook helped them greatly, and 3 in 4 said the training was clear (Census 1972).

In 1970, training of census employees proceeded by echelons, and the training of the enumerators differed according to the nature of the job. In the case of enumerators, in mail-out areas where a decentralized organization was operating, training was conducted in four separate sessions related to the four phases of the job: (1) practice exercises on check-in of mail returns; (2) practice in editing short questionnaires; (3) practice in review and editing of long questionnaires; and (4) training in the technique of follow-up by telephone and home visits. If 1970 training procedures are followed, the prime responsibility for the training of enumerators will fall on crew leaders.

Organization of Work and Remuneration

The recruitment, selection, training, productivity, and turnover of enumerators and other temporary staff are related in important ways to the manner in which the work of the enumerators is organized: for example, whether by individual workers or by teams of workers. They are related as well to how workers are paid and when--by the hour, by the piece, or by salary, and at weekly, bi-monthly, or other intervals.

Pay for Enumerators

Clarity about the basis and the frequency of payment of enumerators is probably as important a factor in affecting turnover and morale among enumerators as is the actual rate of pay. There is evidence that some enumerators have quit because they needed work that provided early payment.

Observers of the Camden and Oakland pretests have reported that the informational aspects and the procedures with regard to pay for enumeration need a great deal of improvement. Robert Hill of the

National Urban League, who is a member of the Census Bureau advisory committee on the black population, in his appearance before the House Subcommittee on Census and Population in June 1977, said (U.S. Congress 1977b, pp. 123-4):

> Perhaps the most difficult problem in conducting the census in inner-city areas is the high turnover rate among enumerators... This problem has been evident in all pretest operations and especially in Oakland. Our discussions with census personnel as well as community leaders revealed that deficiencies in recruiting procedures are a major factor in the high turnover rates.
>
> Hundreds of unemployed persons flocked to the recruiting centers ... as a result of newspaper ads stating that hundreds of census jobs were available at about $3.50 an hour or more. The ad did not make clear that the hourly rate was only a hypothetical average rate for persons completing a minimum number of questionnaires on a piece-rate basis. Moreover, the ads did not even make clear that office workers would be paid on an hourly basis, while enumerators would be paid on a piece-rate basis...
>
> Consequently, many persons felt that the Census Bureau had deliberately deceived them... Their anger and resentment took on an added intensity in Oakland because they often did not become aware of this "deception" until after they had been subjected to a 2 1/2-3 hour test. Clearly, Bureau ads in the future must distinguish between hourly and piece-rate opportunities.

Use of Team Enumeration

The Census Bureau appears to have backed into the use of team enumeration, and its approach to team enumeration in 1980 is cautious. One suggestion for overcoming the various problems associated with enumeration in the inner city was to form teams of enumerators to work in these areas. In the 1970 census, that use was based on considerations of safety and related to problems of recruiting and retaining enumerators for inner-city areas. In "Plans for Improvement of Coverage in the 1980 Census," the rationale and questions about the procedure are presented (Census 1977d, p. 10):

> The hypothesis is that teams can do the work faster; members of teams will feel safer working together rather than alone and so will be more likely to enter the areas as required; and we will be better able to recruit qualified staff.
>
> There are a number of things we will want to look at in this procedure. (a) How does one pre-identify areas where team enumeration is required (since this is a costly procedure we would want to use it only where required)? (b) At what stage in the field work do we implement the procedure? (c) How does one implement the procedure to make it most effective -- size of team, how they work together in an ED, how assignments are made and progress evaluated?

Tests to try to answer some of these questions about team inteviews were conducted in Camden and Oakland. The key concerns were: production rates, enumerator turnover, and coverage by teams. In Camden, two types of teams were formed: teams of two enumerators (pairs) teams of about 8-10 enumerators in which the crew leaders accompanied the enumerators into the area and coordinated the work assignments (Census 1977f, p. 13).

> Preliminary indications are that production rates were similar among the two test procedures and the control procedure, that is, a single enumerator working alone. There is some indication that the turnover rate in the pairs was higher than in the control procedure or the crew leader-accompanied procedure.

Thus it appears that the Census Bureau rightly sees the team approach or technique not in "either/or" terms, but as one of a battery of accepted techniques.

Summary

Both representatives of minority groups and Census Bureau regular staff are committed to making the 1980 census count as complete and accurate as possible. In light of evidence that blacks have been seriously undercounted and the likelihood that other minorities have been undercounted, it is clearly important to recruit minority enumerators who will be accepted by members of their own group, who are qualified and motivated to perform, and who will be adequately trained to obtain and record the information called for on the census questionnaires.

Review of the 1970 experience and plans for recruitment and selection of enumerators and other temporary staff for 1980 indicates that the Census Bureau is attempting to improve selection procedures, particularly as they affect members of minority groups, whose participation is recognized as essential for the successful completion of the census in hard-to-enumerate areas, and that the Bureau is aware of the factors that exacerbate the turnover of temporary staff, with its attendant costs and other problems. The Panel wishes to encourage research that is in progress on staff selection aids and planning for cooperative programs using colleges and high schools in recruitment as well as general informational efforts.

The Panel's necessarily brief review of the staffing problems of enumeration recognizes the complexity of the issues--the intricate interplay and tension between political and technical considerations in decisions about who the enumerators are, how they are selected, and how they are organized and used in work situations. In view of the complexity of the issues and the short time available for study, the Panel offers only a few relatively minor and tentative suggestions on this topic.

Recommendations

4. In order to ensure competent temporary staff, improve morale, and reduce turnover, the Census Bureau should emphasize a number of actions already planned, including the following:

a. Provide more explicit information in recruitment about the types of work and work schedules, the different bases of payment (piece work versus hourly or other time rates), and the frequency of payment. The Census Bureau should also provide more information about the products of the census and what is done with them that has importance for the temporary worker, the workers' family, and the worker's community.

b. Monitor the staffing, mechanics, and content of the selection interview, which is possibly the most critical link in the chain of selection devices in view of the variety of referral sources used. The Census Bureau should also extend its reseach on selection tests in an effort to find better ways of identifying those applicants who are most likely to be effective interviewers in challenging situations.

c. Experiment further with various types and sizes of teams for enumeration, including peer groups among young adults, and the relationship of team enumeration to other ways of organizing enumerators' work under certain conditions.

5. As a means of improving the performance of enumerators and other temporary staff, the Census Bureau should make every effort to improve the materials and logistics for training. As a complement to these efforts, the Census Bureau should give added attention to selection and training of crew leaders, whose pivotal role as members of the field staff includes training of enumerators.

6. The Census Bureau should try to make the experience of the temporary employee more satisfying by making some concrete gesture when the work is completed, perhaps a certificate that would indicate that census work is an investment in the individual's future; this would be particularly valuable to young workers in applying for other jobs.

THE PUBLIC INFORMATION AND COMMUNITY RELATIONS PROGRAMS

In a broad sense, the census involves the government's attempt to communicate with the people in a detailed and specific way--by sending out a set of questions (messages) and by receiving replies to those questions (feedback) from the people. Incompleteness of coverage, viewed in this way, may be thought of as a failure or breakdown in the communicative process. The failure may involve any stage of the process: (1) a failure to deliver the messages to the people; (2) a failure to attract the attention of the people to the messages; (3) a failure to send messages that are properly perceived or understood, as for example, sending the forms in a language that some people cannot read or sending forms that contain questions that are too difficult for people to answer; (4) a failure to send messages that properly motivate people to respond, as for example, giving inadequate explanations of why detailed information is needed; (5) a failure to send messages that can be acted on in the social setting in which the potential respondent lives--is it reasonable to assume, for example, that undocumented aliens in the American Southwest live in a social climate that will permit them to answer the kinds of questions included in the census?

The communicative process may also break down from the effect of adverse publicity. Last-minute unfavorable or sensational news stories ridiculing the questions asked or highlighting charges of discrimination could seriously reduce the mail-back rates. Thus, the information program of the census involves not only the attempt to publicize the census favorably through the mass media, but all aspects of the census process that involve sending messages that may or may not be received, understood, accepted, or acted upon.

An attempt was made by the Panel to examine the communication plans for the 1980 census. As our staring point, we summarized the recommendations about communication found in America's Uncounted People (NRC 1972):

1. That a nationwide study of attitudes toward privacy and anonymity be conducted.

2. That a survey be made to gain a better understanding of how the census is perceived.

3. That census public informational material be thoroughly pre-tested.

4. That a content analysis be made of the national media effort.

5. That the effects of the public information campaigns be carefully evaluated.

6. That sufficient funds be provided for research to permit purchase of advertising.

In summary, that the utility of communication research as an instrument for gaining a better understanding of the reasons for census and survey undercoverage should be fully explored.

In general, we found Census Bureau knowledge of communications, broadly conceived, to be relatively unchanged from the time of the 1972 report, although some recent and encouraging advances have been made. In particular, we examined Census Bureau activities in light of the 6 recommendations of the 1972 study.

1. The Census Bureau sponsored an exploratory study by the National Research Council (1979) on the effects that aspects of privacy and confidentiality, and people's perceptions of them, have on the ability of federal statistical agencies to collect full and accurate information from individuals and households. Some of the results of this study have already been published (Goldfield at al. 1978). The Census Bureau is studying the findings of this study to determine what they suggest about the public's perception of confidentiality provisions.

2. The same study also contained questions bearing on the public's image of the census and its understanding (or lack of understanding) of the purposes and methods of the census. Surveys and interviews to test the effectiveness of advertising themes were made by the Census Bureau or on contract for the Bureau in connection with the Oakland pretest and the Richmond dress rehearsal. The findings from these studies are being carefully examined and may have some impact on the 1980 census.

3. Some testing is now going on in the census pretests and dress rehearsals of census public information materials. In Camden, for example, a small-scale sample survey was carried out ". . . to evaluate the effectiveness of the public information program and to examine the possible intervening effects of attitudes and knowledge

about the census" (Census 1976a). Also in Camden, two versions of a "Dear Friend" letter accompanying the census form were tested to see whether differential effects on mail returns could be detected (Census 1978a). Such beginning efforts should continue to be encouraged in the census. The Panel could find little evidence to suggest that formal pre- or post-testing of news releases and public service advertising using quantitative methods was planned for the dress rehearsals or for the 1980 census itself.

4. So far as the Panel was able to learn, no comprehensive content analysis of public media in the 1970 census has been carried out. While there are estimates that public service advertising carried in newspapers in 1970 amounted to 939,500 lines of newspaper space and that network "home impressions" of spot television ads totaled 652,130,000, such impressive figures fail to include details such as the timing of the television advertising and the placement of the public service advertising in the newspapers (Census 1973). The estimate that the campaign was worth $10 million in media space and time must therefore be regarded with gentle skepticism until better documentation is presented. Studies that could provide such documentation were made in connection with dress rehearsal census in 1978, however, and the Panel hopes this will be done for the 1980 census.

5. As mentioned above (3.), the Panel in its brief review did not find any Census Bureau plans for a quantitatively based evaluation of commuication materials for the 1980 census. Quantitative as well as the qualitative evaluations made in past censuses are needed.

6. The question of purchased advertising for the 1980 census was raised in the planning process, but, apparently, no tests were made and paid advertising has been left out of budget planning for 1980. The Census Bureau plans to use again the voluntary efforts of the Advertising Council to produce its advertising and will rely on the generosity and public spirit of the media to carry it at no cost. The cost of advertising is the primary reason for accepting the service of the Advertising Council.

There are significant disadvantages associated with the choice of the Advertising Council. First, the Census Bureau will be dependent on the willingness of the particular advertising agency chosen by the Advertising Council to devote sufficient energy and resources to the campaign so that it will be effective and on the chosen agency's experience in relevant branches of advertising. The experience in 1970 demonstrates that this disadvantage is real. If it paid for advertising, the Census Bureau could purchase the services of outside consultants ad exercise control over the content and quality of their output. Second, the Census Bureau will have little control over the placement or media used. An otherwise effective campaign can be buried in the back pages of newspapers or in obscure time slots on television. Third, the Census Bureau will not have control over the timing of the compaign. The campaign should be relatively concentrated in a few weeks surrounding the census; by accepting the services of the Advertising Council, the Census Bureau loses the ability to control the momentum of the campaign. Finally, the publicity should be concentrated disproportionately on the groups likely to be underenumerated, but there is evidence that the press and radio serving ethnic minorities can least afford to carry free advertising (Census 1977a).

The cost of paid advertising, though large in absolute numbers of dollars, would constitute only a small percentage of the cost of the 1980 census. If mail return rates would be increased by just a few percentage points by means of effective paid advertising, these costs might be largely offset by reduced costs of census field work. Advertising, which can be very productive if it is properly done, is a highly specialized field. In the judgment of the Panel, the benefits of the use of the Advertising Council are clearly outweighed by the disadvantages.

Various suggestions for publicity that could be implemented outside of the realm of paid or unpaid advertising were advanced in the course of the Panel's discussions. For example, the Census Bureau might collaborate with the Children's Television Workshop, which produces "Sesame Street" on public television, to present segments of the show on the census activity. The Census Bureau's work could be demonstrated either through the character of "the Count," who counts everything (and so introduces children to the concept of numbers) or in a street scene sketch. This publicity would not only inform children of their civic responsibility in future censuses, but might also expose their parents to the message. Whether or not this particular suggestion is feasible, similar imaginative approaches might pay off.

The Canadian concept of an intense, short-term publicity campaign peaking at April 1 was suggested by one Panel member as likely to arouse greater public interest than a long-term, low-key campaign. Another idea was a "practice census" to be used in elementary and secondary schools during the week before the census. It was urged that greater awareness of the census among children might result in better enumeration of hard-to-reach families. A third suggestion was that the mailing package itself be looked upon as an advertising medium and that the envelope, the "Dear Friend" letter, and the questionnaire be carefully reviewed by outside advisory groups for their communicative impact. The Panel members also observed that a considerable literature has emerged in the past decade on the media habits of various population subgroups and that this literature could profitably be reviewed by the Census Bureau's public information office in planning the final aspects of the 1980 information campaign.

Although there are encouraging signs that Census Bureau attitudes toward "soft" research are changing in fields such as communication methods and effects and that attempts are being made to keep abreast of the relevant literature, it is fairly obvious that further change must take place before the recommendation of the earlier panel will be carried out: "that the utility of communication research as an instrument for gaining a better understanding of the reasons for census and survey undercoverage be fully explored" (NRC 1972).

In addition to examining the follow-up to the recommendations of the earlier advisory committee, the Panel also noted some other aspects of the communication plans for the 1980 census.

The Census Bureau has improved its direct communication with minority communities in the last decade. In particular, we note with interest the appointment of minority advisory committees, which have been active in making recommendations to the Census Bureau (Census 1978c). While the recommendations of those committees have not always been followed, we believe that a channel has been set up and that communication is taking place. In addition, the Panel notes that community service representatives are scheduled to be on duty in the 12 Census Bureau regional offices in advance of and during the 1980 census. These representatives will have special responsibility for aiding attempts to reach minority groups with census messages (Census 1977c). These regularized procedures seem to us to be improvements over the ad hoc arrangements set up in 1970.

Of special concern to the Panel is the probable minor use in 1980 of the specially prepared Spanish-language questionnaires. If current plans are followed, 90 percent of all households will receive by mail questionnaires in English that contain a notation in Spanish telling them how to obtain a Spanish-language version of the questionnaire. In the Travis County (Austin, Texas) pretest, only 50 requests for Spanish-language forms were received (Census 1977e). In a county with 15,106 households with Spanish-speaking heads, the number of requests for the Spanish form intuitively seems small. (In Oakland, 94 requests were received for Spanish-language forms; in Camden, there were 133 requests [Census 1977e].) Procedures for getting Spanish-language versions of the questionnaire into the hands of the people who need them require the urgent attention of the Census Bureau.

In 1976 and 1977 the Census Bureau called together several ad hoc advisory groups on communications. These groups included staff of magazines and periodicals, newspaper industry officials, communications research experts from industry, broadcast media officials, advertising and market media officials, and others (Census 1977g). Memoranda from the groups seemed to our Panel to contain many sound suggestions for the public information program. In view of the need, as perceived by the Panel, for continued improvements in communications, the Census Bureau could benefit from having a communications advisory group on a more permanent basis.

Throughout all the census materials we studied, we encountered promising ideas for improving the communicative aspects of the census. What seemed to be lacking was a regularized way of testing these ideas through research. As one speaker on a media advisory committee remarked: "There's not one national company in the U.S. that doesn't take that step (research) before it markets a product" (Census 1976c). The Panel concurs and recommends that the Census Bureau continue to develop its research program on communications.

Recommendations

7. The Census Bureau should continue to develop its research program on communication aspects of the census, broadly conceived, as well as research on operational aspects of the communication program.
8. The Census Bureau should shift to paid advertising in 1980, rather than the free publicity provided through the efforts of the Advertising Council.
9. In view of the need for continued improvements in the Census Bureau's communications, we recommend that the Census Bureau establish a permanent communication advisory group.

THE QUESTIONNAIRE AND ITS EFFECT ON RESPONSE

The questionnaire used in a survey or census constitutes the central point of the operation. A great deal of thought goes into the selection of topics and the wording of particular questions. Other antecedent steps are directed at establishing the motivation for people to be included in and to cooperate with the census. Logistical activities related to the questionnaire include the delivery of the blank form and the retrieval of the completed one. After the questionnaire has been filled out, the forms are retrieved, the data are processed, and statistical summaries are developed and interpreted.

While much effort goes into the logistical and statistical activities, it is the questionnaire itself that is the personal link between the individual and the government. A person may understand the purpose of a census, its usefulness to the country, its importance to him or her, and the effort being made to obtain information and so may wish to comply with the request to cooperate. Yet this knowledge and understanding are mere abstractions. When the respondent is confronted with the questionnaire, he or she becomes personally involved. This is the moment when, for certain segments of the population, the decision about whether or not to cooperate is made. As Senator John Glenn stated in a letter to Dr. Nathan Keyfitz (January 5, 1978):

> We cannot attribute the undercount solely to negative views of the government. Incentive to cooperate may be lost anywhere during the process, such as when the questionnaire itself is received.

Decision points occur not only upon the initial receipt of the questionnaire, but also in the process of filling it out. Noncooperation may be reflected in casual, careless, or incomplete reporting as well as in non-return of the questionnaire. The former may be difficult to detect; the latter would require an enumerator visit and is therefore costly.

This section of the report deals with the effect of the questionnaire upon the completeness of coverage in the census. Although the main thrust of our comments relate to this factor, we have also examined the questionnaire in terms of related factors, such as the burden on the respondent and also the accuracy of responses that can be expected from the wording of particular questions. We have examined and reviewed much of the current literature and comments concerning the role of the questionnaire. Many of those comments are found in the recent hearings before the Subcommittee on Census and Population of the House Committee on Post Office and Civil Service (U.S. Congress 1977a, 1977b, and 1977c). Statements by legislators, city managers, representatives of planning commissions, the director of research of the National Urban League, spokesmen of varous other minority groups, social scientists, and a former and the present director of the Census Bureau were examined. (In addition, the report of the Commission on Federal Paperwork was studied.)

Although many divergent views were expressed concerning the role of the questionnaire per se in the completeness of coverage, it became apparent that other factors--social, economic and legal--may have an overall effect greater than the form and content of the questionnaire itself. Former Census Bureau director Richard Scammon said (U.S. Congress 1977a, p. 17):

> I would suggest that the problems of undercount that I saw indirectly, because I did not myself direct the census during the physical taking of a population census, were largely related to social circumstances in the area in which, whether you ask 5 questions or 50 questions and whether you have system A, scheme B, plan 4, or whatever it may be, you are really dealing with people problems rather than institution problems.

Much of the discussion in this section focuses on the long form, which will go to about 20 percent of the population (one-half in communities with less than 5,000 population, one-sixth in larger communities) and on which the economic and social characteristics and detailed housing data will be collected. Some of the comments also apply to the short form.

The questionnaire itself may affect the census operation in several ways. One occurs when the recipient does not fill out the questionnaire at all for reasons inherent in the format itself, requiring follow-up by personal visit. This may happen for several reasons. For some people, the initial visual impression of the questionnaire may make it seem more formidable than it actually is; for others, the format may be an obstacle: as a result, some people may not even attempt to fill out the form. Dr. Robert B. Hill, director of research of the National Urban League, commented on this in the congressional hearings (U.S. Congress 1977b, p. 121):

> Unfortunately, we do not feel that the form and content of the census forms will enhance the ability of less-educated households to respond. In fact, the proposed format for the forms in 1980 does not significantly differ from that used in 1970, although there are significant differences in some question content. But, overall, once again, we feel that greater consideration was given to facilitating computerized data processing than to significantly increasing response rates from less educated individuals and groups.

Other people may get started but will give up either because they find it difficult to understand the meaning of certain questions, are unable to answer certain questions, do not know how and where to put responses, or do not see the usefulness of certain questions. Dr. Hill also commented on this (U.S. Congress 1977b, p. 122):

> Unfortunately, the format of the income question currently in use in Oakland evokes unnecessary anger, hostility, and resistance because of its confusing format. Not only are individuals asked to write in their precise annual income, in not clearly specified spaces, but they are also asked to go through a rather complex coding procedure of filling in FOSDIC circles, supposedly below each income integer. Although a similarly formatted question on age and birth was also confusing, many more individuals, especially less-educated minorities, found the income question even more baffling. Many persons became angry with the question, not because they did not want to answer it, but because they could not understand how to properly answer it. Thus, it was left either completely blank or in various stages of incompleteness. At a minimum, the Bureau should leave the coding of this question to specially trained office clerks after the amount of income has been written in.

A greater likelihood of underenumeration arises when the completed questionnaire does not include the names of all persons who should be included. The problems of enumeration are affected by ambiguities in the role of the household as a social entity (see NRC 1972, pp. 57-68, and below). Household members will be omitted from the count if the respondent does not understand correctly who is to be included or consciously does not include certain persons. On the latter point, Richard Scammon, said (U.S. Congress 1977a, p. 16):

> I give you a specific case. My wife was a census taker in 1960, and she was told that many people, many families with large numbers of children or with extended family relationships, were very reluctant to identify the total number of people living in apartments because under many public health codes and under the housing codes, you are only allowed to have x number of people in the apartment. If you have got 2x, you are going to get thrown out of your apartment. So suddenly the family loses one uncle, one child, and grandmother because they want to stay there.

While ambiguity of definition and concealment of persons does not often arise, they may occur in those segments of the population that traditionally have been underenumerated.

Nonresponse to mailed questionnaires does not necessarily result in underenumeration because a follow-up by personal visit is made when the questionnaire is not mailed back. Nevertheless, an adverse reaction to the questionnaire could affect the completeness of enumeration in two ways. First, it could motivate incomplete listing of household members, either because the respondent omits listing a person to save time and trouble or because a household member does not want to be listed and forced to answer certain questions. The fact that the questionnaire has space for reporting details on only 7 persons may encourage omissions. Second, in more extreme cases respondents may be motivated to avoid enumeration of the household altogether by making themselves scarce when enumerators visit. If the case is closed out and information from neighbors relied on, the information might be incomplete as to number of persons in the household.

The same factors that influence respondents to return or not to return the questionnaire influence other behavior, including the care and thoroughness with which information is reported and the number of items not reported. Our comments and review of the long form used in the 1978 Richmond dress rehearsal (see Appendix B) relate to these broader response issues. We considered questionnaire factors that may affect: the response rates, including the overall return rate of the completed form and the frequency of nonresponse to individual items; the quality of the data, including the level of accuracy with which items of information are reported and the completeness with which the household members are listed; and the attitudes engendered toward the decennial census, toward the Census Bureau as an organization, and more generally toward the government and its data-gathering functions.

Some Background Concepts

Investigators are always concerned about ways to ensure the "willingness" of respondents to participate in surveys, whether by personal interviews or by self-administered questionnaires. Frequently overlooked, however, are the cognitive demands of the questionnaire itself and the effects of these demands on respondent motivation. It is too easily assumed that if the questions are clearly stated in easily understood language and specify precisely stated concepts, respondents will be both willing and able to provide the requested information. But the evidence is that, while these question characteristics have basic importance, they represent only some of the variables relating to the quality of respondent performance.

The nature of the task as perceived by the respondent--its complexity and acceptability--is a central element underlying the quality of the respondent's participation. Sudman and Bradburn (1974), in an analysis of several hundred surveys, found that variables relating to the task, and the demands made of the respondents, were central to an understanding of what determines the quality of the responses. (Although their analysis included only personal interview surveys, their conclusions relate perhaps even more strongly to self-administered questionnaires.)

Responding to questions requires effort and the willingness to expend this effort; it requires as well that the information requested be readily accessible to the respondent. Some questions require little in the way of effort, for example, "Is there a passenger elevator in this building?" Others require considerably more, such as total wages, salary, commissions, and bonus or tips from all jobs in 1977. Methodologists are coming to realize that responding to questions is often more cognitively and motivationally demanding than has been thought. A "job description" for the respondent's task would include the following:

1. The respondent must comprehend the question and related instructions. Comprehension requires both linguistic understanding and an unambiguous interpretation (understanding) of the variable underlying the question. Only if the respondent and the investigator have a shared interpretation of the question can one expect the response to meet the intended objective.
2. The respondent must search for and process information requested by the questions. For the census questions, this most frequently requires memory retrieval. Some information may be relatively inaccessible and may require considerable thought and effort to recall.
3. The respondent must evaluate the information in terms of whether it meets the question's specification. For example, "Is this really all of my income from salaries or have I overlooked something?" "Do I need to try to recall additional information?" If the answers to such questions suggest the need for additional information, more work is required of the respondent.

If the respondent can perform these tasks smoothly and easily, the result is good information. But often the processes are not performed adequately. One problem is the level of difficulty of the task and the respondent's willingness to work hard enough to perform well. Analysis of nonresponses and the quality of information reported in response to self-administered questions (mostly mail surveys) demonstrate that respondents perform well only those activities that are easy and acceptable. Higher-educated respondents consistently perform better both in responding and in the quality of the information reported for several reasons, including their acceptance of surveys and their greater skill and experience in reporting behavior (Scott 1961). The education-level effect reflects the fact that questions will pose different levels of difficulty for respondents of different educational levels and motivation. Lower-educated respondents have less expertise: they find it more difficult to read and grasp complex questions and instructions and to retrieve and organize the information needed. Higher-educated people have also been found to have a better appreciation of why they are asked to participate: they have more knowledge of the role of research and information acquisition and a greater acceptance of this role. Thus, higher-educated respondents find it both easier to perform the task and are more willing (motivated) to undertake it.

The difficulty of the task not only relates to how well it is likely to be performed, but also influences the willingness of the respondent to perform--whether the person finds it easy to comply with requests or becomes irritated or frustrated, developing negative attitudes toward the task and toward the agency conducting the survey.

Questionnaires and data-collecting instructions need to be considered from two frames of reference: cognitive and motivational. The cognitive frame can be examined by asking: Are questions and response-category instructions clear and readily understood? Is the perceived meaning what the investigator intended? The following specific factors are included:

Language: sentence structure, word difficulty, or ambiguity.

Sentence syntactic or structural complexity.

Concept complexity and clarity. Does the question clearly specify an unambiguous concept? How complex is the concept? Is it a single or multiple variable?

Response mode complexity. Do the response categories fit the respondents' information? Do the categories require a level of specificity or detail which increases the demands of the task?

Instruction complexity.

Format or layout clarity.

Although these factors are cognitive, they have major motivational implications. The more demanding the task, the greater the effort needed to perform it adequately and, consequently, the greater the motivation required to elicit the effort. When the demand is high, respondents are likely to do a poor job of reporting or may fail to respond at all. Resistance is generated when the task requires more effort than a respondent is willing to give. Thus, elements in the questionnaire and instructions that make the task difficult will reduce a respondent's willingness to exert the effort to report adequately.

There are other factors that are also powerful determinants of respondents' performance. A major positive force is the participation in a function specified in the U.S. Constitution. For many people, however, this is not sufficient to invoke the wholehearted cooperation needed. Research findings show that, in general, appeals to citizen responsibility and national welfare are not particularly powerful in inducing people to work hard at a reporting task. This means that such an appeal is adequate for obtaining easily accessible information, but often inadequate for information-reporting tasks that require greater effort.

Two particular types of tasks require especially strong motivation: questions requiring an effort to recall the information and to organize responses and questions asking for information considered to be personal or in some way threatening. Such items not only create resistance to providing the specific information requested, but may also create a general negative attitude toward completing the form and toward the government in general for asking such questions. The resistance potential is especially great when the respondent cannot see how a "difficult" question is related to a legitimate request for basic information about the population.

In personal interviews, the interpersonal interaction develops positive forces that encourage cooperation; these forces are missing in self-administered questionnaires. In self-administered questionnaires, the role of encouraging good performance must lie in the characteristics of the questionnaire itself--in questions that are convenient, easily responded to, and engage the person's interest.

This background sets out a frame of reference for considering the census questionnaire. It explains our concern about length and complexity of questions, attractiveness of layout, readability of format and type face, and the extent to which questions may appear to be difficult for some respondents.

It explains also the consideration of factors other than the response rate. From this frame of reference, the central issue is the respondent's involvement in the reporting job. There are several degrees of cooperation or effort in reporting. At one end of a continuum, the respondent fails to fill out or return the form. Along the continuum, the respondent may complete the form for the easily reported information and return it with a varying number of incomplete items, or the respondent may return a form that appears complete but the information may not be carefully evaluated since the respondent relied primarily on estimates or guesses. At the other end of the continuum is the ideal respondent who considers each question carefully, studies the instructions, evaluates each response, and responds completely and accurately.

Evaluation of the Questionnaire

The Panel studied the long form used in the Richmond dress rehearsal census question by question, looking for potential problems. We have not made a distinction between changes that might be implemented in 1980 and those that would not be possible until 1985, since these matters depend on administrative practicalities with which we are unfamiliar. In our discussion, we have assumed that the questionnaire will reach the household by a mail-out system (as is intended for 90 percent of the households in 1980), rather than being dropped off by an enumerator. We believe that the latter system would give much better results in low-response areas, and there are comments on this topic in other parts of this report.

We recognize that there are some persons who will not fill out a census form, no matter how well designed and attractive. Clearly a major effort has been made over the years by the staff of the Census Bureau to develop effective forms, and experiments with alternative formats are continuing. Our suggestions in many cases may therefore be ideas that have been considered and rejected for good reasons. Nevertheless, as interested outsiders we may be able to identify difficulties that have not occurred to those involved in the census.

The census is a major point of contact between the government and the individual. It is important not only to get a response, and to obtain complete and accurate information, but also to evoke a constructive attitude toward the Census Bureau and toward the government. The questionnaire is the point of contact, especially in the absence of any personal contact by an enumerator. If it appears to a somewhat confused recipient to be deliberately difficult or unclear, then the government will have lost not only facts but also a desirable rapport with those people who may need it most.

The Cover

The present cover is completely matter-of-fact and bureaucratic. (The short and long forms used in the Richmond dress rehearsal are reproduced in Appendix B.) It does nothing to persuade and interest the respondent and achieves nothing by way of rapport, which are matters of great importance, as discussed above. While the cover of the questionnaire might serve as a communication with a business firm or as a basis for an enumerator-administered inquiry, there is little that reflects the fact that it is self-administered and is addressed to individuals. Its arrival a few months after households have received their income tax forms in the mail, and not long before those returns must be filed, will not help its reception.

We understand that a covering letter will accompany the census form. However, a friendly communication with the respondent on the form itself, where it can be seen by all those who are expected to use the questionnaire, would be much better.

The Panel suggests that the cover of the questionnaire be modified to include a letter detailing 4 key facts about the census:

1. the census is an important occasion, for specified reasons;
2. it is obligatory (by law) that all respondents reply;
3. the information provided will be held confidential; and,
4. the form is not really difficult to fill out.

In addition, the letter should provide a general justification for the kinds of questions asked. The letter should also tell a respondent who desires further information how to obtain an explanatory booklet from the Census Bureau by a telephone call, a coupon, or some other easy and quick way.

The front of the form as now designed contains an item (2) that relates to uncertain information: "If you are not sure of an answer, give the best answer you can." The Panel has doubts about the wisdom of this statement since it may encourage individuals to conceal embarrassing information. We therefore recommend that consideration be given to omitting this item entirely.

Inside the Questionnaire: The Layout

An unsophisticated respondent opening the census long form between pages 6 and 19 (see Appendix B) could be pardoned for assuming that it was beyond his or her capacity, especially if the respondent has difficulty in reading. Such respondents are normally surveyed by enumerators and are seldom confronted with this mass of questions. In addition, such people often live on the fringe of the social and economic structure and are reluctant to disclose details about sources of income and family arrangements. Thus, they are unlikely to have a strong desire to overcome difficulties that exist in responding to the census.

There is undoubtedly a good deal of trade-off between the number and detail of census questions and the degree of response reaction. The Panel believes that the long form of the questionnaire represents a substantial burden on the respondent. We wonder whether the Census

Bureau has made an adequate balance of the cost and benefit of each additional question, which it is undoubtedly under pressure to add. For instance, is there sufficient additional advantage in adding question 10 (on highest school grade completed) to the form? Are housing questions H24, H25, and H26 (on condition of the building) all necessary? The Panel recognizes the pressures on the Census Bureau to obtain information on many subjects and supports its efforts to restrict questions to information that cannot be satisfactorily obtained by other means.

The initial impact of the form is confusing. The type is light and thus may be difficult for some to read; the use of slightly heavier type, especially where there is a blue background, would be an improvement. The Panel suggests that the location and register of the blue coloring should be re-examined generally and, in particular, in headings 29-31 and 33 where there are gaps (see Appendix B; the blue coloring, however, does not show in the facsimile).

The Panel considers the placement of the housing questions on the long form (between questions 10 and 11) unfortunate because a respondent may not complete the questions for all persons in the household. We recognize, however, that moving the housing section to the end of the form would create another problem; respondents with small households may never reach this section to respond to the questions.

Another difficulty is the location of space for office coding, which sometimes appears on the right-hand side of the page and is not clearly demarcated from the rest of the form. A respondent can confuse the office coding space with the column for responses. For example, on page 7, this coding area is too close to both columns of questions; on page 6, they are suitably separated.

It is worth re-examining the layout of the questionnaire, particularly the location of office coding space, and testing alternative layouts. This re-examination might involve modification or replacement of the present FOSDIC system by machinery with more flexible capability.

Presentation of Questions

We believe that further critical examination of the questions on the form would indicate scope for improvement; some examples follow.

Confusing Language. There may be a better way of expressing the idea in question 9 of high school being "finished by equivalency." It would be better to place "equivalent" in association with coding mark 12. In question 8 there is no indication of what a "regular school" is.

Complex Instructions. Question 5 imposes a duplicating task on the respondent in coding age. The instructions on the top of page 5 are quite demanding.

Complex Questions. The first question has a very complicated footnote that gets the respondent off to a reluctant start. The "skip" instruction in H13a is not necessary. In H10b it is not clear how to handle a business simply run from the house without special quarters. Under this heading also come problems with race and origin or descent (questions 4 and 7), which are discussed below.

Unknown Details. In the cases of tenants and multiple dwellings, many of the questions about date of construction and heating may not be known; a "Don't know" answer might be provided.

The Panel recommends that the Census Bureau simplify and make clearer the questions and instructions on the census form.

Pretesting the Questionnaire

Our emphasis in this section is on the questionnaire as it fosters or diminishes the respondent's willingness to report and the level of task difficulty posed by the questions, instructions, and format. Pretesting is one way in which such determinations can be made. We consider here one type of pretest, described below, that is particularly useful in evaluating the questionnaire from a respondent's point of view. This pretest is especially helpful with people who are likely to have response problems, such as the elderly and less-educated people. In our experience, this procedure, used before by the Census Bureau, is helpful in developing a respondent-oriented questionnaire.

In this type of pretest, a respondent is given the questionnaire and asked to complete it while an observer is present. The respondent is requested to verbalize his or her thoughts and questions as the form is being completed. This process provides cues to the observer of where difficulties are encountered; where interpretations of questions differ from that intended; where the respondent had difficulty in understanding the question, in recalling the information, or in understanding instructions. Following the completion of the questionnaire, the observer asks questions to determine what problems existed and the cause of the problems. Frequently, the respondent will suggest solutions. On this basis, questions can be redesigned and again pretested.

The Panel recommends that the Census Bureau conduct more pretests of questionnaires by this respondent-observer method.

Post-Enumeration Evaluation

From this same respondent-oriented frame of reference, we suggest some post-enumeration evaluations to prepare for the 1985 census. For example, the Census Bureau should undertake a comparison of self-enumeration and enumerator-administered procedures: using the same questionnaire, comparable samples will provide information on the relative quality of information and the comparability of task demands made by each of these two procedures. Household listing may be particularly benefitted by enumerator administration.

A method that may combine advantages of interview and self-enumeration is to have the schedule delivered in person, with the enumerator describing the process, answering inquiries, helping as necessary, and then leaving the form to be completed and mailed by the household member. We see this procedure, being used presently in the Canadian census, as possibly improving the data quality significantly. The enumerator's presence may be particularly useful in generating a willingness to perform well. Comparative costs of the two methods are obviously a relevant consideration.

Conclusion

In general, we recognize and endorse the efforts made by the Census Bureau to prepare a questionnaire that is clear and attractive to the respondent and that will provide the requested information. Among the Census Bureau staff responsible for tabulating the census information, however, it may be that primary consideration is occasionally given to convenience in processing or to the limitations imposed by the FOSDIC system. Our suggestions are intended to contribute to a balanced compromise to a difficult situation.

In the Panel's opinion, the length and apparent complexity of the long form of the questionnaire now being used in dress rehearsal censuses could discourage or reduce a respondent's willingness to exert the effort to report adequately and completely. The Panel has a number of recommendations on the format of the questionnaire itself and the clarity of, and rationale for, certain questions. These are discussed in the body of this chapter without attempting to identify positively which changes are practicable for 1980 and which could not be implemented until 1985 or later. Although the Census Bureau has had long experience in designing questions and questionnaire formats, new and changed questions are frequently introduced, and the juxtaposition of questions creates difficulties for respondents. With so large a proportion of the 1980 census depending on self-enumeration, we recommend that the present format and wording be reviewed with a view to facilitating respondents' understanding of and ability to respond to the questionnaire.

Recommendations

10. The Census Bureau should conduct more pretests, not as part of any dress rehearsal but in small surveys, in which the respondent is asked to complete the questionnaire in the presence of an observer, verbalizing thought processes, and questions, as the form is being completed. Following completion of the questionnaire, the observer would ask questions to determine what problems existed and the cause of the problems. Results from this type of pretest would facilitate question redesign for fuller respondent comprehension.

11. To prepare for the 1985 and later censuses, the Panel encourages the Census Bureau to conduct more tests, especially in difficult-to-enumerate areas, comparing self-enumeration and enumerator-administered procedures. These tests would provide valuable information on the relative quality of responses, the comparability of task demands made by each procedure, and on relative costs.

RACE AND ETHNIC ORIGIN

The census count for members of ethnic or racial groups may be too low if they are simply not included in the actual count (underenumeration) or if, although counted, they are not identified correctly as members of their particular group. The concern of many racial and ethnic groups that their members are undercounted could be directed at either or both of these causes. This section focuses on the question of racial and ethnic identification.

There are a number of reasons for interest in an accurate count of racial and ethnic groups. The most obvious is the desire and need for information on the number of members and on the social and economic characteristics of each group. In addition, minority groups perceive important advantages in getting the fullest count possible: these advantages include recognition, political influence, the setting of goals in affirmative action programs, and support for bilingual or bicultural education. Insofar as members of a racial or ethnic group have a higher-than-average underenumeration rate, any cities or states with high proportions of residents in that group will have high undercount rates and may therefore receive less funds or legislative representation than they should. Finally, racial and ethnic data from the census are necessary for the demographic techniques used to estimate the undercount, as well as for intercensal estimates of population used for revenue sharing. If there are misclassifications of race or ethnicity, or at least differences in such identification between the census and vital records, some procedures to reconcile these differences must be developed in order to use the demographic techniques to estimate the undercount, especially the differential undercount by race, and to estimate intercensal population size.

For these reasons, we gave specific attention to the race and ethnic origin questions in our review of 1980 census plans.

Race

The question on race plays an important role in the estimation of the undercount and especially in estimating differentials in the undercount and intercensal population. The information on differential undercount by race, along with similar information on age and sex, gives important clues on why people are missed and has led to programs to try to reduce the undercount. The Census Bureau is to be congratulated on its evaluation programs and the professional integrity it has and continues to exhibit in evaluating its performance and publishing the results.

The race question for the Richmond dress rehearsal actually includes racial and national origin categories.

4. Race *Fill one circle.*	White Black or Negro Japanese Chinese Filipino Korean Vietnamese Indian (Amer.) *Print tribe* →	Asian Indian Hawaiian Guamanian Samoan Eskimo Aleut Other — *Print race*

Most Panel members therefore considered the use of the term race inappropriate. The national origin groups mentioned in the race question include several individual Asian and Pacific island groups, American Indians (with instructions to print the particular tribe), Eskimo and Aleut, and finally "Other" (with instructions to print the race).

There are grounds for concern with the nationality groups of Asians included in the race question and the instructions for coding write-in answers for the "Other" category. The justification for the nationality listing of Asian countries was the experience in pretests that many failed to identify with the single category "Asian and Pacific Islander." However, the current list does not include "Other Asian," so Indonesians, Malayans, Thais, Cambodians, Burmese, and others would write in their nationalities and would have to be coded by hand during data processing. Addition of an "Other Asian" category would yield quickly a total for Asian and Pacific Americans.

The Census Bureau has performed some awkward lumping and splitting in an area of great sensitivity in American society. Although there are nuances of the white/black boundary, it is generally assumed that those two categories are socially well defined. The social importance and physical differences connected with the designation of race have been presumed to lend validity to a race question, whether an enumerator or the respondent made the decision as to racial classification. In fact, however, some Spanish-origin persons who might be expected to classify themselves as white or black report themselves as "Other" in response to the question on race. In the Oakland pretest a large number of persons of Spanish (primarily Mexican) background also listed themselves in the "Other" race category. A special sample of early mail returns and enumerator-filled questionnaires from Oakland indicates that about one-third of the persons reporting Spanish origin did not identify themselves in a special racial group but marked either the "Other" circle or no circle on the new version of the race question. The comparable proportion on the old version was 47 percent; most provided a Spanish write-in entry.

The coding instructions for the Richmond dress rehearsal provide that write-in answers for some Spanish-speaking countries under the "Other" race category be retained. The instructions also contain some changes, probably minor in their numerical impact, from past practice (e.g., Asian Indians are no longer classified "White"). There will be a problem in reconciling the results from self-identification in response to question 4 with data from earlier censuses. If it is assumed that vital records or other records used to evaluate coverage will contain an identification along more traditional lines (e.g., a child of Colombian background parents will be classified white), then it will be necessary to make some adjustments to the count that use the present version of coding instructions in order to employ demographic techniques to estimate undercount and to estimate intercensal population.

To a large extent, any recommendation rests on whether the current instructions lead to large difference in estimates as compared to allocation of write-in answers to different categories. If differences are very small, a sound judgment may well be to follow the proposed procedures. If the effect on the demographic estimates of undercount and intercensal population are small, the availability of documentation of a social change regarding racial identity may be well worthwhile, especially if comparisons can be made among answers to race, Spanish origin, ethnic ancestry, and nativity of parents by individual respondents.

Pretest experience and Richmond dress rehearsal instructions indicate that the social category "race" is not as clear for some as it is often assumed. It also seems clear that no matter what categories are printed on the forms, some hand coding of the "Other" category and editing for consistency will be required. It will be possible, for example, for a person to mark "Not Spanish" on question 7 (see below) and mark "Other" on question 4 and write in "Puerto Rican."

The definitional and data processing problems raised here are important for the interpretation of the data reported by race. Moreover, the changes in classification proposed in the coding instructions for 1980 raise questions, as yet unanswered, about their impact on the evaluation of the undercount and the development of intercensal population estimates.

Finally, there is a question about whether the federal government should label as "races" the whole list of categories in question 4. The responses to this question might be classified into "racial categories" by printing an "Asian and Pacific Americans" heading above the specific national origin groups, without a circle to mark. An alternative suggestion is to drop the word "race" and ask: "Is this person: (Fill one circle)." (Such a procedure is to be tested in the Lower Manhattan dress rehearsal.) Such a suggestion merely implies that racial identification is changing in more than marginal ways; this avoids governmental creation of new "races" and may provide information that, when compared to other answers, will document a social change in the concept of race for important parts of the population.

The issue, it seems to us, is whether the Census Bureau will recode write-in responses in more traditional ways or will respect personal preference and not code persons in a racial category they avoided in answering the question. The answer is not simple. Any recommendation we give could hardly be a definitive answer. As we suggested, a decision rests partially on information on the effects of recoding and on a judgment about the usefulness of data to be reported in either format. But we must point out that to carry out studies of the impact of proposed coding instructions on the evaluation of coverage and for intercensal estimates, adjustments will have to be made from the proposed coding and publishing decisions to recode as "White" some groups who reported their race as "Other." If the impacts are judged large enough to affect significantly the evaluation of coverage or intercensal estimates, and these adjustments are published, then two sets of "racial" data will exist. If the adjustments are not published and their effects are large, then replication of estimates of coverage and of population size between censuses by non-Census Bureau personnel will vary widely among themselves and with Bureau estimates.

As noted above, some recoding from "Other" to "White" or some other category was performed in 1970, on the assumption that some mistakenly reported their race. Such an assumption of a mistake is difficult to justify if race is defined as a self-identity question. We are again faced with the problem of a definition of the concept of "race" that question 4 is trying to measure.

Ethnic Ancestry and Spanish Origin

The questions on ethnic ancestry and Spanish origin or descent in the questionnaire for the Richmond dress rehearsal census were 7 and 13:

7. Is this person's origin or descent – *Fill one circle.*	Mexican-Amer. / Mexican or Chicano / Puerto Rican / Cuban / Other Spanish / Not Spanish

13. What is this person's ancestry?

If uncertain about how to report ancestry, see instruction sheet.

(For example – Afro-Amer., English, French, German, Honduran, Hungarian, Italian, Jamaican, Korean, Lebanese, Mexican, Nigerian, Polish, Ukrainian, Venezuelan, etc.)

It is clear that these questions are self-identity questions. There are no conceptual definitions of "origin or descent" and "ancestry" available from the Census Bureau. Guidance to respondents was given on the instruction sheet mailed with each census form:

Question 7. Origin or descent refers to a person's nationality group, lineage, or the country in which the person, or the person's parents or ancestors were born.

Question 13. Ancestry (or origin) refers to the nationality group, the lineage, or the country in which the person or the person's parents or ancestors were born before their arrival in the United States. Ancesry may be based on the origin of the person, near relatives, or some far-removed ancestor. Print the ancestry group with which the person most identifies. Do not report a religious group. If specific ancestry is "Indian," specify whether American Indian, Asian, or East Indian.

For persons who are of more than one origin, and who cannot identify with a single origin group, print the multiple origin (for example, Scotch-Irish).

As Census Bureau officials emphasize, the "truth" is whatever a person answers. These questions allow any individual with a strong sense of group consciousness--however removed by generational distance--to identify as a member of that group. The implications of the fact that there are no "objective criteria" (i.e., unrelated to the respondent's answer) against which to check the answers are discussed below.

Not all of the data developed from these questions, however, represent self-identification: one respondent may fill out the questionnaire for a household without consultation or the consent of other adults or children in the household. Given the variety of possible individual and cooperative efforts to fill out the form, it is not possible to gauge the effect on the response. Thus, these questions will yield data on self-identification and respondent identification of other members of the household, using unknown criteria. (This comment applies to other questionnaire items involving an element of self-identification, such as occupation, whether the person was seeking work, and disability.)

The nature of the questions raises serious doubts about validity and reliability. Validity and reliability are dependent on the precision of the concept being measured. The phrases "origin or descent" and "ancestry" can refer to having one or more forebears from a particular country, or to nationality of a multinational country, or to an ethnic identity (the referent most encountered in discussions of these questions). The discussions in the Panel made it clear that there were different interpretations of, or one could say confusion about, exactly what was being measured (validity). In the concrete, the answer will be what the respondent decides he or she is, or wants to be identified as, etc.

It is by no means clear that persons in similar situations and with similar characteristics will answer in the same way. For example, two third-generation persons with Italian ancestors, with similar family, education, economic, and other characteristics may give two different answers: "Italian" and "American." Each answer is "correct." Similarly, an immigrant man from Poland who still uses the Polish language at home and has values and behavior patterns that an ethnographer or anthropologist would identify as ethnically Polish may answer "American" to the question for himself or his children out of pride and loyalty to his adopted country. On the other hand, a fourth-generation person with some or mostly Polish ancestors and a Polish surname may reply "Polish" in response to the current reawakening of ethnic consciousness. Thus, the conditions or threshold level leading to a particular response are not necessarily uniform or even close to uniform. We are speaking here not of splitting hairs, but of possibly wide variations in respondent behavior across and within generations and cultural groups leading to serious doubts about what the question measures or what its objective referent is. Although the examples above refer to the ancestry question, the Spanish-origin or descent question has some of the same problems (Census 1974c, 1974d).

Reliability is important in two respects in regard to these questions. First, even if we accept the contention that the "truth" here is self-identification, would those in the household, especially adults and adolescents who do not fill out the census form, agree with the respondent? As we will see, this has implications for allocation procedures. Second, would the respondent identify himself or herself in the same way at a later time, if the census were taken at a different time of year or if the respondent were not exposed to organized efforts to educate people to answer ethnic origin or ancestry questions in particular ways? Since Census Day is April 1st, will more "Irish" responses result due to the closeness to March 17th? What would happen to "Italian" responses if Census Day were moved to October 15th?

This abbreviated review of questions of validity and reliability raises serious doubts about the meaning and interpretations of the data to be collected. We now turn to their processing, reporting, and interpretation.

In discussing the processing of the data, we will limit ourselves to two items: allocation for nonresponse and allowable categories in the ancestry questions. Decisions on an allocation program have not been made. If a question is blank, the first decision is whether a follow-up visit or telephone call should be made. In 1970, more than one item had to be missing to initiate follow-up procedures; this may also be the procedure in 1980. Nonresponses on Spanish origin or descent or on ancestry become candidates for follow-up; however, if the respondent is not willing to specify origin or ancestry, is not such a nonresponse as "meaningful" as a response? There has been some discussion on using responses by other persons in a household to allocate for nonresponse to these questions, but different answers within the same household are not unreasonable if they reflect differences in identity. In short, there seem to be no reliable criteria for allocation.

Ancestry categories to be coded for tabulation (at least as currently determined) include "American" and exclude "Jewish." We do not argue with these decisions but raise them here to emphasize the questionable usefulness of some of the information that will result. "American" does emphasize that some people do not identify with an ethnic group or, if they do identify, do not want to be thought of as not American. Others may write "American" to protect their ethnic identities or to avoid identifying themselves as "hyphenated-Americans." The Jewish category is purposefully not to be used as a reporting category even if filled in by the respondent because of avoidance of religious questions in the census, as directed by Congress. Nevertheless, the realities of the situation are that many religious and non-religious Jews think of themselves as ethnically (as a people, a culture, a language) Jewish, not German, Polish, Ukrainian, etc. Because of the overlap of ethnicity and religion in this case, the decision not to use "Jewish," while understandable and defensible, means the self-identification basis for the ethnic distribution will not be used in this case and, to that extent, will not reflect social realities.

The Panel sympathizes with the desire of ethnic groups to get information about their members--their number, location and characteristics--but some of us have a great deal of uneasiness and hesitancy about the origin and ancestry questions. That uneasiness stems from the validity and reliability problems and the possible variety of uses in cross-tabulation and of interpretations that might be questionable. Others on the Panel were less concerned about validity. They held that the questions would yield a measure of the size of groups in the population who identified themselves with various ethnic groups; thus, a self-reported ethnic profile would be available. There was some concern over reliability if the census were "politicized" in the sense that some groups might try to organize people to respond to the origin and ancestry questions in a way that does not reflect their usual self identity. But ethnic consciousness can build and decline in response to various events, including a decennial census.

The uneasiness of some of the Panel members concerning these questions stems not from an objection to the goal of counting the population by "ethnic heritage" or "ethnic identity," but to the self-identification questions to be used; this uneasiness is based at least partly on experience with ethnic identification. The data in Table 3, from the 1970 evaluation program, for example, shows large differences in reporting Spanish origin between responses in the census and the reinterview. The size of the difference varies according to whether one or both sides of the family were of Spanish origin and the recency of the Spanish connection. The questions involved can only be dealt with at face value. In the absence of a conceptual definition (and therefore, of criteria according to which a person is or is not to be classified in a category), the "truth" is what the answer is. Consequently, by definition, no error in the measurement of the size of ethnic groups is possible, except perhaps the errors resulting from reporting by one respondent the "self-identification" of other household members, which could be measured by a reinterview in the household. It sould be made explicit that this means that any charge that a group was undercounted (in the sense that some persons who were counted "should" have identified themselves in a particular way) is without grounds since self identity means that "objective criteria,"

Table 3. **Distribution of Census Responses for Persons Reported as being of Spanish Origin or Descent in the Reinterview, by Selected Demographic Characteristics**

Reinterview classification	Total in category in reinterview[1]	Spanish origin reported in census		95-percent confidence interval on percent
		Number	Percent	
Total of Spanish origin or descent	369	280	76	72 to 80
Spanish on both sides of family	266	258	97	95 to 99
Spanish on one side of family only	103	22	21	13 to 29
Father's side	44	9	20	8 to 32
Mother's side	59	13	22	11 to 33
Which ancestor from Spanish-speaking country:				
Sample person	77	76	99	97 to 99
Parent(s)	90	75	83	75 to 91
Grandparent(s)	89	65	73	64 to 82
Great grandparent(s)	27	12	44	25 to 63
Further back	18	1	6	1 to 17
NA in reinterview	68	(X)	(X)	(X)
Mexican, Puerto Rican, Cuban, or Central or South American origin or descent	282	252	89	85 to 93
Other Spanish origin or descent	86	27	31	21 to 41
NA in reinterview	1	(X)	(X)	(X)

(X) Not applicable.

[1]This total does not include census NA's (not available).

SOURCE: U.S. Bureau of the Census. *Accuracy of Data for Selected Population Characteristics as Measured by Reinterviews.* 1970 Census of Population and Housing, Evaluation and Research Program, PHC(E)-9. Washington, D.C.: U.S. Department of Commerce, 1974. Table C.

like place of birth of the respondent or respondent's parents, are irrelevant.

The advantage of the Spanish-origin and ancestry questions is that each allows individuals with a sense of group consciousness or belonging--however removed by generational distance--to identify as a member of that group. The census provides the opportunity to collect data from a large sample for ethnic identify and from the whole population on Spanish origin or descent. (The need for information on a small-area level dictated the inclusion of the Spanish-origin question on a 100-percent basis.)

Ethnic measures, and the racial measures discussed above, are fraught with methodological issues that are not easily resolved, as we have emphasized in our discussion. The Panel's own deliberations reflected the tension between the advantages of the data and the methodological problems that could vitiate the value of those data.

There was agreement among Panel members that the proposed ethnic questions are something of an experiment. We need to evaluate the information obtained to shed light on its meaning. Do some groups maintain an identify over more generations than do others? Are there regional differences? What is the effect of intermarriage on identity, particularly of offspring? For this reason, the Panel strongly endorses the plan to use the current population survey (CPS) for November 1979 to investigate such questions regarding ethnicity and ethnic identity. We recommend that the Census Bureau carefully plan to use the CPS for that month to shed light on the issues surrounding the ethnic ancestry, Spanish-origin, and race questions proposed for the 1980 census. This may require expansion of current plans for the November 1979 CPS, but we think the possible payoff warrants expanded efforts.

Place of Birth of Parents

Present plans for the 1980 census include the self-identity ethnic ancestry question just discussed, while a question that has generated useful data in the past--place of birth of parents--is to be dropped. The Panel is concerned about the loss of the data on place of birth of parents, which has been collected since the 1870 census. This question has provided information on second-generation Americans (native-born of foreign or mixed parentage), which, combined with the information on the foreign-born population, is the source of significant studies on the first two immigrant generations (Kritz and Gurak 1975, Bean and Wood 1974).

The Census Bureau has approached the situation as if the ancestry write-in item, which is a multi-generational question, were an adequate replacement for the question on place of parents' birth. The Panel believes the two-generation data have been undervalued by the Census Bureau: significant comparative studies of ethnic fertility, inter-generational changes in fertility, education, occupation, etc., as well as data on ethnic changes in neighborhoods and on differences in ethnic behavior and immigrant adaptation will come to a sudden halt. Many members of the Panel believe that there is no justification for breaking a hundred-years' series of data that has practical applications, especially with increased awareness of the continuing role of immigration to the United States.

Recommendations

12. Because of the validity and reliability concerns about the origin and ancestry questions, the following limitations are recommended:

a. No imputation procedures should be used in field or computer editing of these two questions, and a "not stated" category should be accepted.

b. Census publications (including those in forms like public use tapes that allow user manipulation of individual records) should clearly specify the limitations of the data.

13. The Panel supports the current population survey planned for November 1979. This survey should include both self-identity and objective multi-generational origin questions in order to provide an opportunity for analysis of responses on ethnicity. The Census Bureau should also use the origin and ancestry information to evaluate responses to racial categories other than white or black.

14. The question on place of birth of parent should definitely be included, if at all possible, in the 1980 census; it should be included in the Lower Manhattan dress rehearsal. The Census Bureau should use the data in cross-tabulations with the responses to questions, 4, 7, and 13 to provide users with additional insights on the meaning of those responses, and appropriate tabulations of social and economic characteristics of the foreign stock should continue to be made.

15. The instructions for enumerators and coders on handling write-in responses to the "Other" race category should be reviewed for consistency and should be specified in detail to conform to federal guidelines. For this purpose, the list of American Indian tribes should be reviewed for both completeness and comparability of level of taxonomy. Terms in current use by American Indian tribal persons should be considered for inclusion (see list on the following page).

16. The effect of the proposed 1980 census racial categories and instructions to enumerators (which differ from those used in previous censuses) on the demographic techniques used to evaluate underenumeration and to develop intercensal estimates should be investigated.

HOUSEHOLD COMPOSITION

The Census Bureau's plan to use a mail-out/mail-back procedure in 1980 for about 90 percent of the population assumes that most Americans are sufficiently literate to understand the questionnaire, are willing to respond completely and accurately, and can return the forms in a timely manner. As is also true of traditional methods, the census procedure assumes further that the majority of Americans are members of a nuclear family with a habitual residence in a fixed structure referenced by the postal system. To maximize compliance in completing and returning the questionnaire, the Census Bureau has designed and worded it for mainstream middle-class, educated family members.

For enumerating most of the population, census procedures are built on the basic assumptions inherent in the following formula: one address = one housing unit = household = one family (or one-person household or group of unrelated individuals) = one or more persons to be recorded and summed in the enumeration.

The following list of American Indian groups, in use by the groups themselves, should be considered for inclusion in the Census Bureau's present list of American Indian tribes.

Acoma
Agua Caliente
Alabama/Alibamu
Alturas Rancheria
Appalchiola
Arapaho
Arikara
Bannoc
Barona
Blood
Caddo
Cahto
Catawba
Cayuse
Chehalis
Chickahominy
Chitimaca
Challam
Coahilla
Coeur d'Alene
Cpharie
Colville
Coushatta
(Alabama Coushatta)
Cree
Cuipeno
Delaware
Edisto
Flathead
Goshute
Gros Ventre
Haliwa
Hassamanisco
Havasupai
Hidatsa
Hoopa
Houma
Hulapai
Iowa
Jemez
Jicarilla
Kalispel
Keetoowah
Kickapoo
Kootenai/Kutenai
Laguna
Lummi
Makah
Mandan
Maricopa
Mattaponi
Mescalero (Apache)
Metis
Miami
MicMac
Mission
Mi-Wuk
Mohave
Mohican/Mohegan
Muckleshoot
Narrangansett
Nanticoke
Nespelem
Nisqually
Ojibwa
Ottawa
Paugusett
Pawnee
Peoria
Pomo
Ponca
Powhatan
Quapaw
Quilente
Quinault
Rappahanock
Salish
Scaticoke
Seneca
Shawnee
Snokomish
Spokane
Squamish
Squaxin Island
Swinomish
Tache
Taos
Tigua
Tonkawa
Tsimshian
Tule River
Tunica Biloxi
Tush
Umatilla
Upper Skagit
Walla Walla
Warm Springs
Wasco
Washoe
Wichita
Wintun
Yavapai
Yuma
Zuni

The Panel finds good reason to accept the assumptions made by the Census Bureau at each step between a mailing address and the enumeration of individuals, but also good reason to note exceptions at each step. Somewhat simplified, the series of steps are: address/structure; housing unit; household; family, if present (as determined by relationship to the first person listed on the form, designated householder); and number of individuals.

In addition to the increasing proportion of persons who live alone, three other trends in contemporary society make the one-to-one relationship between housing unit and household and between household and family especially subject to question. First, the American population is highly mobile, and an indeterminate number of persons have alternative residences or are away from home for some period of time. Second, the group house of two or more unrelated persons is an increasingly common mode of accommodation, largely among middle-class persons (younger and older). Third, the housing unit/household boundary is not entirely meaningful for household networks most commonly found among low-income persons.

The Census Bureau clearly recognizes that for some people different procedures are necessary. There are some places that are particularly difficult to enumerate using the regular census mail procedures. These "special places" are where people have living arrangements other than the standard apartment or house, where the Census Bureau has no knowledge of the number of questionnaires to mail. Special places include hotels, campgrounds, prisons, hospitals, college dormitories, military installations, marinas, tents, wigwams, flophouses, orphanages, rooming and boarding houses, etc. Special places may contain housing units, non-institutional group quarters, and institutions. In 1970, specially trained enumerators canvassed residents of such special places, who numbered more than 3 percent of the national population.

Names and locations of special places are compiled from lists of military installations, Indian reservations, prisons, hospitals, migrant worker camps, nursing homes, homes for domiciliary and custodial care, directories of colleges and universities, and from hotel and motel listings in the Yellow Pages. Additions are made by enumerators and by district office personnel from their knowledge of other local special places. Particular difficulties may be encountered in getting census questionnaires to all mobile dwelling units, such as boats, trailers, wigwams, in either the address list or precanvass areas.

In the effort to obtain census information from each person in the United States, the Census Bureau also has special procedures to collect information from transients or guests in a housing unit, motel, or other group quarters, who have no one at their home addresses to report them on the census. For such people, individual census report forms have been used, and special nights designated for enumeration: T-night for hotels and other establishments with 50 or more rooms for transient guests, and M-night for missions, flophouses, jails, and similar places where people usually reside or are detained for 30 days or less. Despite all efforts, however, some such persons may be missed.

Housing Units and Household Membership

A housing unit is defined by the Census Bureau as a house, apartment, group of rooms, or single room that is occupied as a separate living quarters or, if vacant, intended for occupancy as a separate living quarters. Separate living quarters are those in which the occupants do not live and eat with any other person(s) in the building and that have direct access to the outside of the building or through a common hall, as in an apartment building. While the majority of living quarters in the United States are easily recognized as housing units, single-family or two-family houses, or apartments and flats, housing units may also be found in unexpected or unusual places: in a penthouse, loft, office building, factory (as for a watchman), behind a family store, in railroad cars, houseboats, tents, etc., if occupied as a usual residence.

Households are of two main types: those containing two or more related persons (families), which account for about 75 percent of all households (Census 1977b), and those containing persons living alone or with non-relatives only. About 90 percent of the latter contain only one person. (The number of single-person households has increased very rapidly in recent years.) Close to 85 percent of all families include a husband and wife, while only slightly more than 50 percent include one or more children under 18.

Even when a housing unit is identified, there may be uncertainty as to who is to be enumerated at that unit. A detailed list of residence rules prepared for the guidance of enumerators and editors (see Appendix C) illustrates the kinds of problems frequently encountered. For example, college students away at college, even if at home on vacation, are enumerated as residents of the college, while students away attending regular school below college level are reported as residents of the household. In general, persons only temporarily away are enumerated at the household; it is assumed that others will be enumerated elsewhere. As the population becomes more mobile, the opportunities for misapplication of the rules increase.

It had been customary for the Census Bureau to ask who is head of household and then record the relationship (or non-relationship) to the head of all others in the household. However, whenever the household contained a married couple, the man was arbitrarily designated head, regardless of the financial relationship. Because some now see this as sexist, the Census Bureau is dropping the term "head" from enumerations and tabulations. The questionnaire planned for the 1980 census instructs the respondent to start in column 1 with the household member (or one of the members) in whose name the home is owned or rented, and in subsequent columns to specify how each person is related to the person in column 1. Together with responses to questions 3 and 6 on sex and marital status, this will provide the information needed to determine household composition: Are co-residents related? Is the household a single-person household? Do household members constitute a family, and more specifically, a nuclear family? And is a sub-family present? As a result of this effort to properly recognize women's roles in today's society, some people fear a loss in the historical continuity of data on families and households. Census Bureau officials are confident, however, that bridging tabulations are feasible.

Two well-documented recent trends in American life also do not conform to the historic pattern of the nuclear family with male head residing in its own household: the household network, primarily (although not exclusively) found among lower-income blacks; and the group house, primarily found among middle-class younger persons.

The household network typically contains more than 50 persons and is centered on adult women, their children, and the families of the children's fathers. The network encompasses more than one house and involves sharing and exchange for income sources, cooking, sleeping accommodations, child care, and emergency help. The household network is the focus of current research in Chicago, New York, Boston, and Durham and in Appalachia and several other rural areas. Informal reports from these research efforts support the documentation of Stack and Lombardi (1974, p. 124):

> Black families...and the non-kin they regard as kin have evolved patterns of co-residence, kinship-based exchange networks linking multiple domestic units, elastic household boundaries, lifelong bonds to three-generation households, social controls against the formation of marriages that could endanger the network of kin, the domestic authority of women, and limitations on the role of the husband or male friend within a woman's kin network. (Emphasis added.)

Such household networks occur among the population most commonly subject to underenumeration, and the existence of the networks is relevant to examine for the implications it has for means of reducing the underenumeration. The results of the work cited above show that adult black males participate in household networks, as do their mates and their children. This fact as well as the fact of underenumeration is also supported by the results of the ethnographic work sponsored by the Census Bureau: adult males who regularly participate in households or families may still not be reported on the Census Bureau's forms. In the opinion of researchers on this topic, the "father in the house" rule means that many adult men will not be reported accurately on census forms. These researchers believe that it would be expensive and time-consuming to design and conduct a survey to document the existence and frequency of networks in a satisfactory manner. It may be worth testing the use of the question "Who eats here?" rather than the implied "Who sleeps here?" to identify the existence of networks.

Although the numbers of such types of networks is unknown, research is now confirming their existence in rural and urban areas, in towns and in cities. These networks are more prominent among blacks than whites in comparable low-income categories, suggesting that network formation is to some extent a cultural as well as an income phenomenon. The Panel notes with interest the consideration being given by the Census Bureau to using a family network approach in a post-enumeration survey to identify people missed in the census and to develop estimates of the undercount (Census 1978b).

Group houses, composed of individuals who are not readily recognized in census category terms as family members, accommodate between 2 and 9 persons. Many group house members are students. Group houses may subsume couples and may or may not include children. It is expected that most rural and religious communes, which are usually larger than group houses, will be prelisted as communes and classified as a form of group quarters.

Finally, the Panel wishes to comment on households of 8 or more persons. Families of 7 or more persons accounted for 2.2 million families in 1977 or 4 percent of all families (Census 1977b). In 1970, there was space on the long form for 7 household members (8 on the short form), and it appears that people were sometimes missed when enumerator or clerical failures in the Census Bureau office resulted in not picking up information on the presence of more than 7 (or 8) household members. In an effort to ensure that all members of large households are counted in 1980, the procedure now planned is for an enumerator to call regarding each census form returned that lists 7 members to inquire whether there are additional members of the household, and if so, to collect the additonal information. The Panel strongly endorses this plan.

Ethnographic Study

Instead of relying on ad hoc studies that fortuitously document the occurrence of household networks and the persons who form these networks, the Panel supports the recommendation of the advisory committee's 1972 report (NRC) for more ethnographic research.

A trained observer, who lives in an area and participates in its life over a considerable period of time, should be able to locate all of the people who frequent that area. If this were done in a city block of 100 or so households over a few months, for example, a complete list could be developed to compare with a list developed by a census-type enumeration. Comparison of the two lists would identify residents who were not enumerated and yield information not only on their race, age, and sex, but probably also on their income, language, and many other characteristics. At a minimum, such research should provide valuable insights into causes of underenumeration. At the maximum, participant-observer research might provide a basis for estimating what percentage of certain subgroups are missed. The latter would be possible, however, only if a large survey were undertaken with a systematic sample.

The Panel considered a proposal to develop a list of the difficult-to-enumerate areas of the country, and, from this list, to chose a random sample of such areas where people trained in ethnographic investigation would be located, the majority of them to be graduate students in anthropology hired and supervised by their faculty advisors. Although attracted by the possibility that information so obtained on characteristics of the uncounted might be used with regression techniques to adjust for the undercount in such areas, the Panel does not recommend that such an ambitious project be undertaken. The sample involved in such a project would have to be substantial in size to secure the results desired, and this would, of course, be costly because of the amount of time that observers would have to spend in each area. In addition, there might not be enough anthropologists or other suitably trained people in the country to do the work.

More serious, however, is the concern of some Panel members about invasion of privacy and the possibility that an extension of participant-observer studies under Census Bureau sponsorship, particularly if conducted in direct conjunction with a census, might be misunderstood. Although the purpose would be to obtain clues as to the characteristics of persons missed, some people might assume that the Census Bureau would obtain names and seek out individuals appearing on an ethnographer's list who had not been enumerated in the census-type survey. Because of the possibility that such research by the Census Bureau might incorrectly be preceived as unwarranted governmental intrusion, the Panel suggests that further ethnographic research--beyond the three small-scale studies now under way--should be conducted by a private or university research group and supported by sources other than the Census Bureau. The Panel also proposes that some independent research organization or foundation develop a research program on this topic to enhance understanding of the social and cultural correlates of the undercount in hard-to-enumerate communities.

Recommendations

17. Further research should be undertaken on means of identifying and enumerating members of kinship networks that tend to occur among the population most subject to underenumeration.

18. A program of participant-observer studies has great potential for providing insight into the cultural and social problems associated with census-taking, especially in difficult-to-enumerate areas, and for providing clues to characteristics of persons missed in household surveys. To avoid any possible implication of invasion of privacy by the Census Bureau, the Panel recommends that additional studies not be sponsored or funded by the Bureau, but rather be conducted under the aegis of an independent research organization.

REFERENCES

Azores, Tania (1977) "Participation in the Pretest of Camden, New Jersey," Memorandum to the Acting Director, Bureau of the Census, January 25.

Bean, Frank D. and Charles H. Wood (1974) "Ethnic Variations in the Relationship between Income and Fertility," Demography, Vol. 11, No. 4, November.

Goldfield, Edwin D., Anthony Turner, Charles D. Cowan, and John C. Scott (1978) "Privacy and Confidentiality as Factors in Survey Response," in 1977 Proceedings of the Social Statistics Section, American Statistical Association, Part I, pp. 219-231. Washington, D.C.: American Statistical Association.

Kritz, Mary M. and Douglas Gurak (1975) "Foreign Stock, Minority and Native White Fertility Differentials," paper presented at the Population Association of America annual meeting.

Lacey, Barbara, Larry Love, and Maria Urrutia (1977) "Validating the 1980 Census Selection Procedures: A Report to Census Advisory Committees," November.

Lancaster, Clarise, and Frederick J. Scheuren (1971) "Counting the Uncountable Illegals: Some Initial Statistical Speculations Employing Capture-Recapture Techniques," in Proceedings of the Social Statistics Section, American Statistical Association, Part I, pp. 530-535. Washington, D.C.: American Statistical Association.

National Research Council (1972) America's Uncounted People, Report of the Advisory Committee on Problems of Census Enumeration. Washington, D.C.: National Academy of Sciences.

National Research Counci (1979) Privacy and Confidentiality as Factors in Survey Response, Panel on Privacy and Confidentiality as Factors in Survey Response, Committee on National Statistics. Washington, D.C.: National Academy of Sciences.

Scott, Christopher (1961) "Research on Mail Surveys," Journal of the Royal Statistical Society, Vol. 124, No. 2, pp. 143-205.

Stack, Carol A., and John Lombardi (1974) "Conclusion" in All Our Kin, ed. Carol A. Stack. New York: Harper & Row.

Sudman, Seymour and Norman Bradburn (1974) Response Effects in Surveys: A Review and Synthesis. Chicago: Aldine.

U.S. Bureau of the Census (1972) Investigation of the Census Bureau Interviewer Characteristics, Performance and Attitude: A Summary, prepared by Gail Poe Inderfurth, Working Paper No. 34. Washington, D.C.: U.S. Government Printing Office.

U.S. Bureau of the Census (1973) "The Public Information Program" (Advance issuance of Chapter 6), in Procedural History: 1970 Census of Population and Housing, PHC(R)-1A. Washington, D.C.: U.S. Government Printing Office.

U.S. Bureau of the Census (1974a) Effect of Special Procedures to Improve Coverage in the 1970 Census, 1970 Census of Population and Housing, Evaluation and Research Program, PHC(E)-6. Washington, D.C.: U.S. Government Printing Office.

U.S. Bureau of the Census (1974b) Estimates of Coverage of Population by Sex, Race, and Age: Demographic Analysis. 1970 Census of Population and Housing, Evaluation and Research Program, PHC(E)-4. Washington, D.C.: U.S. Government Printing Office.

U.S. Bureau of the Census (1974c) Consistency of Reporting of Ethnic Origin in the Current Population Survey, Technical Paper No. 31. Washington, D.C.: U.S. Government Printing Office.

U.S. Bureau of the Census (1974d) Accuracy of Data for Selected Population Characteristics as Measured by Reinterviews, 1970 Census of Population and Housing, Evaluation and Research Program, PHC(E)-9. Washington, D.C.: U.S. Government Printing Office.

U.S. Bureau of the Census (1976a) "Description of Public Information Evaluation Survey," prepared by Jean Foster. 1976 Census of Camden, New Jersey, General Memorandum No. 9, December 9, 1976.

U.S. Bureau of the Census (1976b) Procedural History, 1970 Census of Population and Housing, PHC(R)-1. Washington, D.C.: U.S. Government Printing Office.

U.S. Bureau of the Census (1976c) "Summary Report on Conference on the Media and the 1980 Census," memo from Henry H. Smith, Chief, Public Information Office, November 30, 1976.

U.S. Bureau of the Census (1977a) "Broadcast Media Seminar," memo from Henry H. Smith, April 5, 1977.

U.S. Bureau of the Census (1977b) "Households and Families by Type: March 1977" (Advance report), Current Population Reports, Population Characteristics, Series P-20, No. 313. Washington, D.C.: U.S. Government Printing Office.

U.S. Bureau of the Census (1977c) "Minority Statistics Program of the Bureau of the Census," March 9, 1977.

U.S. Bureau of the Census (1977d) "Plans for Improvement of Coverage in the 1980 Census," prepared for the September 1977 meeting of the Census Advisory Committee of the American Statistical Association, Washington, D.C.

U.S. Bureau of the Census (1977e) "Requests for Spanish Language Questinnaires," 1976 Census of Travis County, Texas. Memorandum No. 28, September 28.

U.S. Bureau of the Census (1977f) "Status of Coverage Improvement Procedures in the 1980 Census," prepared for the September 1977 meeting of the Census Advisory Committee of the American Statistical Association, Washington, D.C.

U.S. Bureau of the Census (1977g) Various memoranda from Henry H. Smith. "Meeting with Newspaper Industry Officials" (February 17, 1977); "Meeting with Communications Research Officials from Industry" (February 22, 1977); "Advertising Recommendation for 1980 Census Public Information Program" (March 4, 1977); "Meeting with Magazine and Periodical Officials" (March 22, 1977).

U.S. Bureau of the Census (1978a) "Effect of Alternative Versions of the 'Dear Friend' Letter on Cooperation with the Camden Pretest," memo from Jeff Moore, Response Research Staff, Statistical Research Division, January 4, 1978.

U.S. Bureau of the Census (1978b) "Proposals for Coverage Evaluation for the 1980 Census," prepared for the March 1978 meeting of the Census Advisory Committee of the American Statistical Association, Washington, D.C.

U.S. Bureau of the Census (1978c) Recommendations from Minutes of Minority Advisory Committee Meetings for the 1980 Census, prepared by Eddie N. Williams, January 31, 1978.

U.S. Congress, House (1977a) The Census Reform Act, Hearings before the Subcommittee on Census and Population of the Committee on Post Office and Civil Service, 95th Congress, 1st session, Serial No. 95-46, September 12 & 23, 1977. Washington, D.C.: U.S. Government Printing Office.

U.S. Congress, House (1977b) The 1980 Census, Hearings before the Subcommittee on Census and Population of the Committee on Post Office and Civil Service, 95th Congress, 1st session, Serial No. 95-41, June 9, 10, & 24, 1977. Washington, D.C.: U.S. Government Printing Office.

U.S. Congress, House (1977c) Pretest Census in Oakland, California and Camden, New Jersey, Hearings before the Subcommittee on Census and Population of the Committee on Post Office and Civil Service, 95th Congress, 1st session, Serial No. 95-42, March 25 & May 16, 1977. Washington, D.C.: U.S. Government Printing Office.

4. PLANS FOR LOCAL REVIEW AND PROCEDURES FOR HANDLING CONTESTED COUNTS

The proposed local review program is an important innovation of the 1980 decennial census and the Panel commends it. For the first time, local officials will be given a formal opportunity to review counts both before and after the actual field work on the census and to communicate with the Census Bureau regarding possible errors in time for their information to affect the completeness of the count.

The Panel considers the issue of procedures for handling contested counts to be closely related to the local review program. The latter not only holds promise of making the enumeration more complete, but also may serve as an effective channel for what in the past had perforce been a post-census activity of contesting or appealing the counts. If the local review program works well, the number of subsequent appeals might be reduced.

But local review can be effective only if the local governments are prepared to participate actively. In order to take full advantage of the program, at least in places of significant population size, local officials will have to be prepared with data on residential units and possibly their own independent population estimates with which to compare the Census Bureau's figures. This is a significant problem that may well limit the usefulness of the program in all but a few jurisdictions.

Current Plans for Local Review

As currently outlined, the local review program will have 6 aspects.

1. In January 1979, the Census Bureau will send a letter to the "Chief Executive" or "highest elected official" in each of the 39,000 revenue-sharing jurisdictions in the country. These jurisdictions include cities, townships, counties, and other minor civil divisions as appropriate, state by state. It should be noted that there is overlap in the group: the chief official of a county, as well as the minor civil divisions within it, will receive a letter. This is probably not a serious problem. In the letter, the chief executive will be asked to designate, if he or she wishes, a technical liaison, such as the planning department.

2. Meanwhile, beginning in February 1978, the Census Bureau has been contacting technical people known to be involved in making population estimates or who might know of such activity in their metropolitan areas ("Census Statistical Area Key Persons"). As of mid-March, 162 agencies had been contacted; of these, 64 indicated that they have tract-level population or housing unit estimates while 98 do not. These agencies may represent cities, counties, or councils of government.

3. From mid-January to mid-February 1980, the Census Bureau plans to send the pre-enumeration, mailing-list address counts, with maps, explanations, and instructions, to those of the 39,000 jurisdictions where mail-out procedures will be used. The data will be presented at the city-block level in areas with blocks and at the enumeration-district level otherwise. Aggregations to the census-tract level where appropriate and to bigger geographic levels will also be shown. The local area will have from 6 to 10 weeks, depending on the date of receipt, to review the material and transmit to the census field office any comments or information on suspected errors. In addition to reviewing the address count, the local officials will be able to verify the current city boundaries in Census Bureau records. In this way, the field offices will be able to check out the information immediately and make any necessary corrections and adjustments.

4. Finally, after the field work is completed, the Census Bureau will transmit to the local officials the preliminary population and housing-unit counts from the census itself, also by block or enumeration district. The review period at this stage will be much shorter (perhaps two weeks), but it will provide an opportunity to look for errors and at problems before the counts are made public. Again, the local officials will communicate with the field office personnel so that problems can be attended to, and resolved, on the spot. Census enumerators and local office staff will be available after completion of the field work so that questioned blocks or other areas can be rechecked. In this connection, the Panel assumes that the Census Bureau will not allow local officials access to any records for households or individuals, in accordance with the Bureau's standard procedures for confidentiality.

5. Census Bureau staff will review all counts coming out of the field, for all 39,000 revenue sharing jurisdictions, and will approve the figures if they appear reasonable and consistent with what might have been expected. More detailed review will be devoted to places that have not had the benefit of review by local government.

6. Whether or not a community has participated in the local review program, there is still the possibility that it will be dissatisfied with its count. When the preliminary count has been announced to the press, a complaint of an inaccurate enumeration takes on the status of a "contested count." The Census Bureau currently has no formal procedure planned for handling contested counts, although one is proposed for intercensal estimates. With the hope that the number of such instances will be substantially reduced through the local review program, the Census Bureau is stating simply that if some real evidence is presented, it will be considered--no matter how long after the census is conducted--as long as the evidence can reasonably be investigated.

Comments on the Plans

The local review program is a useful measure on the part of the Census Bureau to involve local communities in improving the accuracy of the census. It should forestall much of the local criticism of the Census Bureau's work. There are, however, several areas of concern that limit the potential benefits of the program.

The most important problem is the lack of capability on the part of most local governments to respond in a positive and constructive manner to the opportunity presented. According to conversations with a few local government officials, only a small proportion of the approximately 2,100 places in the country with more than 10,000 population would now be able to produce independent housing unit or population estimates at the census tract or block level to compare with the Census Bureau's figures.

To prepare such figures (assuming there is no universal local census effort being conducted) generally requires geographic coding of information on residential units. In many cases the best information available will be building permits, which represent changes over time. If geographic coding is done, the new construction and demolition data by small area can be used to adjust the 1970 counts to the expected 1980 counts of housing units. Alternatively, in some cases, a continuing count of housing units reflected in a source such as utility meters or real estate tax records could be used. Regardless of the particular data source, however, the geographic coding operation is essential (since the Census Bureau's data will be arranged in this way), and relatively few jurisdictions are doing it now. Thus, in order to have the local review program operate effectively, local areas (particularly those not in Standard Metropolitan Statistical Areas (SMSAs) should be encouraged and assisted in developing and implementing a capability for geographic coding.

Another problem revolves around the planned timetable. The earlier local governments are made aware of the program, the more lead time they would have if they choose to develop the independent estimates needed to take full advantage of the program. The current Census Bureau position, however, is that the initial letters should not go out until 1979 because of a likely turnover in chief executives in the 1978 elections and because it is "too early" and the local officials will "put it on a shelf." This may be true in a large number of jurisdictions, but it would not be an insuperable problem since a follow-up letter could be sent several months after the first. Meanwhile, for communities that would be interested in developing the capability to respond, the extra several months' lead time could be crucial.

The Census Bureau cannot rely solely on form letters to local officials to publicize the program. It should seek to reach them through other channels, including journals read by local government officials. Because of the effort and cost involved, the officials will have to be effectively motivated to participate.

It would also seem incumbent on the Census Bureau to increase its efforts to assist in the development of the local technical capability needed to participate effectively. One possibility is to hold information seminars or workshops at national or state conventions of relevant organizations, such as the National League of Cities, the National Association of Counties, or the American Institute of Planners. In addition, perhaps the geography division of the Census Bureau could work with local agencies--usually planning groups of councils of governments--to develop tract or tract/block coding guides for use by local governments. Ideally, funding should be made available to a non-government agency, such as the League of Cities, to establish a group of professional experts who could, on request, go to local areas and help them start on the process of developing their own estimates.

As with other aspects of the census, the Census Bureau will need records on the local review procedure so that its cost-effectiveness can be estimated and the planning for it improved for future censuses. Such records will also be needed as background information relevant to appeals of the census count by local governments. The records might include, for example, the number and kinds of local government units participating actively, the nature of the participation, the results of reinterviews to check errors reported by the local government, and the number of people added to the count.

Contested Counts and the Intercensal Estimates

The Census Bureau has issued intercensal estimates of the population of states and many local areas for use in revenue sharing and in other determinations in the allocation of federal funds. Such estimates have been made for 1973, 1975, and 1976, and it is planned to issue a set for 1977. It is possible that by the time the 1980 population census results are available even more recent intercensal estimates will have been issued.

State and local governments will necessarily take these estimates as official and base their planning as well as their claims for federal funds on them. If the actual 1980 census count for any geographical unit is significantly different from what is implied for the census date by these estimates, state and local governments may contest the count, citing these estimates, among other data, as evidence. The Census Bureau should, therefore, accompany its publication of the 1977 and any subsequent estimates with a statement pointing out the uncertainties in these estimates and making clear that they will be superseded by the more accurate 1980 census.

The Panel is especially concerned about intercensal population estimates for local areas, especially for areas as small as tracts, that are produced privately but distributed by the National Technical Information Service (NTIS) of the U.S. Department of Commerce. The potential difficulty is not that competing estimates exist, but that the government is marketing figures that appear to have an official stamp of approval; these privately produced figures are being distributed by the same department that conducts the census and issues its own intercensal population estimates.

Procedures for Handling Contested Counts

The question of whether the Census Bureau should implement a formal procedure for contested counts is difficult to answer; the Census Bureau is prepared to handle questions and issues of the count on an informal basis. Its basic position is: "Give us evidence; we'll evaluate it and make the corrections if justified." The experience of one Panel member with numerous suggestions for correction following 1970 indicates that the Census Bureau has, in fact, done this. To many observers and to some advocates of the cities, however, this position is insufficient. It is too easy, they believe, for the Census Bureau to turn a bureaucratic cold shoulder to possible errors. The current situation provides no means of formal appeals short of lawsuits in court.

Thus, it would appear that, at this time, the weight of the argument falls on the side of establishing a formal procedure, in the interests of fairness to the cities and other governmental entities that may feel shortchanged by the announced count. The informal process currently used by the Census Bureau should be maintained, however, so that the possibility of resolving questions short of a formal contested count remains.

The formal procedure should parallel the one now being established to provide a formal mechanism to state and local governments wishing to challenge the Census Bureau's intercensal estimates of population and per capita income (see the statement by Courtenay M. Slater, before the Subcommittee on Census and Population of the House Committee on Post Office and Civil Service, March 21, 1978). This procedure provides for hearing officers to examine all contested intercensal estimates. In the case of formal challenges to the 1980 census counts, the Panel recommends that the hearing officer also be a professionally qualified employee of the Census Bureau who had not been involved in any way with the preparation of the counts. The officer would be appointed by the director of the Census Bureau to hold an open hearing and receive oral and written evidence relating to the challenge of the census count and to recommend appropriate action to the director. A complete record of the proceeding would be kept. The protesting governmental entity should be required to bear a significant portion of the cost to discourage frivolous or politically motivated protests.

Recommendations

19. The Census Bureau should alert local public officials to the local review program as soon as possible, and well before the planned January 1979 date; it should concentrate sufficient resources to prepare appropriate mailing lists by an earlier date to reach not only the chief elected officials but also appropriate technical staff.

20. The Census Bureau should mount an effective program to assist local areas to take advantage of the local review program, including, but not limited to:

a. Conducting seminars or workshops at national conventions attended by the appropriate local officials and at state conventions of city and county officials;

b. Assisting local communities with geographic coding of local records; and

c. Publishing articles to reach local government officials, through such organizations as the National League of Cities and county governmental associations, with cogent arguments to elicit the interest of readers.

21. The Census Bureau should publish its intercensal local area population estimate for late in the 1970-1980 decade with adequate qualifications to prevent their improper use as a basis for contesting the 1980 population census counts. The estimates being marketed by the National Technical Information Service should be accompanied by an unambiguous statement that they do not represent estimates by the U.S. Department of Commerce.

22. The Census Bureau should establish a formal review process for contested counts of the 1980 decennial census to supplement the informal process currently in place and to provide a route of appeal for dissatisfied local officials short of filing suit in a court of law. The local governments should be required to bear part or all of the financial burden involved when this process is invoked.

5. FEASIBILITY OF ADJUSTING LOCAL CENSUS COUNTS AND POPULATION ESTIMATES

Up to this point, the focus of our discussion and recommendations has been on how to improve the coverage of the 1980 decennial census and reduce the underenumeration. It is the Panel's hope that the measures the Census Bureau has adopted will be effective and that our recommendations will also help towards this goal. Yet as is inevitable in any census, there will not be a complete count. Despite all that can be done, some net undercount will occur in 1980, and, as in the past, it will have a differential impact by geographic area.

Therefore, the issue arises of whether the census results for states and local areas should be adjusted for the undercount. This issue has arisen only infrequently in the past. For 1870, for example, revisions were made for an undercount in southern states long after the data were first published. In recent years, however, a combination of factors has brought the issue sharply to the fore. First, the enactment of a variety of laws distributing large sums in federal grants-in-aid to state or local governments, on the basis of population as at least one of the factors, with the result that correction of errors in the count could mean the gain or loss of millions of dollars to individual cities or states. Second, the publication of Census Bureau estimates of the undercount since the 1950 census has not only made the undercount estimates a matter of public record, but has also, through Bureau studies (Census 1975, 1977), suggested to states and cities the approximate amount that adjustments might mean for them. Third, the increasing activism of minority groups and their realization that the undercount affects them more than others and undercuts public recognition of the size of their problems. It is not only a minority concern, but one of general equity, that a differential undercount by race deprives the very localities that Congress has most in mind in enacting revenue sharing and other financial aid legislation.

A vigorous demand has arisen for the Census Bureau to adjust the decennial census counts and the subsequent intercensal population estimates for local and state areas to reduce the distortion caused by differential underenumeration. This pressure has culminated in a bill currently before the Congress (H.R. 10386) that among other things would require the Secretary of Commerce to establish procedures for correcting census counts for persons missed. In view of this situation, part of the charge given to the Panel by the Secretary of Commerce was to "investigate the feasibility of adjusting census counts, and subsequent population estimates, for underenumeration, and assess the implications of such procedures."

Use of Population Estimates for Allocation

Before looking at the question of adjusting the count, we will review how census data on population of states and areas are used.

The major use under the Constitution is, of course, the apportionment among the states of seats in the House of Representatives and, therefore, also of votes in the electoral college. Data on population for areas within states are used in drawing boundaries for congressional districts and in apportionment of seats in state legislatures. The law governing the population census requires that the count by state be reported no later than 9 months after the census is taken, and the counts for legislative apportionment or districting purposes within states be reported no later than 3 months thereafter.

The Census Bureau is obligated to prepare intercensal population estimates for states and thousands of local areas for use in distributing revenue sharing and other funds (Title 13, U.S. Code, Section 181). Such estimates have been issued for 1973, 1975, and 1976, and a set of estimates for 1978 is planned. For use in general revenue sharing, current estimates of population have to be made for 39,000 geographic units, of which 22,000 had populations of less than 1,000 according to the Census Bureau's estimates for July 1, 1975.

For these estimates, the Census Bureau first estimates the national population starting with the decennial count (and therefore perpetuating any geographical disparities in completeness of enumeration) and using reported data on births, deaths, and net immigration. This is then distributed by state, using decennial census counts, state vital statistics, and information from various sources to estimate net interstate migration or total population change. By a similar process, state estimates are then distributed among smaller geographic areas, as required to meet the needs specified in legislation. Needless to say, the estimates of internal migration or population change could have large, relative errors. The intercensal estimates are checked by the results of special censuses that have been taken in more than 1,000 local areas since 1970 so that users of the data can evaluate their accuracy.

In making the intercensal estimates, the Census Bureau cooperates with state agencies and universities that have expertise or local data that may aid in developing local estimates. But because of the need for consistency among states, the Census Bureau retains responsibility for constructing and publishing the small-area estimates used for general revenue sharing. It sends to state and local governments extensive information on how the estimates are made and has recently advised these governments on how the estimates may be questioned or putative errors called to the Census Bureau's attention (Census 1977b, 1978).

Intercensal estimates of population also enter into other estimates. For example, they serve as "controls" for the estimates of labor force, employment, and unemployment in the current population survey; for this purpose, monthly estimates are made for the country, each state, and large SMSAs. In addition to the labor force estimates, other intercensal estimates for states and local areas required for use in formulas for distributing federal funds include per capita income, numbers of children under age 21, urbanized population, and working-age population.

The undercount of population affects the distribution of federal funds in other ways. In revenue sharing, relative per capita income (i.e., per capita income in the state as a percentage of the national average) is a more significant component of the formula than is population. If, as is plausible, the income of persons missed in the census is below the average for persons enumerated (and this is likely because of the high undercount rate for blacks), an adjustment for underenumeration that does not adjust the income distribution misses one effect of the undercount; since the weight of missed persons in the total population is small, however, the effect on average income is likely to be small. This raises the question of whether an adjustment for the undercount should be made for some or all of the characteristics of the population tabulated by the Census Bureau, instead of being confined to the population estimates alone. As noted in Chapter 1, income data derived from household surveys also are known to be subject to errors resulting from underreporting of income, but this issue is outside the scope of the Panel's work.

The above description of intercensal population estimates (which are mandated by law) suggests that the Census Bureau, responding to an urgent need for data, has issued extensive sets of current estimates of the population of states and local areas, some elements of which rest on tenuous data. The Census Bureau has asked the National Research Council to review the methodology for current population estimates. When the Census Bureau began its program of intercensal estimates, it may have had some of the same hesitations and concerns that it now faces when considering adjustment of the decennial count for underenumeration.

Statistics for Information and Statistics for Allocation

In approaching the question of adjustment of census counts, a distinction may be made between a statistic and a convention, the former providing information, the latter providing numbers to be used in an allocation formula. A statistic is an estimate of a parameter (that is, of a true, although unknown, value or number); in the real world, inferences are made on the basis of statistics and knowledge of their probable errors. For allocation, no uncertainty is permissible; seats in the House of Representatives or dollars have to be distributed exactly. An indeterminancy of even one person in the population of the United States is unacceptable: one missing person could deprive a state of a Representative or of $100 or more in revenue sharing or other federal grants. Distributive legislation that is based on population imposes on the census a requirement that no census can meet. In order to use census statistics in allocation formulas, therefore, a convention is required on how to deal with the error inherent in the counts.

From the size of the undercount in earlier censuses and from the fact that other industrialized countries also have undercounts, it is clear that far from being able to count the population to the last person, a statistical agency cannot count it to the last million persons. Omissions in recent censuses seem to have been of the order of 5 million persons, despite all the effort and expertise applied. And in 1980, the error could well be larger despite all measures taken to reduce it, not primarily because the population is larger, but because of a variety of social changes--especially more variety in living arrangements and more married women working outside the home and so not as available as before to provide information to the census taker or to serve as enumerators.

Attempting to eliminate the undercount presents a classic case of diminishing returns with increasing investment. This may be illustrated by a hypothetical example. With a certain expenditure, say $200 million, the Census Bureau might locate and count 90 percent of the population; with $400 million, it might count 95 percent; with $800 million, it might count 98 percent. As the percentage nears 100, people are harder and harder to find, and the cost per added person counted goes up steeply; it is very possible that a further $200 million might only bring the count up to 98.5 percent.

The search for completeness is also limited by certain constraints other than financial. At present, people are not required by law to step forward to be counted; their only obligation is to respond truthfully to the best of their ability when the Census Bureau finds them. If the law were changed or if everyone could be made to sit still "at home" for a day while the Census Bureau did its work, a higher level of completeness could be attained--the census might even come within 1 million of the true figure. But then, aside from the regimentation, if it were a working day, the economy would lose a day's production at a cost of about $5 billion, which most would judge too high a cost for counting those last people.

The Panel makes detailed suggestions that might improve completeness, but it must be remembered that all this concerns, at most, whether the 1980 census count is within 5 million or within 3 million of the "true" total.

Whatever happens, there will be a margin of indeterminancy in counting the population that cannot be resolved. To ask why the census cannot count 100 percent of the population is the same as asking why books contain typographical errors, why manufactured products often have defects, why the police cannot catch all criminals: the impossibility of determining with certainty the parameters of the real world. But this insight of classical statistics has to be used in a different way for allocation than for estimating the value of a parameter.

The need for an exact number for allocation can best be resolved, in the face of random variation, by establishing a convention or agreement in advance of knowledge of the outcome. Such agreement might be to use the actual census count, as in the past, or to use an adjusted census count arrived at by a specified procedure. The procedure should be publicly known before the enumeration; the Census Bureau should respond to suggestions on procedure as well as it can within cost and other constraints; it should then make revised estimates for April 1, 1980, and the only grounds for contesting the figures after that would be that the Census Bureau failed to follow the agreed-on procedure.

This need for a convention is based on the fact that any enumeration process yields a value plus a random component. How small the random component can be made is discussed below in detail, but it cannot be eliminated. The only way to deal with whatever random component remains after all the improvements in procedure, after all the examination to ensure that the procedure is fair, is to agree in advance to accept the outcome. Protests based on the numbers that result make as little sense here as they do in a lottery. Just as an estimate with known error structure is the answer to an information question, so a convention made in advance is the answer to an allocation question.

Allocations are targeted on problems, which may be substandard housing, pollution of waterways, or unemployed youth. The statistical variable that is used for the allocation is some kind of measure of the problem, but it can never be an exact measure. It is rather, as Bixby (1977) says, a proxy for the variable that the legislators have in mind. Some group in the population is in need of assistance; a certain series of statistical data seems to be correlated with the need; the distribution is made according to that known series of statistical data. The legislation may go further and include provision for collecting more appropriate information, but it is not always possible to develop statistics that measure actual individual need; we must often be satisfied with proxies or indicators of the need the legislation is aiming at.

The fact that an indicator is not identical with a need causes no confusion. Once a law is passed, the distribution of funds is according to the indicator and not the need. The recourse for anyone who objects is to go back to the legislature and argue for some other indicator of need. The distribution will not be exactly on the target the legislators had in mind, but it must be specifiable to the last dollar when checks are to be written.

Unfortunately, the desirable administrative certainty dissolves if the proxy variables are not unambiguously specified. The word "population" in the law can mean two quite different things: the true population and the population as estimated by a given procedure. And since these are inevitably different from one another, the controversy that the legislature tried to contain by specifying some proxy variable for the need breaks out again.

The question that then presents itself is how to develop a consensus for a convention. One possible convention is to use the decennial results without adjustment; others include a variety of technical methods of adjustment. At this stage, even the first alternative, although it is the traditional one, may require a consensus because the issue of adjustment has been so sharply raised.

This is an issue in which technical questions and public policy concerns intersect. It therefore requires input by both technicians (including staff of the Census Bureau and technical advisory committees to the Census Bureau) and those concerned with policy.

While the method to be followed if an adjustment is to be made is primarily a technical matter, the question of whether an adjustment should be made at all is in part a policy issue that should be decided at a broader than technical level. If the decision is made before the 1980 census date, knowledge of the effects of different alternatives on legislative apportionment and fund distributions would not unduly prejudice consideration of the issues. Post-censal estimates that will be available through 1978 make it possible to guess the direction and amount of population changes that will occur in the decade, but the effects of various adjustment techniques cannot be known with assurance until the basic data becomes available after the 1980 census is taken.

There are a number of ways in which the issues could be considered and the decision made. Within the Administration there are channels for consultation and decision making, such as the Cabinet-level Statistical Policy Coordination Committee. Appropriate committees of the Congress could be consulted. Public hearings would elicit the views of interested groups. Publication of a proposed procedure in the *Federal Register*, with opportunity for objections to be filed, is another way in which the views of various groups could be obtained. Achieving public acceptance of the use of the census figures for distributing funds is also advanced by other measures the Census Bureau is following, including the local review program, the extensive program of public communications and public relations, the work with advisory committees and community groups.

Methods for Adjusting Census Counts

A number of methods for estimating undercount and for making adjustments are available. Specifically, three methods of adjustment have been proposed--synthetic, demographic, and matching (described below)--and each can be applied to yield adjusted figures. Both levels and geographical patterns of estimated underenumeration differ according to the method employed. This section considers the choice of methods in terms of general questions: Does any method appear to be superior to the others and, therefore, does any particular set of estimates appear to be more soundly based? Even if one method is judged superior, can it be judged accurate enough to warrant its use in the face of possible criticism of "tampering" with the reported census count?

There are several criteria by which a method is judged. The most obvious criterion is an evaluation of how well the method works. Unfortunately, there is no standard by which to judge the correctness of the three proposed adjustment methods since the true undercount for any geographic area is not known.

Another criterion is that of plausibility. If the level or pattern of estimation appears to be patently implausible or absurd, then the method may be immediately rejected. The major problem with this criterion is that what may be implausible to some may be very plausible to others.

A third criterion is that of robustness. Each method is based upon certain assumptions. If the results are not sensitive to the particular choice of assumptions (i.e., if the results change little when alternative assumptions that are equally plausible are used), then the method is said to be robust. Such a criterion makes political as well as scientific sense. By nature, assumptions are not ordinarily subject to verification; thus, if alternative assumptions produced estimates that differed substantially from one another, the Census Bureau would be hard-pressed to justify the particular choice that formed the basis of the official adjustments.

Synthetic Method

The synthetic method is simply a way of distributing an undercount estimate for a large area (nation or state) among its component areas. It requires independently obtained estimates of the completeness of coverage for the larger area. Estimates of coverage by age, race, and sex can be obtained by demographic methods; others (e.g., for income, education, ethnic origin) must be based on matching studies. If one assumes that the national estimates of net undercount by age, sex, and race (derived as described in Chapter 1 and in the section on the demographic method, below) or by another characteristic hold for all geographic units, then an estimate of enumeration completeness for any geographic unit can be obtained by applying the national undercount rates to the enumerated population by age, sex, race, etc. in that unit (Census 1975). If E_{hij} is the estimated completeness of enumeration or coverage rate (for the United States) of individuals with age h, sex i, and race j, and P_{hijk} is the number of persons counted of age h, sex i, and race j in geographic unit k, then the enumeration completeness of unit $k (E_k)$ is given as:

$$E_k = \frac{\Sigma_h \Sigma_i \Sigma_j P_{hijk}}{\Sigma_h \Sigma_i \Sigma_j (P_{hijk}/E_{hij})} \qquad (1)$$

In equation (1), the numerator is simply the number of persons counted as living in unit k and the denominator is the true population corrected for underenumeration by age, sex, and race.

Use of the synthetic method involves the assumption that a person of age h, sex i, and race j (e.g., a black male 20-24 years of age) is as likely to be missed by the census if he lives in Alaska as if he lives in Alabama. However, the 1970 census-CPS match study indicates that coverage rates for persons of the same race and sex vary by geographic region (Census 1977a). Hence, one needs estimates of that are specific to each region. Other factors thought likely to influence the probability of being omitted, such as income and education, might be added in the estimation scheme. In adding such factors in an actual adjustment, as distinct from some illustrative ones made by the Census Bureau, it would be necessary to have some empirical information on the association between the factor and the extent of the undercount.

The sensitivity of adjustments of state population estimates to the assumptions used can be seen in a calculation made by the Census Bureau of the distribution of the adjusted 1970 population by states (and of a hypothetical $1 billion distributed according to population), using each of four sets of assumptions: one using the age, sex, and race undercount ratios for the national population; the other three using only the race undercount ratio and adding median income, proportion of the population in families below the poverty income level, and educational attainment, respectively. The effect of the alternative assumptions on each state's share of population or money may be seen in the following tabulation (calculated from Table 2 in Appendix A):

Highest of the four estimates divided by the lowest	Number of States (including the District of Columbia)
Less than 1.005	32
1.005 and less than 1.010	13
1.010 and less than 1.020	3
1.020 or more	3

The three states in the last row are Mississippi, 1.037; the District of Columbia, 1.023; and Arkansas, 1.021: that is, the highest estimate of Mississippi's share of the total population (or of any given total of funds distributed according to population) was 3.7 percent (not percentage points) more than the lowest estimate. In 45 of the states, the highest estimate was no more than 1 percent higher than the lowest; thus, the method was not very sensitive to the alternative assumptions tested.

Other factors that might be associated with differences in enumeration completeness include quality of enumeration in each area (as indicated by the percent of the population imputed because of non-interview or the percent for which some characteristics had to be allocated because of partial response), the unemployment rate, and the percent of families receiving public assistance income (both to be collected on the 1980 sample census questionnaire). Since there are no data by which to estimate an undercount rate for Spanish-origin or other minority groups (except blacks), an effective proxy reflecting the likely undercount in states and areas where they live might aid in achieving greater equity in fund distribution.

The synthetic method can be used to adjust population for areas of any size, but the smaller the area the more unstable the adjusted data would be because the assumptions become less valid. If, as seems plausible, there are wide variations among local areas in undercoverage rates for persons of the same race, sex, and age groups, the simple synthetic technique (without adding factors associated with an undercount) would have low reliability.

Demographic Method

The technique of demographic analysis gives the estimates, cited in Chapter 1, of the size of national undercounts in 1950, 1960, and 1970. This technique involves the comparison of the expected number of persons, estimated independently, with the actual number enumerated. The demographic method estimates the "true" population for each state on the basis of actual independent data for that state, rather than from national undercount ratios, applied to the local population, as does the synthetic method.

The expected number can be described as the number born minus the number who have died, adjusted to account for the number who have moved into or out of the country. The demographic method involves a number of steps. Accurate records of births are available for all states only since 1935; hence direct estimates of births can be obtained only for the population under age 35 in 1970 (under age 45 in 1980). Medicare enrollments (after adjustment for those legally unable to enroll) provide a good estimate of those 65 and over. For the middle group, aged 35-64 in 1970, there exists no independent body of data with which to compare the census. Data from previous censuses are used, with estimates of the undercount derived from the 1950 post-enumeration survey and other sources, as well as a variety of assumptions, to get the female population; sex ratios based on birth and survival estimates are used to derive the male population. Immigration and emigration data are used to develop estimates of net immigration by age, sex, and race (Census 1974). For 1980, the same techniques would be used for a smaller age group, 45-64.

A modified demographic method, similar to the national analysis, has been applied to states (Census 1977a). The major modification is to account for interstate migration. By employing information on state of birth obtained from the census and information on births obtained directly from birth registrations, the number of persons who could be expected to list a particular state as a state of birth (the number born minus the number who should have died plus an adjustment for net overseas migration) was compared with the number who actually reported having been born in that state. Differences were assumed to result from omission of persons from the census. This analysis applies to omission by state of birth, however, when what is wanted is omission by state of residence. Some assumption is needed to make this conversion. Two extreme assumptions are available: omission is a function of the state of birth, or omission is a function of the state of residence. These assumptions lead to different estimates of completeness of reports by state of residence; the Census Bureau used as the final estimate an average of the two.

Demographic analysis can yield fairly good estimates of the underenumeration of the entire population by sex and age (Census 1974). Nevertheless, it must be emphasized that a not insignificant band of error surrounds even these national estimates. This is due to the uncertainty surrounding estimates of emigration from the United

States, the net movement of government and private sector personnel to foreign assignments, net migration to Puerto Rico and United States dependencies, and undocumented immigration. Emigration of native-born persons seems to have been undercounted until 1957, when the Immigration and Naturalization Service ended attempts to collect emigration statistics, and underestimated since then. Statistics of births by state are not complete and have to be adjusted for underregistration.

Because of the relatively poor quality of the available data, a large number of assumptions are required for any estimates. In general, the data for blacks are much worse than those for whites, particularly the state-of-birth data, so that the estimates of undercoverage for blacks are more suspect than those for whites.

Reasonable alternative assumptions produce somewhat different estimates for states. Illustrative estimates of the distribution of the population by states were made by the Census Bureau from data on the undercount ratios calculated, using five alternative assumptions and two composite methods (see Table 3 in Appendix A). The sensitivity of the adjusted figures for the alternative assumptions may be seen in the following tabulations prepared for the Panel by the Census Bureau:

Highest of the four estimates divided by the lowest	Number of States (including the District of Columbia)
Less than 1.005	4
1.005 and less than 1.010	22
1.010 and less than 1.020	19
1.020 or more	6

The two highest estimates were for Alaska, 1.030, and for Nevada, 1.026: that is, the highest estimate of Alaska's share of the total population was 3.1 percent more than the lowest estimate. In 25 of the states (the bottom two rows above), the highest estimates were more than one percent higher than the lowest.

Figure 2 is a scatter diagram of net undercount rates for the states estimated by two of the seven methods, a variant of SOR-1 and composite-2.

Since no data are available on migration by county and city of birth, the method cannot be applied to areas smaller than states (unless bold assumptions are made about the within-state distribution of the birthplaces of migrants). Distribution of the state totals to areas within the state by the synthetic method, however, would be possible.

Matching Method

Matching techniques (Marks et al. 1974, Bishop et al. 1975, Blacker 1977) are sometimes called "dual systems" techniques. (They are also called "capture-recapture" techniques when the same mathematical approach is used by biologists to estimate the size of an animal, bird, or fish population by capturing, tagging, and releasing

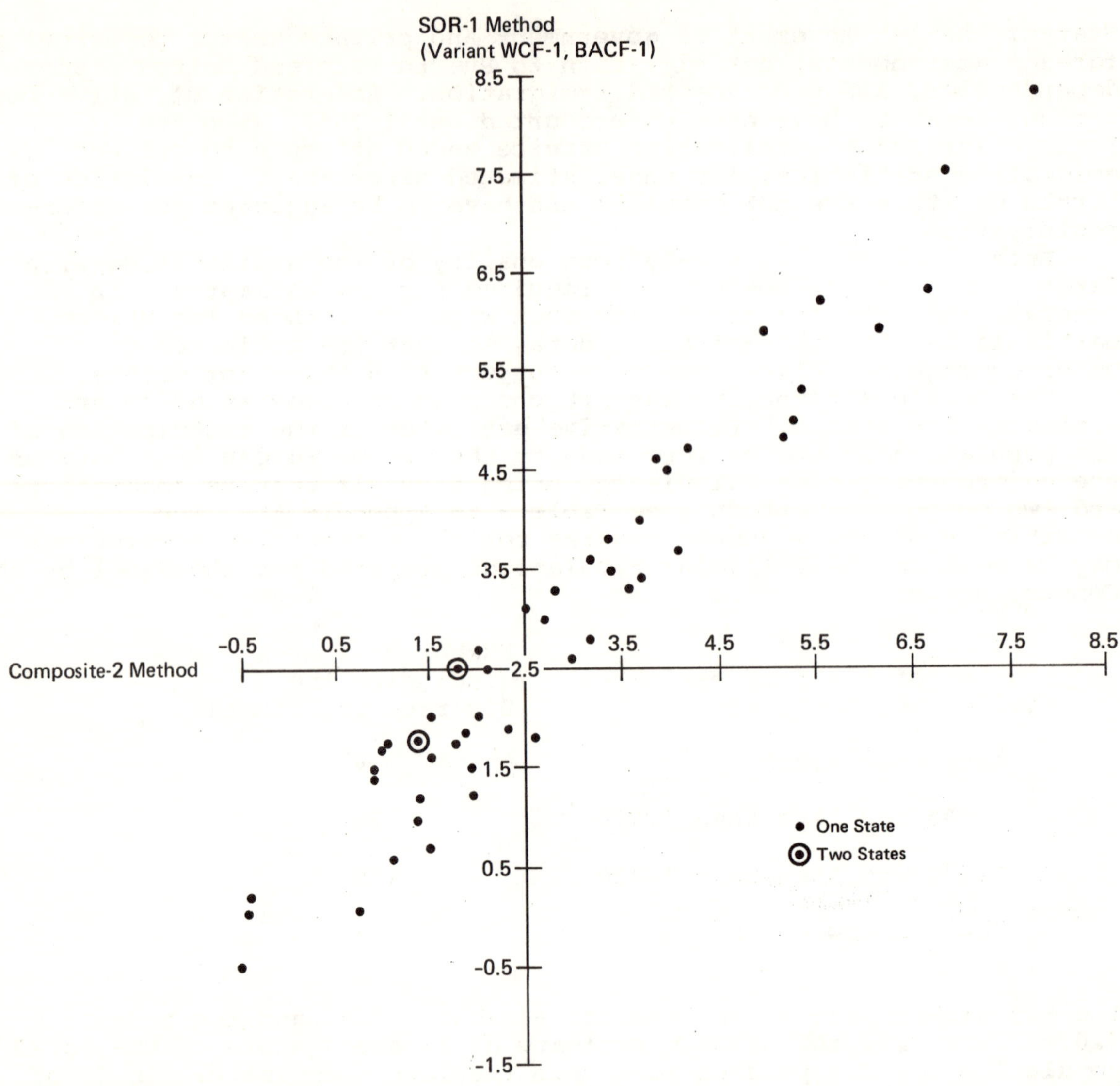

SOURCE: Appendix A, Table 3; Explanation: Appendix A.

FIGURE 2 Net underenumeration rates for 1970 total population of states estimated by two methods.

a sample of the subjects and shortly thereafter capturing another sample and determining how many had previously been captured.)

If two independent surveys are made of a population at about the same time, the total population would be composed of those who were counted both times (N_{11}), those who were counted in the first survey but not in the second (N_{10}), those who were counted in the second survey but not in the first (N_{01}), and those who were counted in neither survey (N_{00}). The object is to estimate the unknown number (N_{00}) who were not counted at all. If it can be assumed that the probability of being counted the first time $(N_{11} + N_{10})/(N_{11} + N_{10} + N_{01} + N_{00})$ is independent of the probability of being counted the second time $(N_{11} + N_{01})/(N_{11} + N_{10} + N_{01} + N_{00})$ and that N_{11} is not zero, then the unknown N_{00} can be derived as follows:

$$\frac{N_{11}+N_{10}}{N_{11}+N_{10}+N_{01}+N_{00}} \cdot \frac{N_{11}+N_{01}}{N_{11}+N_{10}+N_{01}+N_{00}} = \frac{N_{11}}{(N_{11}+N_{10}+N_{01}+N_{00})} \qquad (2)$$

hence

$$N_{00} = \frac{N_{01}\,N_{10}}{N_{11}} \qquad (3)$$

The assumption of independence is crucial. If the persons missed by one survey are likely to be missed by another, then the independence assumption will be violated, and a more complex formula has to be used, involving an estimate of the degree of correlation (El-Khorazaty et al. 1977).

The matching method has been used to estimate the undercount in census data, and it was the principal means of evaluating the 1950 census. In 1970, the census was matched to the current population survey (CPS) and estimates of underenumeration were obtained. (This study has not been published, but results are cited in several publications, including Census [1974], Census [1975], and Census [1977a].) The match estimates failed to show a higher underenumeration rate for males than for females even though this difference is firmly established by demographic analysis. The reason for the discrepancy is most likely correlation bias; those persons who were missed in the census were more likely to be missed in the CPS. Correlation bias can be reduced by matching a survey to an independent list of people, such as a register of persons holding drivers' licenses, if the factors causing underenumeration in surveys do not apply to the list. A characteristic problem in matching techniques is the difficulty in matching individuals; erroneous matches reduce the estimates of undercounts, while erroneous non-matches inflate the estimates. Finally, if an independent list of persons is used it must be made to conform in time to the census; failure to exclude from the survey or record system those who could not properly be counted in the census (deaths, emigrants) produces overestimates of the undercount.

There is no reason, however, why the method has to be limited to only two lists (i.e., the census plus one other). In fact, the larger the number of supposedly independent lists or surveys, the smaller will be the unknown residual of persons missed in all lists. Hence, the reliance that can be placed on an estimate will increase. Furthermore, a number of alternative estimates are available, depending on the assumptions made about independence among the several lists. Unfortunately, the matching bias will probably also increase.

The Census Bureau is currently evaluating a match of the Oakland pretest census to the Oakland post-enumeration survey and a combined Social Security Administration-Internal Revenue Service-Medicare file.

The Census Bureau currently plans to conduct a three-way, person-by-person match following the 1980 census, consisting of: (1) the 1980 census; (2) a post-enumeration survey, which may be an expanded CPS; and (3) a composite file consisting of names from the Social Security Administration file on current earnings, a file of 1979 income tax returns, and a Medicare file. (In the actual conduct of the 1980 census, names from other independent sources, such as drivers' licenses or alien registration records, will be matched with census records from households to pick up persons missed in the enumeration; therefore, these files could not be used in a post-census record match.) Of course, two-way matches of the census to either of the other two files will also be available. The Census Bureau hopes to reduce correlation bias by making separate estimates for race-sex-age-income-education-geographic groups among which coverage rates may be supposed to vary. The characteristics associated with being missed in the census can be learned either from the independent survey or records or by inquiry in the household about the characteristics of persons identified as having been missed.

Since the absence of correlation bias cannot be taken for granted, it is possible that not all the uncounted people will be estimated by this method. The extent to which matching methods are successful can be evaluated by comparing the undercount at a national level estimated by this method with the undercount estimated by demographic methods. The matching method, if reasonably successful by this test, could be used to distribute among states and areas the national undercount estimate derived by demographic analysis.

A sample size of approximately 250,000 households in the post-enumeration survey will be required for estimates of underenumeration in states and large cities or SMSAs; this sample would provide estimates of the adjusted population by state with a sampling error of 0.25 percent. Considering the sample size required, this method cannot be expected to yield estimates of underenumeration for small areas.

A method will be explored, however, that might make it possible to adjust the population of small areas for underenumeration. This is the proposed regression method. The post-enumeration survey sample could be so designed that it would yield, together with the results of record matching, estimates of the undercount ratios for a sample of small areas (as well as for the states and nation as a whole). The undercount ratios for each of the areas sampled could then be used as dependent variables in regression equations in which the independent variables were such demographic characteristics of the population as age, sex, race, and ethnic identity, such economic characteristics as income or unemployment, and even census operating data that may serve as a proxy for the degree of difficulty in enumerating the areas. From these regression equations, it might be possible to estimate the undercount ratios in areas not included in the post-enumeration survey or record-matching samples, since the independent variables will be available for all areas.

Summary Appraisal of Adjustment Methods

The above review of three methods by which state and local census data might be adjusted for the undercount shows that they are generally feasible. The following discussion summarizes their features in terms of accuracy, robustness, ability to adjust for all geographical areas, ability to provide adjusted estimates of the characteristics of the population of areas, the amount of time after the census before adjusted data could be issued, and the extent to which the method could be specified in advance of the census date.

Accuracy

Two of the methods, demographic and matching, appear a priori to be technically superior in that they use independent empirical data on the undercount in each geographic area rather than national undercount ratios applied to an area population. It is possible that as local data on factors associated with the likelihood of an undercount are added to the synthetic method this a priori difference would diminish.

An empirical test of how well each method actually works would be difficult to design because, as noted above, the true undercount for any geographic area is not known. A partial and not entirely conclusive test would be to see whether the estimates for states and areas derived by a method add to the total national undercount, but this test would be valid only for the matching method, since both the synthetic and the demographic methods start with an estimate of the total national undercount, and the comparison would be circular.

Another test is to see whether two independent methods give similar results. Comparison of the changes from the distribution shown by the original census count that would result from 7 different adjustment methods--4 variants of the synthetic method (Table 2 in Appendix A) and 3 variants of the demographic method (Table 4 in Appendix A)--shows that for 31 states and the District of Columbia all the changes in the state's share of national population were in the same direction. For the other 19 states, some adjustment methods raised and some lowered the state's share. This suggests the likelihood that, on the whole, the data on the geographical distribution of population would be somewhat improved by adjustment by either the synthetic or the demographic method, but the figures for some geographical units would be further from the true population after adjustment than before. No similar comparison is now possible for the matching method.

Robustness

The synthetic method appeared to be less sensitive to changes in the assumptions made than the demographic method. This comparison has to be made cautiously, however, since the assumptions tested for each of the methods do not exhaust the full range of plausible assumptions. No test was possible for the matching method.

Size of Area

The synthetic method permits adjustment of the population for even the smallest areas within states, although with results that become less reliable the smaller the area. The demographic method could be used for states only (unless rather bold assumptions as to within-state variations in migration were made), and the matching method could be used only for states and large SMSAs. Estimates for states made by either of these methods could be distributed among areas within the states by a synthetic method. In addition, on the basis of the matching techniques, regression methods might be developed to make small-area adjustments possible, but their reliability cannot be estimated until the regression equations are developed and tested with empirical data.

Characteristics

Only the matching method holds promise of obtaining characteristics of persons missed (other than age, sex, and race). The significant characteristics that might be obtained (either from households when the missed person has been identified or from the independent records) include ethnic origin, race other than white and black, and such economic characteristics as income and employment status, which would be relevant to the data needed for various formulas for the distribution of funds.

Neither the demographic method nor any synthetic method relying on the demographic method for its national undercount ratios permits an adjustment of the count of the Spanish-origin population, which is probably substantially undercounted, or indeed, for any other ethnic group, since birth and death statistics with a consistent definition of ethnic origin are not available. The effect of adjusting by race, but not ethnic origin, would be to raise the proportion of the national population in states with many blacks and to reduce the proportion in states with few blacks, including those in the Southwest with many Spanish-origin people.

Racial differences themselves may not be the major cause of the undercount: it is likely that an important factor is the social and economic status associated with being black--the higher proportion who are poor and subject to educational and other disadvantages. The same factors probably affect most other minority groups in the population, as well as non-minority persons who are poor and disadvantaged. An adjustment by race alone would over-adjust the population of areas with preponderantly middle-class black residents, who are likely to have a low undercount rate. This argues for using an adjustment method that includes either some economic or social variable associated with the likelihood of being missed or census operating data reflecting the difficulty of enumeration in an area. Such an adjustment method may be more defensible than a suggestion that has been made to adjust the counted population in the Spanish-origin or other groups believed to be underenumerated by a proxy factor (in the absence of a direct measure of their undercount ratio), for example, the undercount ratio for blacks. This would be questionable, and, as with the blacks, would overadjust the population for areas with preponderantly middle-class residents. It should be clear that while such a proxy adjustment for these groups might be considered as a way of achieving a more accurate geographical distribution of total population, it would not be defensible to estimate the total population in any one of the groups themselves because the relative error of the adjustment would be much larger for the subgroups than for the total population of an area.

Time Required for Adjustment

The amount of time after the census date that is required for completing estimates of the undercount for states and areas and adjusting the count depends on the availability of data from the tabulations of the census itself, from the independent statistics on births, deaths, and net immigration, and from the post-enumeration survey and record-matching studies. A simple synthetic method using national undercount rates developed by demographic analysis and the census tabulations on the population by age, sex, and race might take about a year and a half. A synthetic method using in addition such variables as income or education could not be completed until the state and area data on these characteristics had been tabulated and relationships between the variables and undercount rates had been shown by a post-enumeration survey. Adjustment of state population counts by the demographic method requires data on state of birth, which also would not be available until the sample data were tabulated. Adjustment using the findings of a post-enumeration survey or record matching would also take substantial additional time. As a rough estimate, about three years after the census date would be required for adjustment by any method but the simple synthetic method.

Advance Specification

If the synthetic or demographic methods were to be used (or a combination of the demographic method for states and the synthetic method to distribute state totals among areas), it would be possible to state in advance of the census the method of adjustment. It would also be possible if a matching method were to be used for states and large areas and synthetic methods were to be used for the smaller areas within the states. If, however, a matching method were to be combined with regression estimates for small areas, it might be difficult to specify the method in advance, before the reliability of the regression equations could be tested. In proposing that the method of adjustment be specified in advance of the census to aid in gaining public acceptance, the Panel recognizes that this procedure requires the Census Bureau to select a method before it can examine the results of the census.

Conclusion

On balance, on the basis of its brief study, the Panel has not identified a specific method that would clearly be superior technically and would meet the other requirements for an adjustment method. Further examinations of the issues by the Census Bureau, and research, particularly on the development of matching techniques and regression methods for estimating the undercount in local areas, might make it possible to reach more decisive conclusions.

Once the concern with local area information goes beyond total numbers of people to numbers in special groups, such as the poor or school children, the reliability of the data defining these groups becomes important. Adjusting for underenumeration makes far less difference for these estimates than adjusting for item nonresponse or response errors and biases, especially as they affect income. This calls for much more investment in research on the causes of and solutions to the problems of accurate data about individuals. Such research requires individual validity or reliability studies and experiments and better ways of adjusting for the remaining biases and omissions of such crucial data items as income and family composition.

Imputation and Adjusted Estimates

If a convention involving adjustments to the count for states and local areas should be adopted, a question arises concerning the relation of the resulting adjusted totals of the population to the unadjusted, original decennial census count, which includes data on the population distribution by many demographic, social, and economic characteristics: Should the adjusted figures be separate from the major body of data and created solely for purposes of allocating funds or should the census as a whole be adjusted for the undercount?

It is possible to envisage two alternative situations. In the first, there would be two sets of figures on the population of the country, each state, and each local area: one set, for purposes of allocating funds, based on the adjusted counts, with no data on characteristics; and another set, for all other purposes for which census data are used, based on the original count, for which the characteristics are tabulated. In the second situation, there would be only one set of population estimates, the adjusted counts, with full detail for all characteristics; in order to create this set, the full panoply of characteristics would have to be allocated to each person added to the count by the adjustment.

Under the first of these alternatives, some problems would arise from the existence of two sets of 1980 census data. Users would be unable to ascertain the composition of the estimated total population of the United States or any state or local area with respect to any characteristic--such as industry of employment, distribution of income, etc.; they would know only the characteristics of that part of the population that was counted. The intercensal estimates of population for states and local areas would, of course, use the adjusted counts as a base.

The second alternative would be generally more convenient for users of the 1980 census data, even though they would have to recognize that the characteristics for a small percentage of the population were obtained not by actual enumeration but by systematic allocation on the basis of the characteristics of similar persons for whom data were more completely reported. In the published reports of the 1970 census, users were cautioned about the percentage of responses to any question that had to be supplied by imputation. In micro-data files (samples of individual census records used for analytical purposes), "flagging" each item of imputed data further cautions users. The convenience in using one set of data for 1980 would, however, be offset by the loss of comparability with earlier censuses that were not adjusted for underenumeration. Only comparisons of the percentage composition of the population with respect to various characteristics would be appropriate. This is an important consideration in view of the immensity of the task of adjusting earlier censuses for the undercount and allocating characteristics to the added population. Analysts of historical trends through the decennial censuses and census-based data, such as the current population survey, would face difficult technical problems as a result of adjustment of the 1980 count and imputation of characteristics to the population added.

Allocating characteristics to the people added to adjust for the undercount would be an extension of what the Census Bureau has done in the past. In 1970, for example, 4.9 million persons (2.4 percent of the census total of 203 million persons and a number about equal to the estimated undercount) represent people whose existence was inferred and whose characteristics were imputed. The manner in which this was done (described below) suggests how it could be done for the people added to the count by an adjustment procedure. Thus, the Census Bureau has published data that go beyond what it collected by actual enumeration, the development of which involved an extensive system of imputations. The procedures followed and the number of cases involved are fully described in the published census reports. The users of census data have generally accepted this practice as providing improved information.

The imputation of 4.9 million people in 1970 was done for four principal types of situations: to correct for people missed by counting as "vacant" some dwelling units that were really occupied (as estimated by the national vacancy check); to correct for people living in dwelling units whose existence was determined only after the enumeration by a post office check; to include people whose households could not be visited during the census because they were not found at home by repeated visits or refused to cooperate, but for whom some information could be obtained from neighbors; to correct for cases in which a questionnaire page was not properly microfilmed or read by the FOSDIC (i.e., processing failures). Altogether, of the reported population of 203 million, 1.3 percent were imputed because of failure of enumeration and 1.1 percent because of processing failures.

The basic method by which characteristics were allocated to these 4.9 million people was by programming the computer to store a continually updated set of records for individuals and households; when a missing or deficient record came up in the processing, the most recently processed record was duplicated or partly duplicated to fill the gap. This method means that characteristics for the missing persons were imputed from the characteristics of other individuals or households in their neighborhoods. As a result of the vacancy check, for example, every n^{th} non-seasonal vacant unit in each enumeration district was selected by the computer, mechanically converted to an occupied unit, and the number of persons in the preceding occupied housing unit, together with their characteristics, was inserted into the record for the converted unit.

The purpose of the imputation procedure was to make the census statistics closer to what complete and accurate enumeration and processing would have produced and also to make the census more convenient to use because of the elimination of the "unknown" categories.

In most cases, the Census Bureau had evidence that some people (although often an unknown number) really lived in each household identified, and therefore the population was augmented in the enumeration district where it was known that some people were missed. The 1,069,000 people added by the vacancy check, however, were not known to be in the locations to which they were assigned; instead, inhabitants were allocated to a certain proportion of the "vacancies" in each enumeration district on the basis of findings for a broad region as to the proportion of the units reported as vacant that were really inhabited. Among the four types of situations in which imputation of persons was done, this one comes closest in its tenuousness to the imputation procedure that would have to be used if a decision were made to impute characteristics to population allocated to states and local areas to adjust for the undercount.

There are two ways in which the imputation of characteristics to people added to each local area by adjustment for the undercount would be different. First, the adjustment resulting from the vacancy check in 1970 began with a household to which people and their characteristics were imputed. An attempt was made to make a reasonable estimate of the household composition and personal characteristics by duplicating the composition and characteristics of other households in the same enumeration district. The adjustment for the undercount, however, begins with a number of people, possibly by race, age, and sex, allocated to an area; they could not be grouped into households, since the uncounted people have characteristics that are not typical of any household (they include nearly twice as many males as females, for example). An imputation procedure would have to be devised to deal with this fact. One possibility would be to multiply the number of persons in each race-sex-age group that appears in each tabulation of economic or social characteristics by the uniform adjustment factor for that race-sex-age group. The critical question is how different the characteristics of the uncounted people are from those of the people who were counted. The second difference is the incompatibility of the adjusted population count with the count of housing units, which are cross-tabulated in some census tables.

Cost of the Census in Relation to Possible Adjustment for the Undercount

We have noted that an attempt to make the most complete enumeration possible runs into diminishing returns. The extra efforts planned by the Census Bureau to improve the enumeration for 1980 will be costly, and they will depend in part on extra efforts by community groups to ensure participation in the census and by local governments to check the housing unit and population counts. The question may be raised whether, in view of the possibility that the count may be adjusted for underenumeration anyway (if that should be the convention that is adopted), a less perfect count should be accepted to begin with, thereby saving a substantial amount of money and work.

The Panel strongly believes that a major effort should be made to get the most complete initial enumeration that is feasible with the resources available and that at this stage in the census-taking process there should be no drawing back from the resolve to do so. First, the original count is needed for legislative apportionment. Second, with as close to a complete intial count as possible, adjusted estimates would be closer to the true total of the population, both nationally and for states and local areas. This would be true not only for the simple reason that there would be less of an undercount for which to adjust, and therefore less room for error, but also because efforts to improve coverage directed at those in the population most subject to being undercounted would, if successful, have the effect of reducing differential underenumeration.

Conclusions

Historically, the census enumeration, as tabulated and published, has been accepted as accurate and appropriate for legislative apportionnment and for distributing funds. Its general acceptance has avoided pointless argument and unnecessary confusion. Now, however, such general acceptance is less because of the Census Bureau's forthright publication of its estimates of an undercount and by the widespread perception, with which the Panel concurs, that the differential undercount creates inequities in the distribution of federal funds and penalizes particularly those areas with large proportions of the very people that many grants-in-aid programs are designed to help. Considerations of equity, therefore, require that a convention be reached on which counts are to be used, including a way in which the original counts for states and local areas could be adjusted.

The Census Bureau, custodian of the method by which representation in our legislatures has been determined for nearly 200 years, is understandably hesitant to do anything that might be interpreted as "tampering" with the population counts, especially when its studies have not been able to identify a clearly preferred method of adjustment. At this time, however, the Census Bureau's concern must be tempered by a number of considerations. One is the widespread public recognition that the count is incomplete in such a way as to be inequitable and the consequent demands that it be adjusted. A second is that, with growing sophisticaiton about the limitations and the potential of statistical techniques, the Census Bureau has been assuming the responsibility not simply of counting the population but also of producing the most accurate estimates possible of the population. For example, the Census Bureau already partially corrects decennial census data for incomplete enumeration and did so in 1970 for almost 5 million people not directly counted, on the basis of scanty information, without serious criticism. And to meet an urgent need, the Census Bureau also issues intercensal population and income estimates for thousands of local areas--estimates that may have as many questionable components as an adjustment of the decennial counts would have. Even though some of the intercensal estimates have been contested, the general public perception of the Census Bureau as a competent, unbiased, professional agency remains untarnished. Publication of a full account of the procedures used in an adjustment and their effect on the results, following the Census Bureau's practice, would reduce the danger of accusations that something improper is going on. As part of such an account, it would be essential to have an evaluation of the accuracy of the adjustment and the degree of uncertainty involved.

The Panel sees the issue of adjusting the count as an extension of the steps the Census Bureau has taken in earlier censuses toward correction of the deficiencies of the enumeration in the course of, and as part of, the census operation itself. The full correction and the imputation of demographic, social, and economic characteristics to the entire estimated population might eventually become an integral part of the taking of the census. At this point, time constraints and technical problems stand in the way of this goal, but as the Census Bureau gains experience and conducts further research, we hope the goal can be attained.

Meanwhile, to meet the urgent demand for some greater degree of equity, a temporary expedient has to be considered. The Panel believes that a greater degree of equity would be achieved if errors resulting from failure to find and collect information about every inhabitant of the United States in the 1980 census were adjusted for, in the best way currently available, in the state and local area figures that are used for the distribution of federal funds.

Use of the adjusted estimates only for distributing funds and not for legislative apportionment or other legal uses might disarm some potential criticism. (As an example of such other uses, a number of states have established classes of communities, based on population, that have different powers and duties. Illustrations of provisions related to size of population are cited in Hauser [1975]). If a demand to use the adjusted estimates for apportionment or other legal purposes should arise, the Panel believe the issue is best left to the Congress or state legislatures.

In certain important respects, the use of population data for apportionment differs from its use for distributing funds. Apportionment for the U.S. House of Representatives is a constitutional matter, and the manner in which it is done has many legal ramifications (which the Panel did not investigate). Moreover, the legal requirement for state population figures to be produced by 9 months after the census date and local figures by 3 months later would preclude adjustments by any of the methods available. The law also specifically rules out the use of the mid-decade census for congressional apportionment. Intercensal estimates, used in distributing funds and probably embodying greater margin for error, are not used for apportionment. It is for distributing funds that the greatest demands for an adjustment to the census are made. Estimates by the Census Bureau show that if an adjustment had been made to the state population data for 1970, there would have been only a small effect on congressional apportionment, although apportionment in state legislatures or city councils is somewhat more likely to be affected (Census 1975).

The Panel's review of the Census Bureau's research on methods of adjusting for the undercount, and of attempts by various people to do the adjustment, shows that the methods so far devised have limitations. The demographic and matching methods cannot be used for all areas; they would have to be supplemented by synthetic methods for estimates within states. Matching methods using regression to make estimates for small areas are untested and could not be specified in advance of the 1980 census. Only a simple synthetic method lends itself to adjusting the counts for small areas in less than about 3 years after the census is taken. While it is plausible that adjustment would generally improve the data on the geographic distribution of population, it is also quite likely that the figures for many areas would be further from the true population after adjustment than before. In the past, some communities that believed their population had been undercounted complained to the Census Bureau or took the issue to court; if the population data were adjusted, communities that would lose funds as a result might do the same. On balance, however, the Panel believes that it would be better to make even a modest improvement in general equity through crude methods of adjustment than to continue the present situation.

Adjustment of the population figures of states and local areas would have a greater effect on some formulas for distributing funds than on others. In one major program, general revenue sharing, income has a greater weight than population, and adjusting the population count without simultaneously adjusting the income data for underenumeration (or underreporting of income) could result in little or no improvement in the equity of the distribution of funds under this program (Census 1975). For other programs, adjusting the population count would have a greater effect in improving the equity of distribution. Research should continue on how to adjust income data, as well as other characteristics, for the effects of the undercount.

Whether to adjust the census counts is, in part, a policy issue, while how to do it is primarily a technical one. The Panel believes that the decision on whether to adjust should be made by policy officials in the Administration, who are answerable to the Congress; the technical advice of the Census Bureau should be used in that decison. Under law, the Secretary of Commerce is responsible for taking the census. If the Secretary agrees with the Panel's view that greater equity would be achieved by adjusting the census results for states and areas for underenumeration, she should, after appropriate consultation, direct the Census Bureau to do so. The directive should be sufficiently specific so that the Census Bureau will not be subject to pressure from various interested groups.

If adjustment is decided upon, the methods should be determined by the Census Bureau, with technical advice from such sources as it may seek. The Panel considered whether the Census Bureau should be relieved of this responsibility, but concluded, on balance, to support the principle that these decisions should be made by the technically competent agency charged with making the best estimates it can.

Three additional obligations might be imposed on the Census Bureau in this connection. First, it should publicly state the methods it proposes to follow in making these adjustments, with a procedure for obtaining comments from the public; the procedure finally decided upon should be announced in advance of the census date of April 1, 1980. Second, it should make the estimates within a reasonable time, which can be defined by the Secretary of Commerce on the basis of the needs for data for determining the distribution of funds. Third, the Census Bureau should publish a full account of the way it made the adjustment and the effect upon the estimates, including if possible an assessment of the accuracy, or degree of uncertainty, in the adjusted figures, following its traditional practices.

The Census Bureau would thus have full technical responsibliity for the methods used, within the limits prescribed by the Secretary of Commerce. It will in theory have a variety of technical options, ranging from such simple procedures as a basic synthetic method to elaborate techniques involving the results of a post-enumeration survey, record matching, and regression methods for making estimates for individual areas. The Panel recognizes, however, that constraints of time and resources may limit the options. Different methods could be introduced for future censuses if they prove better.

At the present time, adjustment for underenumeration is considered by the Panel to be essential in the figures used for the distribution of funds, i.e., in the census figures offically designated as appropriate for this purpose in Directive No. 13 of the Office of Federal Statistical Policy and Standards (Commerce 1978). The adjustment should be made only in the total population and the distribution of the total among states and areas, not in any of the characteristics of the population of states and areas (except those for which the adjustment method is clearly appropriate). The adjusted total population counts for states and areas should serve as a basis for the intercensal estimates used for the distribution of funds. The Panel does not recommend adjustment of the census counts used for legislative apportionment.

As a goal, some members of the Panel believe it would be desirable if an adjustment could be applied to the social and economic characteristics of the population, not only because some of these affect the distribution of funds, but also for the development of better data on characteristics for analytical uses. Reaching this goal will, however, require further technical and methodological research, and it may not be achieved for some time to come.

The Panel recognizes that adjustment of population data would have implications for series such as the employment and unemployment data developed from the current population survey for states and localities. The distribution of federal funds under the Comprehensive Employment and Training Act would be affected by changes in the unemployment figures; at the same time, there would be a problem of discontinuity in the employment and unemployment series.

The Panel considered the possibility that efforts to achieve the most complete enumeration possible might be undercut by the knowledge that the count might be adjusted for underenumeration. A major effort should be made to get the most complete initial enumeration feasible, to reduce the amount by which adjustments would have to be made and thus leave less room for error. The Panel firmly believes that neither in the funding of the census operation nor in the work of community groups or local governments to achieve a complete count should there be any relaxation of effort.

Recommendations

23. The Panel concludes that inequities resulting from the geographic differentials in the decennial census undercount could be reduced by adjustment of the data for underenumeration. Methods of adjustment with tolerable accuracy are feasible. While the application of these methods has some arbitrary features and while the figures for some areas would not be made closer to the correct distribution of population, the Panel believes that on balance an improvement in equity would be achieved.

If the Secretary of Commerce agrees with the Panel's conclusion, the Panel believes she should direct the Census Bureau to adjust for underenumeration the counts for the total population of the United States, the states, and local areas, for use in distributing funds. The adjustments would not be applied to the counts used for legislative apportionment nor to the body of census data on the characteristics of the population. The adjusted data for the decennial census would serve as the basis for intercensal estimates of the population of states and areas prepared for use in distributing funds.

24. The technical responsiblity for the adjustment procedure should reside in the Census Bureau. In carrying out this responsibility, the Census Bureau should: publicly state, in advance of the census date, the general methods it will follow in making the adjustment so that interested parties may comment on them; prepare the adjusted figures within a reasonable time after taking the census and at least in time for their use in the first intecensal population estimates for small areas; and publish a full account of the methods it followed in making the adjustments and the effect of those methods on the estimates for states and local areas. This account should include, to the extent feasible, an assessment of the accuracy of the adjustments.

25. The Census Bureau should continue research on methods for improving both the enumeration of the population and the evaluation of its completeness; on methods of adjustment for underenumeration, including methods of assessing the accuracy of the adjusted estimates at the state and substate levels; and on methods for full imputation

of characteristics to the uncounted population. Finally, the Census Bureau should continue research and data improvement work that are needed to provide a firmer underpinning for the national demographic estimates that are believed to be the best method for estimating the total population, especially for the weakest elements, emigration and undocumented immigration, both of which are difficult to measure.

COMMENTS BY PANEL MEMBERS
EDDIE N. WILLIAMS AND LEOBARDO F. ESTRADA

While we concur with the Panel's findings, we regret that the Panel report does not pursue those findings to their logical conclusion: that the Secretary of Commerce should direct the Census Bureau to make a synthetic adjustment of the 1980 census data to correct for underenumeration.

The failure to pursue such a specific recommendation is based, we understand, on the nature of the charge given to the Panel by the Department of Commerce. The Department asked us "to investigate the feasibility of adjusting census counts, and subsequent population estimates, for underenumeration, and assess the implications of such procedures." The Panel has fulfilled this responsibility. In doing so, however, the Panel has not told the Department or the Bureau anything either did not already know. What is missing, it seems to us, is a Panel comment on the advisability of making an appropriate adjustment in 1980 in order to assure greater equity in the distribution of funds.

Given our findings that an underenumeration creates inequities and that there are feasible methods of adjustment to reduce such inequities, we cannot avoid the inevitable conclusion that the Department of Commerce should make an adjustment for underenumeration.

We think we do the Department a grave disservice by hiding our views on this subject behind a narrow, literal interpretaion of our charge.

REFERENCES

Bishop, Yvonne, Stephen Fienberg, and Paul Holland (1975) Discrete Multivariable Analysis: Theory and Practice. Cambridge, Massachusetts: MIT Press.

Bixby, Lenore E. (1977) Statistical Data Requirements in Legislation. Prepared for the Committee on National Statistics, National Research Council. Washington, D.C.: National Academy of Sciences.

Blacker, John (1977) "Dual Record Demographic Surveys: A Re-Assessment." Population Studies, November, pp. 585-597.

El-Khorazaty, M. Nabil, Peter B. Imrey, Gary G. Koch, and H. Bradley Wells (1977) "Estimating the Total Number of Events with Data from Multiple-record Systems: A Review of Methodological Strategies," International Statistical Review, Vol. 45, pp. 129-157. Great Britain: International Statistical Institute.

Hauser, Philip M. (1975) "On Population", Chapter 2 in Social Statistics in Use. New York: Russell Sage Foundation.

Marks, Eli, William Seltzer, and Karol Krotki (1974) Population Growth Estimation. New York: The Population Council.

U.S. Bureau of the Census. "Estimate of Coverage of Population: Census-CPS Match." 1970 Census of Population and Housing, Evaluation and Research Program. Unpublished.

U.S. Bureau of the Census (1974) Estimates of Coverage of Population by Sex, Race, and Age: Demographic Analysis. 1970 Census of Population and Housing, Evaluation and Research Program, PHC(E)-4. Washington, D.C.: U.S. Government Printing Office.

U.S. Bureau of the Census (1975) Coverage of Population in the 1970 Census and Some Implications for Public Programs. Current Population Reports, Special Studies, Series P-23, No. 56. Washington, D.C.: U.S. Government Printing Office.

U.S. Bureau of the Census (1977a) Developmental Estimates of the Coverage of the Population of States in the 1970 Census: Demographic Analaysis. Current Population Reports, Series P-23, No. 65. Washington, D.C.: U.S. Government Printing Office.

U.S. Bureau of the Census (1978) Form letter from Meyer Zitter, Chief, Population Division, to local officials, dated February 1978, enclosing the Census Bureau's July 1, 1976 estimates of population for each city and supporting data.

U.S. Department of Commerce, Office of Federal Statistical Policy and Standards (1978) Statistical Policy Handbook, Washington, D.C.: U.S. Government Printing Office.

6. EVALUATION OF THE 1980 CENSUS AND STEPS TO IMPROVE FUTURE CENSUSES

For each decennial census it has conducted, especially since 1950, the Census Bureau has made a major effort to evaluate quality and completeness. Decade by decade, the scope of its research program has grown as the Census Bureau seeks both a systematic and cumulative understanding of the size and seriousness of census-taking errors.

The Census Bureau's evaluation programs have three objectives: (1) to evaluate specific census operations and procedures; (2) to provide data users with measures of response variance and bias; and (3) to understand the various kinds of errors made in order to take corrective steps in future censuses and surveys. For 1980, there is a greater appreciation than previously of the need to evaluate also the interrelationships among census routines or practices and a greater sensitivity to the possibilities of providing different kinds of data users with evaluation measures suited to their particular purposes.

At this point, the Census Bureau's evaluation plans for the 1980 census are still being formulated, and what the Panel reviewed were the drafts of the plans that were prepared for review by the Census Bureau's advisory committees. Some of these drafts were early-stage lists of a variety of evaluation projects, with few priorities indicated, put together for the purpose of getting initial reactions from the advisory groups. The Panel's comments are made with the tentative nature of the program in mind. These comments concern the direction and emphasis of the Census Bureau's plans and call attention to some important features of census work that are relatively neglected.

The Census Bureau's 1980 evaluation program can be conveniently divided into four categories: experimental projects, content assessments, coverage improvement assessments, and coverage evaluations. Each of these is examined separately, both to clarify the Census Bureau's concerns and hesitations about each category and to provide a background for the discussion that follows, which emphasizes alternative approaches and different concerns that the Panel has identified.

Experimental Projects

The experimental projects category is the least homogeneous part of the evaluation program. It is oriented toward procedures that might be followed in 1985 or later. Perhaps the leading high-priority project is a proposal to try a two-stage enumeration approach in selected areas, with short forms first mailed to everyone and long forms later obtained from a sample of respondents, either by mail or personal visit. Another project will test the list-leave procedure: an enumerator hand-delivers the questionnaire, completes the household listing with the respondent, and leaves the form to be filled out and returned (in contrast to the current mail-out/mail-back procedure). An assessment would be made of the effects on coverage, costs, and response rates of the list-leave procedure. These experimental projects have been identified as optional approaches to basic census design; each clearly has significant ramifications for the overall design of the enumeration process.

Other projects in this category are an experimental design to evaluate 3 or more proposed methods of editing questionnaires and a separate proposal to compare computerized editing methods with conventional editing.

A third, clearly important project would seek to test alternative and presumably simpler versions of census questionnaires, including a non-FOSDIC form. The aim would be not only to see if mail return rates are substantially different, but also to discover if instructions are less confusing, formats easier to understand, incomplete returns less frequent, and responses more accurate by some independent criteria.

Some of these projects touch on this Panel's concerns about the present plans for the 1980 census, particularly the two-stage enumeration, the list-leave procedures, and the non-FOSDIC questionnaire, and the Panel would be glad to see these experiments pursued. (Whether the best way to conduct them is in the context of the 1980 census in which experiments might divert attention of Census Bureau management from the main business at hand is a question best left to the Bureau.) Because questionnaire content changes, different formats and routines for editing questionnaire forms also need to be tested. Variations on the mail-out/mail-back procedure need to be systematically explored.

There is a quality of belatedness in the Census Bureau's own documents describing some of the large-scale, high-priority experiments being currently considered; the criteria to measure how worthwhile each would be are not specified. The opportunity for genuine experimentation in adequately monitored contexts during the actual census enumeration can be most productive for projects that have had extensive prior testing. The process would be helped by evaluation by the Census Bureau's advisory committees and through other institutionalized arrangements by which social scientists in various disciplines can contribute their judgments to the design and selection of experimental projects and to the analysis and interpretation of the results.

Content Assessments

A quite different part of the 1980 evaluation program is the work on accuracy of response. One large project calls for a re-enumeration of a sample of households, probing extensively for various kinds of response bias. Other content-error studies being considered involve matching census long-form responses with records for the same structures or individuals to be found in other surveys (e.g., about 15,000 housing units in the annual housing survey for 1979 or the full sample of persons interviewed in the current population survey for March 1980). Other such studies would use matched records found in specialized files, such as the tax and escrow records in selected localities (to check mortgage, tax, and insurance costs reported in the census), the disability benefits file of the Social Security Administration (to check reports of disability on the census), or the individual taxpayer files of the Internal Revenue Service (to check income). There would be no attempt to reconcile disparities by reinterview.

Many of the content assessment studies involve collecting data during the enumeration stage of the 1980 census. This is the case, for example, of studies of the effectiveness of the Census Bureau's quality controls used in the prelist, precanvass, and edit phases of field operations. Similar evaluations are being considered on: (a) the use of Spanish-language questionnaires; (b) the results from team enumeration in hard-to-enumerate areas; (c) the use of assistance centers; and (d) various other specialized census procedures.

Taken individually, these projects are often well designed. They are reviewed for feasibility and value not only by Census Bureau specialists but also by consultant panels of experts; often, too, they can be shown to measure the bias or variance effect in the response patterns under investigation. These content assessment studies traditionally have provided a rigorous research basis for Census Bureau attempts to produce unbiased estimates of specific demographic parameters; to keep the response variance between enumerators or betweeen coders within tolerable lists; or to reduce the net error rates on particular counts to negligible levels, even if the gross error rates remain high. However, such studies pay inadequate attention to attitudinal determinants of questionnaire response, the interaction dynamics that occur in enumerator-respondent relationships, the effects of mass belief patterns on the willingness of people to answer personal questions, and the significance of a community's organizational resources in locating census evaders and other missing cases. The kind of respondent observation and interview study recommended by the Panel (see Chapter 3) would address some of these questions.

Again, there seems to be an ad hoc quality about much of the content assessment work proposed for 1980. Each problem is seen as analytically distinct; each project is a feasible and relatively inexpensive way of measuring the error and distortion due to one or more of the intertwined factors affecting the content and quality of specific data items. For this reason, one of the proposed evaluation projects has special appeal: the development of generalized estimates of mean-square errors for areas of different sizes, in which sampling error, non-sampling error biases, and non-sampling error variances would all be reflected. This kind of integrative project begins to give coherence to an evaluation research program, although it is very difficult to do.

Coverage Improvement Assessments

A third part of the 1980 evaluation program is devoted to coverage improvement assessments. Numerous procedures and operations to be used in 1980 have never before been part of the decennial census, although they may have been tested under less extensive conditons. It is manifestly important to assess the "yield" from such new operations and thus to gauge their success in improving coverage. Some are very necessary operations: for example, plans have been made to precanvass each enumeration district in areas where questionnaires will be mailed and to correct the address register listings.

Certain procedures that have previously been used as post-censal statistical checks on the accuracy of the count are to become part of the main census operation. These include plans to match driver's license files, Immigration and Naturalization Service files, and similar nonhousehold sources of names and addresses with census enumeration records to identify individuals missed in the household enumeration, with a view to enumerating them in time to be included in the census (before ending the field collection in a given area). Another procedure transferred from the post-censal to the actual census operation stage is a follow-up on all housing units classified as vacant in order to find those that are actually occupied.

New to the census operation will be special handling of whole households found at such places as vacation sites, but having a usual residence elsewhere; listings by the "casual count" method of persons found in bars, pool halls, and other nonhousehold settings, whose living arrangements might make them difficult to enumerate otherwise; and cooperation with local officials in mail-out areas in previewing the count of residential addresses on each block and later in reviewing the enumeration count data for blocks, tracts, and jurisdictions, so that those familiar with the locality will spot anomalies in the address lists and early raw-count tallies. Because these procedures are costly, it will be important to have systematic measures of their effectiveness for the planning of future censuses.

Such measures are also needed for the human input into the census operation. Census-taking is a complex process carried out by a small professional cadre who hire, train, and supervise a large temporary work force. Those in charge of particular districts, offices, or regional headquarters are continually evaluating the performance of enumerators, crew leaders, coders, and other personnel. Often, the routines developed for address listing, checks of movers, missing person traces, close-out decisions, and a host of similar practices are modified in the field as necessary, with work assignments changed, job descriptions revised, and work flow rechanneled.

Many of the "in process" quality controls used to identify poor performances, falsification of data, and other enumerator-specific faults leave no trace once corrective actions are taken. They are simply a necessary part of the personnel management practices that are selectively invoked as circumstances require them. However, a measure of the "enumeration complexity" found to characterize a given enueration district would be useful. It could start with some of the quality-control barometers that are maintained by Census Bureau administrators (e.g., flags that indicate editing-phase complications or completion-rate difficulties). Imputation rates for each enumeration district, both for missing persons and for partly incomplete questionnaires, could also be included. Measures, even crude ones, might be added to ascertain how newsworthy events were responded to in a particular locality at the time of the census. Adverse publicity about the census may inhibit public cooperation and thus seriously affect mail return rates as well as the validity and completeness of responses to particular questions.

In 1980, special organized efforts are to be made by the Census Bureau's community services program to increase the willingness to be counted, especially in minority communities. Such efforts seem likely to be intensive in hard-to-enumerate areas and less strenuous in other areas. Measures of the duration and penetration of such efforts could also be devised, as another factor affecting the "enumeration complexity quotient" of a given block, district, or tract.

In 1980, then, a wide variety of statistical measures can and will be generated in the field operations stage of the census. On one hand, these measures can provide a basis for assessing the efficacy of newly installed data collection and processing procedures; on the other hand, they can also be used to assess the impact of field performance on census coverage (Census 1978, p., 27):

> The current monitoring programs (such as quality control operations) provide answers to such questions as "How well was a given procedure carried out?" but do not answer such equally important questions as "What effects do specific field operations have on coverage?" or "Does the amount of coverage improvement from some procedure vary with the type of area?" or "Are district offices with good performance records located in areas with good census coverage?"

In the past, little has been done to analyze the relationship of field performance to census coverage. In 1980 the Census Bureau is considering a significant effort--which the Panel strongly endorses--to design the post-enumeration survey (PES) so that a number of coverage estimates for household and population characteristics can be produced for a national probability sample of small areas for which data on operating problems in enumeration and on the results of various coverage improvement assessment projects will be available.

Four types of data for each sampled unit would thus be available in the same data base, in proportions representative of the nation as a whole: (1) census data on population and housing; (2) coverage estimates on age, sex, race, or other characteristics computed from PES data; (3) yields for different coverage improvement procedures studied in the evaluation program; and (4) quality control data about the work of the district staff, field performance information about all phases of the enumeration process in each area, and, perhaps, a composite measure of "enumeration complexity" in a given area. These data would permit study of underenumeration correlates, the links between field performance and coverage, and a wide variety of interactional and contextual factors that could be useful in planning and conducting future censuses.

Coverage Evaluation

The fourth part of the 1980 evaluation program is the estimation of the completeness of coverage at both national and subnational levels. This is related to the important issue of whether and by what method census counts for states and local areas could be adjusted for underenumeration.

The Census Bureau's current plans rely principally on demographic techniques to provide estimates of census coverage for the country as a whole; on the dual (or multiple) systems technique--matching--and demographic methods to develop estimates for states; and on dual (or multiple) systems and statistical techniques (such as regression) to develop estimates for local areas.

The demographic method, discussed in the previous chapter, involves estimating the population on the census date by adding to a corrected population estimate for the previous census period the number of births and immigrants and subtracting the number of deaths and emigrants--all by sex, age, and race. When this is done at the state level, estimates of interstate migration must also be made.

The Census Bureau's plans for demographic estimates include tests of the accuracy of the characteristics reported on birth and death records and the Medicare enrollment data used to estimate the older population. The most serious deficiencies--the incompleteness of the migration statistics because of the influx of undocumented immigrants and the lack of satisfactory data on emigrants-- are recognized, and there are plans for research on them. As long as these gaps remain, there will always be a nagging question on the accuracy of the demographic method in estimating total population and the completeness of census enumeration.

A costly but essential method of coverage evaluation is the dual or multiple systems technique, which depends on matching census results with those of independent surveys or record systems to identify the numbers, location, and characteristics of missed persons. This method may make it possible to adjust state and area population counts for undercoverage on the basis of estimated differential coverage rates rather than by crude allocation of national undercount estimates. By identifying the characteristics of missed persons, this method also provides insights into the reasons for undercounts and aids in planning coverage improvement. It does not, however, yield estimates of total undercoverage and so has to be used together with demographic analysis.

The major alternatives for an independent survey are either a specially designed post-enumeration survey or the current population survey for a date close to census day, April 1. The former is the preferred: the CPS sample is far smaller than what is needed to produce estimates of underenumeration for states and large SMSAs. A large-scale PES should yield undercoverage estimates for persons of Hispanic origin, at least in areas having substantial Hispanic-origin populations.

To reduce the bias resulting from estimating the number of people missed by another household survey that is subject to some of the same difficulties as the census, a matching of the PES with the combined Internal Revenue Service-Social Security Administration-Medicare files is being considered. Another method being considered is "network" or "multiplicity" sampling, in which an individual is picked up not only in the household where he or she resides, but also in the enumeration of households where a specified relative (e.g., parent, sibling) resides. This method, which is still being tested, may improve the enumeration of such frequently missed people as black males.

In the Canadian census of 1976, a "reverse record check" was used: people were identified from the last previous census, birth records, immigration records, and persons missed in the last previous census but found in its post-enumeration survey, and the current census records were checked to see if persons so identified were enumerated. The major problem with this method is in tracing individuals and matching names and other identifiers: in trying this method for the 1960 census, the Census Bureau was unable to match 16 percent of the persons whose names they started with and therefore was unable to determine whether they were enumerated in the census. It is plausible that the undercount rate for the people who could not be matched is higher than for those for whom a match was made. The undercoverage estimates made by this method will therefore vary greatly according to the assumptions made about the enumeration of those unmatched. Because of the Canadian experience, the Census Bureau may find it worthwhile to explore this method further.

The Census Bureau is further hoping to develop regression equations for small areas that would show the relationship between rates of underenumeration (as shown by PES-derived estimates of coverage) and such independent variables as: relevant data on community characteristics such as racial composition or median family income; measures reflecting the quality of the census operation in the area, such as percentage of persons with one or more missing-data allocations or percentage of forms requiring telephone follow-up; and coverage improvement assessment results, such as number of persons added by searches of non-household record sources. Using such equations, coverage estimates could be made for areas not falling within the PES sample. The research could not only make it possible to develop estimates of underenumeration rates for all areas (and therefore more solidly based adjustments to the census count), but could also provide insight about the concomitants of underenumeration and possibly point to ways in which coverage can be improved. The success of such research will depend on the ability of the PES to provide reasonably accurate coverage estimates for a sample of small areas.

An important part of coverage evaluation projects is record matching. This can be done economically and with acceptable precision only if there is enough identifying information on the census and the matching lists. All lists need to be sorted on an ordered set of identifiers starting with the most reliable and stable and have to include a redundant set of identifiers to allow for errors, multiple possiblities, and changes. Actual names are rather far down on such a list since people can, and in the case of women often do, change names, and there are frequently alternative spellings. In the case of Orientals, and some people of Spanish origin, even determining the last or family name is difficult. Social Security numbers, not now on census questionnaires, are probably better than surnames, and have less duplicates, although people can have more than one number.

The long-run implications of all this are that a serious attempt to improve the census count, to improve the detailed estimation of the undercount, and to improve the census methods would require adding more identifiers to the census itself, particularly alternative surnames for women (maiden names or married names), alternative addresses, and the Social Security number or numbers. If Congress wants more accurate counts by small areas, or ways of estimating populations and special subpopulations (the poor, for example) by small areas, it must consider that the price of such data is the use of identifiers, probably including Social Security numbers.

There can be safeguards against the potential invasion of privacy. There would be no permanent transfer of information from other lists to the census list and the data retained about the cases missed by the Census Bureau would easily be limited to the basic census demographic characteristics or such of them as were on the other list. For some small-scale studies of the reasons for missing people, some people might be approached for additional information about where they were on the census day and other facts or opinions relevant to understanding their exclusion.

Nor would there be a serious cost problem, although some of the identifiers, those to be used in mechanical sorting and matching, would have to be on the data tapes, not just on the census forms. The advantages of being able to sort on Social Security numbers, rather than on an overlapping set of names and addresses or ages, is obvious.

Indeed, since no single identifier is totally reliable, the process of matching to locate individuals missed in the census might well involve matching first on Social Security number, but separately by state, then matching with a national alphabetic or Social Security number-ordered census file for those not found in the first match. Computers would be required if any of this matching were to be economically feasible, which means that the basic census computerized files would have to contain, and be sorted by, such things as name,

Social Security number, and perhaps zip code or state. A separate file of secondary names or addresses given on the census might be useful to resolve cases where the individual is in other files under another name or address, but was actually enumerated. (It should be clear that the Social Security individual account records themselves do not include a current address of the worker; only if the Social Security number is included in some other file that has a current address [e.g., drivers' license records or personal income tax reports] would a current address be available to match to census records.)

Very little such file matching is economically feasible for the 1980 census except on an experimental basis to develop hypotheses about the demographic groups most subject to underenumeration and the reasons for it. But if there is to be a mid-decade census in 1985, Congress should consider seriously whether an investment in collecting and computerizing the information necessary for matching to build up full counts would be worth the cost in operations and in explaining to the public that this offers no real threat to privacy because of traditional Census Bureau practices and legal safeguards.

General Comments

The Census Bureau's 1980 evaluation program is broad and varied; in important respects it is also innovative and imaginative. But many of its high-priority experimental projects (such as trials of a two-stage enumeration, computerized editing, and testing of alternative questionnaire versions) seem to be justified too largely on ad hoc grounds. A greater sense of the interdependence of census-taking practices is evident in the plans for selected content appraisal projects (e.g., evaluating coding practices, quality control procedures, and response error rates) and especially in the efforts to view each distorting and complicating factor as a contribution to the total net error index that characterizes the quality of particular data. The need to study a variety of evaluation problems in the same sample universe is recognized by the Census Bureau in their work on coverage improvement assessment.

What remains is to give consideration to the distinctive difficulties of 1980 and the historically emerging problems facing the Census Bureau in its future census and survey work. This discussion in turn should raise again a number of questions about how the Census Bureau might improve its clientele and constituenecy contacts by cultivating more durable and penetrating work relationships and what the Census Bureau needs to do to capitalize and consolidate its research program more systematically and extensively than in the past. One way to improve the research program is by continuing to strengthen the Census Bureau's staffing in the social sciences. The Census Bureau can also work more closely with the social science community in the design and analysis of program components, so that the individuals and groups consulted are more likely to make substantive contributions rather than merely to voice reservations or suggest minor changes and the like. In the future, as the work of the Census Bureau becomes more difficult, it will have to rely more on outside advice and consultation. Recent developments clearly foreshadow the complexities--changing American lifestyles, heightened public suspicion, and group pressures--under which future national enumeration efforts must be conducted.

The last few years have seen a dramatic escalation in the Census Bureau's consultative relationships. Very simply, this has meant that significantly larger numbers of outside voices have affected what the census takers will try to do in 1980. Demographers and social scientists have made professional appraisals; federal program administrators and state and local government officials have made critical as well as constructive evaluations; legislators have held hearings at which they have challenged Census Bureau plans and policies; representatives speaking for the housing industry, the marketing community, agriculture, and other economic sectors have had effective consultative opportunities; and those who directly speak for the interests of cultural and ethnic minorities have been able on a regular basis to suggest improvements in what the Census Bureau does.

Moreover, it is the exemplary practice of the Census Bureau--in its various meetings with advisory committees of all kinds--to compile and disseminate the minutes of virtually all sessions. Groups are encouraged to make recommendations, touching on highly specific points as well as on general practices. Most impressive is the evidence of Census Bureau responsiveness contained in such records. Almost without exception, recommendations are thoughtfully and often extensively examined by staff, and written replies are provided to the group in question. Improvements could be made, to be sure, especially by speeding up the preparation of minutes. At least occasionally, some of the questions seem ill-conceived, just as some of the answers seem diplomatically vague.

The Census Bureau should seek effective ways to increase the continuity, sustain the amount of interaction, and raise the level of mutual awareness of relevant concerns on the part of both its personnel and the members of its advisory groups. The best payoff comes from arrangements that bring more fresh and thoughtful perspectives to bear on Census Bureau problems.

Recommendations

26. The Census Bureau should improve its clientele and constitutency contacts by strengthening the work relationships between its personnel, the members of its advisory groups, and representatives of the social science community. Specifically, the Census Bureau should devise ways to increase the continuity, sustain the amount of interaction, and raise the level of mutual awareness of relevant concerns and contributions among these people, so that the participation of outside groups is less confined to reactive patterns, voicing reservations, suggesting minor changes, and the like.

27. In the Census Bureau's research programs, designs for seriously considered individual projects should be systematically formulated so that they can be profitably reviewed by advisory groups. The apparently ad hoc nature of the research efforts would be better understood and evaluted if projects were placed within a systematic framework that shows their linkage to others in an overall research program, sets project priorities, and provides a timetable for experimental and evaluation work.

28. The Census Bureau should continue its efforts to design evaluation programs so that many of them will be carried out in the same test sites. For example, the 1980 post-enumeration survey should include some of the same geographical areas as those sampled for various coverage improvement assessment projects. Thus, data from both the PES and the evaluation projects would contribute to the same data

base; this would facilitate future study of underenumeration correlates, the links between coverage and field performance, and a wide variety of other factors, which could be worthwhile in planning and conducting future censuses.

29. The orientation of the Census Bureau's evaluation research program should be examined, with particular emphasis on developing innovative and imaginative projects to deal with some of the census-taking problems arising out of life patterns that do not conform to standard or typical life styles and on developing ways to measure the attitudes and motivations that determine response.

REFERENCE

U.S. Bureau of the Census (1978) "Proposals for Coverage Evaluation of the 1980 Census," prepared for the March 1978 meeting of the Census Advisory Committee of the American Statistical Association, Washington, D.C.

7. CONCLUSIONS AND RECOMMENDATIONS

The 1980 census will be more costly than ever and probably more difficult than any in a century. The important uses of its results, including allocation of funds among states and local areas, intensifies the pressures on the Census Bureau to make the census as complete as possible. At the same time, changes in life styles and other social changes increase the difficulty of enumeration: for example, with more women working, fewer are available for temporary census jobs, and there are fewer housewives to answer the enumerator's knock during the day, and a larger number of undocumented aliens increases the number of persons averse to being identified by the authorities and skeptical of assurances of confidentiality. Meanwhile, costs generally have risen, and special measures to improve the completeness of the enumeration will further raise the costs of the census.

The Census Bureau's general plans for the 1980 census are responsive to this situation. These plans are well considered, reflect the concerns expressed by advisory and other groups in the community, and can be expected to be generally effective. Several innovations have the potential for considerably improving the enumeration: the development of improved mailing lists; the inclusion in the actual census of record matching and vacancy checks that had previously been used for post-censal statistical evaluation; and plans for active participation by local government officials during the course of the census. The Panel is concerned, in fact, that these plans may not be fully and effectively carried out in view of their costs and difficulties. The Panel also is concerned about a few elements of the plans.

Procedures to Improve Completeness of Coverage

The present plans for procedures to improve the completeness of enumeration represent a distinct step forward. The plan for mail delivery and return of the census questionnaires in areas where 90 percent of the population lives takes advantage of the fact that a majority of residents are literate and civic-minded so that efforts can be focused on those who fail to return the forms or who are difficult to enumerate. There is a further advantage in accuracy when the form is filled out at a time that is convenient for the household so that records and household members can be consulted.

The Panel is impressed with the advantages that will result from creating the most complete mailing list of dwelling places possible, since it serves as one control over enumerator error. Gains in enumeration completeness should result from incorporating in the actual census process two procedures formerly used only after the census had been taken to make statistical corrections: a check of apparently vacant dwellings for possible occupants and the matching of records from nonhousehold sources. Matching is costly and difficult, but has a potential for yielding substantial gains in completeness.

The Panel is concerned, however, that reliance on postal delivery will result in the loss of personal contact with households in difficult-to-enumerate areas, possibly resulting in incomplete listing of household members; less use of Spanish-language questionnaires than would be desirable; and special difficulties for other people who do not read English easily.

Recommendation 1. Experiments with an enumerator dropping off the questionnaire, describing the census process, answering inquiries, listing household members, helping where it may be necessary, and then leaving the form to be completed and mailed in should be conducted in difficult-to-enumerate areas, either before or during the 1980 census. Tests should be made to see if this procedure results in a higher mail return rate, a more complete listing of persons living in the household (as judged by matching records and post-enumeration surveys), and more requests for a Spanish-language questionnaire.

Recommendation 2. With the cost of the 1980 census projected to be close to $1 billion, the Census Bureau will want to consider the cost-effectiveness of various procedures to improve enumeration. To aid in this consideration, the Census Bureau should compile data, as in some test censuses and as in 1970, on the cost and the effect of each procedure in increasing coverage.

Recommendation 3. The Census Bureau should study the pros and cons of more extensive matching than is now planned for use during the enumeration process and undertake experiments in a few places to provide guidance for 1985 and later. The difficult issue of privacy that is involved has to be balanced against the opportunity to improve the count.

Census Staffing Problems and Issues

A competent and well-trained temporary staff is essential to achieving a complete and accurate enumeration, and the Census Bureau is aware of the factors that exacerbate costly turnover. The Panel's review of plans for the recruitment, selection, and training of enumerators and other temporary staff indicates that the Census Bureau is attempting to improve hiring procedures, particularly as they affect minority groups whose participation is recognized as essential for successful completion of the census in hard-to-enumerate areas. The Panel is also encouraged that research is in progress on effective selection methods and that plans are being developed for cooperative recruitment programs with colleges and high schools.

Recommendation 4. In order to ensure competent temporary staff, improve morale, and reduce turnover, the Census Bureau should emphasize a number of actions already planned, including the following:

a. Provide more explicit information in recruitment about the types of work and work schedules, the different bases of payment (piece work versus hourly or other time rates), and the frequency of payment. The Census Bureau should also provide more information about the products of the census and what is done with them that has importance for the temporary worker, the workers' family, and the worker's community.

b. Monitor the staffing, mechanics, and content of the selection interview, which is possibly the most critical link in the chain of selection devices in view of the variety of referral sources used. The Census Bureau should also extend its reseach on selection tests in an effort to find better ways of identifying those applicants who are most likely to be effective interviewers in challenging situations.

c. Experiment further with various types and sizes of teams for enumeration, including peer groups among young adults, and the relationship of team enumeration to other ways of organizing enumerators' work under certain conditions.

Recommendation 5. As a means of improving the performance of enumerators and other temporary staff, the Census Bureau should make every effort to improve the materials and logistics for training. As a complement to these efforts, the Census Bureau should give added attention to selection and training of crew leaders, whose pivotal role as members of the field staff includes training of enumerators.

Recommendation 6. The Census Bureau should try to make the experience of the temporary employee more satisfying by making some concrete gesture when the work is completed, perhaps a certificate that would indicate that census work is an investment in the individual's future; this would be particularly valuable to young workers in applying for other jobs.

The Public Information and Community Relations Program

The Panel believes that the extensive community relations program planned for 1980 is worthwhile and likely to help in gaining public support, even though no direct measure of effect on completeness of coverage appears feasible at this time; but more research on the effectiveness of various methods of publicity than has been done is needed to guide future efforts in this area. The Panel believes that the Census Bureau should be in a position to determine the tone and content of its information program and to pay for advertising, as appropriate, by media that may find it difficult to carry census material free, such as papers and radio stations directed at ethnic minorities. The Census Bureau is presently limited in its control over those aspects of the information program by its dependence on the free advertising provided through the efforts of the Advertising Council.

Recommendation 7. The Census Bureau should continue to develop its research program on communication aspects of the census, broadly conceived, as well as research on operational aspects of the communication program.

Recommendation 8. The Census Bureau should shift to paid advertising in 1980, rather than the free publicity provided through the efforts of the Advertising Council.

Recommendation 9. In view of the need for continued improvements in the Census Bureau's communications, we recommend that the Census Bureau establish a permanent communication advisory group.

The Questionnaire and Its Effect on Response

The Panel believes the length and apparent complexity of the long form of the questinnaire now being used in dress rehearsal censuses could discourage response or reduce respondents' willingness to exert the effort needed to report adequately and completely. With the 1980 census so largely dependent on self-enumeration, the present format and wording of the questionnaire should be reviewed with a view to facilitating respondents' understanding of and ability to respond to the questionnaire.

Recommendations. The Panel has a number of recommendations on the format of the questionnaire itself and on the clarity of, and rationale for, certain questions; they are discussed in the body of the report (Chapter 3) without attempting to identify positively which changes are practicable for the 1980 census and which for the longer run.

Recommendation 10. The Census Bureau should conduct more pretests, not as part of any dress rehearsal but in small surveys, in which the respondent is asked to complete the questionnaire in the presence of an observer, verbalizing thought processes, and questions, as the form is being completed. Following completion of the questionnaire, the observer would ask questions to determine what problems existed and the cause of the problems. Results from this type of pretest would facilitate question redesign for fuller respondent comprehension.

Recommendation 11. To prepare for the 1985 and later censuses, the Panel encourages the Census Bureau to conduct more tests, especially in difficult-to-enumerate areas, comparing self-enumeration and enumerator-administered procedures. These tests would provide valuable information on the relative quality of responses, the comparability of task demands made by each procedure, and on relative costs.

Race and Ethnic Origin

Accurate and complete statistics on persons by race or ethnic origin require not only their inclusion in the overall count but also their correct racial or ethnic identification. The Panel, therefore, examined the plans for getting information on ethnic origin and race in the census.

The Panel has serious concerns about the validity and reliability of the origin and ancestry questions. Response is based wholly on self-identification, which is closer to a person's opinion or feeling than to an objective fact. As such, it is not a permanent characteristic and could reflect the transitory success of self-awareness efforts by ethnic groups. At the same time, the Panel deplores the loss of the traditional question on birthplace of parents, which, even with its limitations, did provide some objective information on second-generation Americans with various national origins. The Panel therefore proposes certain rules and limitations for the compilation and publication of the data based on the questions on origin and ancestry and the issuance of caution to users of the data. The Panel believes that research on the meaning of the data should be conducted, that data required to supplement and better understand the responses to these questions should be collected in the 1980 census, and that instructions to enumerators and coders should be clarified.

Recommendation 12. Because of the validity and reliability concerns about the origin and ancestry questions, the following limitations are recommended:

a. No imputation procedures should be used in field or computer editing of these two questions, and a "not stated" category should be accepted.

b. Census publications (including those in forms like public use tapes that allow user manipulation of individual records) should clearly specify the limitations of the data.

Recommendation 13. The Panel supports the current population survey planned for November 1979. This survey should include both self-identity and objective multi-generational origin questions in order to provide an opportunity for analysis of responses on ethnicity. The Census Bureau should also use the origin and ancestry information to evaluate responses to racial categories other than white or black.

Recommendation 14. The question on place of birth of parents should definitely be included, if at all possible, in the 1980 census; it should be included in the Lower Manhattan dress rehearsal. The Census Bureau should use the data in cross-tabulations with the responses to questions, 4, 7, and 13 to provide users with additional insights on the meaning of those responses, and appropriate tabulations of social and economic characteristics of the foreign stock should continue to be made.

Recommendation 15. The instructions for enumerators and coders on handling write-in responses to the "Other" race category should be reviewed for consistency and should be specified in detail to conform to federal guidelines. For this purpose, the list of American Indian tribes should be reviewed for both completeness and comparability of level of taxonomy. Terms in current use by American Indian tribal persons should be considered for inclusion (see list on p. 142).

Recommendation 16. The effect of the proposed 1980 census racial categories and instructions to enumerators (which differ from those used in previous censuses) on the demographic techniques used to evaluate underenumeration and to develop intercensal estimates should be investigated.

Household Composition

The Panel notes that the traditional pattern of identification of people with a single fixed household does not hold for some. Instead, cultural patterns have developed involving group living and also household networks with tenuous relationships to any one household. The latter are particularly common among persons most subject to underenumeration--low-income blacks and some other minority groups.

The Panel devoted considerable attention to the possibilities of ethnographic research as a tool for documenting the occurrence of household networks and for identifying the characteristics of persons particularly subject to underenumeration. The Panel is deeply concerned, however, that Census Bureau sponsorship of extensive participant-observer studies, particulary if undertaken in direct conjunction with a census, might be seen as a serious invasion of privacy.

Recommendation 17. Further research should be undertaken on means of identifying and enumerating members of kinship networks that tend to occur among the population most subject to underenumeration.

Recommendation 18. A program of participant-observer studies has great potential for providing insight into the cultural and social problems associated with census-taking, especially in difficult-to-enumerate areas, and for providing clues to characteristics of persons missed in household surveys. To avoid any possible implication of invasion of privacy by the Census Bureau, the Panel recommends that additional studies not be sponsored or funded by the Bureau, but rather be conducted under the aegis of an independent research organization.

Plans for Local Review and Procedures for Handling Contested Counts

The issue of how contested counts should be handled is closely related to two other issues: participation by local government officials in the conduct of the census and how to adjust the census count for underenumeration. The local review program, giving local government officials an opportunity to correct errors at two stages in the census process, could be effective not only in improving the count but also in averting subsequent disagreements. Some of the disagreements that survive this process might later be resolved if the count were to be adjusted for remaining underenumeration (see below). The success of the local review program, however, is endangered by limitations of expertise, data, time, or resources in many local governments. Further, the Census Bureau has to be prepared for the possibility that its own intercensal population estimates for the 1970-1980 period will be used to contest the 1980 census results.

Recommendation 19. The Census Bureau should alert local public officials to the local review program as soon as possible, and well before the planned January 1979 date; it should concentrate sufficient resources to prepare appropriate mailing lists by an earlier date to reach not only the chief elected officials but also appropriate technical staff.

Recommendation 20. The Census Bureau should mount an effective program to assist local areas to take advantage of the local review program, including, but not limited to:

a. Conducting seminars or workshops at national conventions attended by the appropriate local officials and at state conventions of city and county officials;

b. Assisting local communities with geographic coding of local records; and

c. Publishing articles to reach local government officials, through such organizations as the National League of Cities and county governmental associations, with cogent arguments to elicit the interest of readers.

Recommendation 21. The Census Bureau should publish its intercensal local area population estimate for late in the 1970-1980 decade with adequate qualifications to prevent their improper use as a basis for contesting the 1980 population census counts. The estimates being marketed by the National Technical Information Service should be accompanied by an unambiguous statement that they do not represent estimates by the U.S. Department of Commerce.

Recommendation 22. The Census Bureau should establish a formal review process for contested counts of the 1980 decennial census to supplement the informal process currently in place and to provide a route of appeal for dissatisfied local officials short of filing suit in a court of law. The local governments should be required to bear part or all of the financial burden involved when this process is invoked.

Feasibility of Adjusting Local Census Counts and Population Estimates

Despite all the procedures to improve coverage the Census Bureau has planned, it is unrealistic to expect that a complete enumeration will be attained. To raise the completeness of the count from 98 percent to 99 percent would increase costs sharply, and to raise it further would entail proportionately larger cost increases. Short of drastic measures that the American people probably would not tolerate, some undercount will remain. If, as in the past, it has different effects on different groups in the population or on different geographic areas, a serious issue of inequity arises.

The use of the population census and post-censal population estimates for allocating federal funds creates special problems in view of the inherent imperfections of censuses. For allocating funds, controversy can be avoided only if there is a generally accepted convention governing the way in which the census data will be used. The convention might be to accept the original count or to adjust it by a method to be described in advance. The Panel reviewed the characteristics and limitations of several general methods for adjustment and was unable to select any one of them at this time as clearly superior.

In view of the present uncertainty about methods for adjustment, the Census Bureau is understandably hesitant about engaging in anything that might be interpreted as tampering with figures that are used for so many important purposes. Yet the issue of equity cries for attention.

The Panel notes that the Census Bureau already is engaged in other work that involves substantial exercise of professional judgment to develop estimates on the basis of data with severe limitations. One important instance is the development of biennial intercensal population and income estimates for 39,000 geographic areas, many of them small. A second instance is the addition to the population actually enumerated in the 1970 census of several million persons whose existence was inferred from partial evidence and whose characteristics were estimated from those of other persons in the same communities. The adjustment of census data for the remaining undercount may be seen in principle as an extension of these imputation procedures by which the 1970 census data were made more complete.

The Census Bureau is to be commended for responding imaginatively and responsibly to these needs for information. The Panel is confident that the Census Bureau would also be able to respond in an appropriate and competent fashion to a directive to adjust the state and local population data for the undercount if a decision were made to adjust.

The Panel believes that such adjustments in the population totals would lead to greater equity in the distribution of funds among states and local areas. It recognizes the limitations of the methods now available, including the probability that an adjustment that generally improves the estimates of geographic distribution of the population would produce figures for some individual areas that are farther from the true population instead of closer.

Whether to adjust the census estimates is largely a policy issue; how to do it is primarily a technical one. The decision of whether to adjust should be made by the Secretary of Commerce, the policy official responsible for taking the census, who is answerable to Congress; the technical views of the Census Bureau would be available to aid in this decision. The decision as to methods of adjustment should be determined by the Census Bureau.

A decision to adjust the census results should not affect efforts on the part of the Census Bureau, community groups, and local governments to make the 1980 census enumeration as complete as possible.

Recommendation 23. The Panel concludes that inequities resulting from the geographic differentials in the decennial census undercount could be reduced by adjustment of the data for underenumeration. Methods of adjustment with tolerable accuracy are feasible. While the application of these methods has some arbitrary features and while the figures for some areas would not be made closer to the correct distribution of population, the Panel believes that on balance an improvement in equity would be achieved.

If the Secretary of Commerce agrees with the Panel's conclusion, the Panel believes she should direct the Census Bureau to adjust for underenumeration the counts for the total population of the United States, the states, and local areas, for use in distributing funds. (See comments by Panel members Eddie N. Williams and Leobardo F. Estrada, page 115.) The adjustments would not be applied to the counts used for legislative apportionment nor to the body of census data on the characteristics of the population. The adjusted data for the decennial census would serve as the basis for intercensal estimates of the population of states and areas prepared for use in distributing funds.

Recommendation 24. The technical responsibility for the adjustment procedure should reside in the Census Bureau. In carrying out this responsibility, the Census Bureau should: publicly state, in advance of the census date, the general methods it will follow in making the adjustment so that interested parties may comment on them; prepare the adjusted figures within a reasonable time after taking the census and at least in time for their use in the first intecensal population estimates for small areas; and publish a full account of the methods it followed in making the adjustments and the effect of those methods on the estimates for states and local areas. This account should include, to the extent feasible, an assessment of the accuracy of the adjustments.

Recommendation 25. The Census Bureau should continue research on methods for improving both the enumeration of the population and the evaluation of its completeness; on methods of adjustment for underenumeration, including methods of assessing the accuracy of the adjusted estimates at the state and substate levels; and on methods for full imputation of characteristics to the uncounted population. Finally, the Census Bureau should continue research and data improvement work that are needed to provide a firmer underpinning for the national demographic estimates that are believed to be the best method for estimating the total population, especially for the weakest elements, emigration and undocumented immigration, both of which are difficult to measure.

Evaluation of the 1980 Census and Steps to Improve Future Censuses

The Census Bureau has an evaluation program that is both broad and varied, encompassing experimental projects, content assessments, coverage improvement assessments, and coverage adjustment evaluations. In the time available, the Panel could undertake only a limited review of that program. It is clear that there are a number of interesting and worthwhile projects under consideration, but many need more detailed specification. Moreover, there is a need to integrate various parts of the evaluation program so that they contribute more significantly to a common and complex evaluation data base. The data base needed is one that would open up new possibilities for analysis, provide data on which generalized estimates of error can be developed, and yield systematic information on the correlates of local underenumeration that could lead to estimates of undercoverage and to improvement of methods for future censueses.

Recommendation 26. The Census Bureau should improve its clientele and constitutency contacts by strengthening the work relationships between its personnel, the members of its advisory groups, and representatives of the social science community. Specifically, the Census Bureau should devise ways to increase the continuity, sustain the amount of interaction, and raise the level of mutual awareness of relevant concerns and contributions among these people, so that the participation of outside groups is less confined to reactive patterns, voicing reservations, suggesting minor changes, and the like.

Recommendation 27. In the Census Bureau's research programs, designs for seriously considered individual projects should be systematically formulated so that they can be profitably reviewed by advisory groups. The apparently ad hoc nature of the research efforts would be better understood and evaluted if projects were placed within a systematic framework that shows their linkage to others in an overall research program, sets project priorities, and provides a timetable for experimental and evaluation work.

Recommendation 28. The Census Bureau should continue its efforts to design evaluation programs so that many of them will be carried out in the same test sites. For example, the 1980 post-enumeration survey should include some of the same geographical areas as those sampled for various coverage improvement assessment projects. Thus, data from both the PES and the evaluation projects would contribute to the same data base; this would facilitate future study of underenumeration correlates, the links between coverage and field performance, and a wide variety of other factors, which could be worthwhile in planning and conducting future censuses.

Recommendation 29. The orientation of the Census Bureau's evaluation research program should be examined, with particular emphasis on developing innovative and imaginative projects to deal with some of the census-taking problems arising out of life patterns that do not conform to standard or typical life styles and on developing ways to measure the attitudes and motivations that determine response.

APPENDIX A

TABLES OF UNDERENUMERATION RATES BY STATE AND ESTIMATES OF THE DISTRIBUTION OF $1 BILLION BY VARIOUS METHODS

Legend

Tables 1 and 2

Basic Synthetic Method: Makes adjustments for net underenumeration according to national enumeration rates for age, sex, and race groups.

Modified Synthetic Method: Basic synthetic method, and in addition, one of
- proportion at low-income level,
- median family income, or
- educational attainment.

Tables 3 and 4

SOR 3-1, 3-2: Makes adjustments for net underenumeration according to state-of-residence estimates prepared separately for each state by demographic methods, two variants.

Composite-2: Makes adjustments for net underenumeration according to a combination of demographic analysis and matching studies.

Sources:

Tables 1 and 2 from U.S. Bureau of the Census, _Coverage of Population in the 1970 Census and Some Implications for Public Programs_, Current Population Reports, Special Studies, Series P-23, No. 56. Washington, D.C.: U.S. Department of Commerce, 1975. Pp. 25, 26.

Tables 3 and 4 from U.S. Bureau of the Census, _Developmental Estimates of the Coverage of the Population of States in the 1970 Census: Demographic Analysis_, Current Population Reports, Special Studies, Series P-23, No. 65. Washington, D.C.: U.S. Department of Commerce, 1977. Pp. 99, 111.

Table 1. RATES OF NET UNDERENUMERATION ACCORDING TO THE POPULATION CORRECTED BY THE BASIC SYNTHETIC METHOD AND BY VARIOUS MODIFIED SYNTHETIC METHODS, FOR STATES, DIVISIONS, AND REGIONS: 1970

(See text for explanation of methods)

Region, division, and State	Basic synthetic method		Modified synthetic method		
	Age, sex, and race	Race only	Proportion at low income level	Median family income	Educational attainment
United States, total	2.5	2.5	2.5	2.5	2.5
Northeast	2.4	2.4	2.3	2.1	2.3
New England	2.1	2.1	2.0	1.8	2.0
Maine	1.9	1.9	1.9	2.2	1.8
New Hampshire	1.9	1.9	1.8	1.9	1.8
Vermont	1.9	1.9	1.9	2.0	1.8
Massachusetts	2.1	2.1	2.0	1.8	2.0
Rhode Island	2.1	2.1	2.0	2.0	2.1
Connecticut	2.3	2.3	2.1	1.8	2.1
Middle Atlantic	2.6	2.5	2.3	2.2	2.4
New York	2.6	2.6	2.4	2.2	2.4
New Jersey	2.6	2.5	2.3	2.0	2.4
Pennsylvania	2.4	2.4	2.3	2.2	2.3
North Central	2.4	2.4	2.2	2.1	2.3
East North Central	2.5	2.5	2.3	2.1	2.4
Ohio	2.5	2.5	2.3	2.1	2.3
Indiana	2.3	2.3	2.2	2.1	2.2
Illinois	2.7	2.7	2.5	2.1	2.5
Michigan	2.6	2.6	2.3	2.0	2.4
Wisconsin	2.1	2.1	2.0	1.9	2.0
West North Central	2.2	2.1	2.1	2.2	2.1
Minnesota	2.0	1.9	1.9	1.8	1.9
Iowa	2.0	2.0	1.9	2.0	1.9
Missouri	2.5	2.5	2.4	2.5	2.5
North Dakota	1.9	1.9	1.9	2.3	1.9
South Dakota	1.9	1.8	1.9	2.3	1.8
Nebraska	2.1	2.1	2.0	2.2	2.0
Kansas	2.2	2.2	2.1	2.3	2.1
South	3.0	3.1	3.0	3.6	3.3
South Atlantic	3.1	3.2	3.1	3.4	3.4
Delaware	2.8	2.8	2.6	2.5	2.7
Maryland	3.0	3.0	2.7	2.3	2.9
District of Columbia	6.4	6.1	5.1	4.2	5.1
Virginia	3.0	3.0	2.9	3.0	3.2
West Virginia	2.0	2.1	2.2	2.7	2.4
North Carolina	3.2	3.2	3.2	3.9	3.6
South Carolina	3.7	3.7	3.8	4.7	4.5
Georgia	3.4	3.5	3.4	4.1	4.0
Florida	2.8	2.8	2.8	3.2	2.9
East South Central	3.0	3.1	3.2	4.4	3.6
Kentucky	2.3	2.3	2.4	2.9	2.7
Tennessee	2.8	2.9	2.9	3.5	3.1
Alabama	3.3	3.5	3.6	4.8	4.0
Mississippi	3.8	4.1	4.5	7.2	5.1
West South Central	2.8	2.8	2.9	3.5	3.0
Arkansas	2.9	3.0	3.2	4.8	3.5
Louisiana	3.6	3.7	3.8	5.1	4.2
Oklahoma	2.3	2.2	2.3	2.8	2.2
Texas	2.7	2.7	2.6	2.9	2.6
West	2.2	2.1	2.0	1.9	1.9
Mountain	2.0	2.0	1.9	2.0	1.9
Montana	1.9	1.8	1.8	2.0	1.8
Idaho	1.9	1.9	1.9	2.1	1.8
Wyoming	1.9	1.9	1.9	2.0	1.8
Colorado	2.1	2.1	2.0	2.0	1.9
New Mexico	1.9	1.9	2.0	2.2	1.8
Arizona	2.0	2.0	1.9	2.0	1.9
Utah	1.9	1.9	1.9	1.9	1.8
Nevada	2.3	2.2	2.1	1.9	2.1
Pacific	2.2	2.2	2.0	1.8	2.0
Washington	2.0	2.0	1.9	1.8	1.9
Oregon	2.0	2.0	1.9	1.9	1.9
California	2.3	2.3	2.1	1.9	2.1
Alaska	2.1	1.8	1.6	1.2	1.6
Hawaii	1.3	0.8	0.8	0.7	0.7

Table 2. DISTRIBUTION OF ONE BILLION DOLLARS BY STATES, DIVISIONS, AND REGIONS ACCORDING TO THE 1970 CENSUS POPULATION COUNT AND THE 1970 CENSUS POPULATION CORRECTED BY THE BASIC SYNTHETIC METHOD AND BY VARIOUS MODIFIED SYNTHETIC METHODS

(See text for explanation of methods. Numbers in thousands)

Region, division, and State	Census count	Basic synthetic method[1]	Modified synthetic method: Proportion at low income level	Modified synthetic method: Median family income	Modified synthetic method: Educational attainment	Difference from census count: Basic synthetic method[1]: Amount	Basic synthetic method[1]: Percent	Modified synthetic method: Proportion at low income level: Amount	Proportion at low income level: Percent	Median family income: Amount	Median family income: Percent	Educational attainment: Amount	Educational attainment: Percent
United States, total	1,000,000	1,000,000	1,000,000	1,000,000	1,000,000	-	-	-	-	-	-	-	-
Northeast	241,348	241,066	240,863	240,238	240,762	-283	-0.1	-485	-0.2	-1,111	-0.5	-586	-0.2
New England	58,293	58,028	58,011	57,878	57,968	-265	-0.5	-282	-0.5	-415	-0.7	-325	-0.6
Maine	4,889	4,857	4,862	4,873	4,855	-32	-0.7	-27	-0.6	-16	-0.3	-35	-0.7
New Hampshire	3,630	3,607	3,607	3,605	3,604	-23	-0.6	-23	-0.6	-25	-0.7	-26	-0.7
Vermont	2,188	2,174	2,176	2,177	2,172	-14	-0.7	-12	-0.5	-12	-0.5	-16	-0.7
Massachusetts	27,993	27,861	27,853	27,778	27,829	-132	-0.5	-140	-0.5	-215	-0.8	-165	-0.6
Rhode Island	4,673	4,649	4,651	4,646	4,650	-24	-0.5	-22	-0.5	-27	-0.6	-23	-0.5
Connecticut	14,920	14,880	14,862	14,800	14,858	-40	-0.3	-58	-0.4	-120	-0.8	-61	-0.4
Middle Atlantic	183,056	183,037	182,851	182,359	182,794	-18	-	-205	-0.1	-696	-0.4	-262	-0.1
New York	89,754	89,831	89,712	89,426	89,660	+77	+0.1	-42	-	-328	-0.4	-94	-0.1
New Jersey	35,270	35,275	35,218	35,078	35,226	+4	-	-52	-0.1	-193	-0.5	-44	-0.1
Pennsylvania	58,031	57,931	57,921	57,856	57,907	-100	-0.2	-110	-0.2	-175	-0.3	-124	-0.2
North Central	278,382	277,921	277,763	277,122	277,616	-462	-0.2	-619	-0.2	-1,260	-0.5	-766	-0.3
East North Central	198,059	197,928	197,735	197,083	197,680	-132	-0.1	-324	-0.2	-976	-0.5	-380	-0.2
Ohio	52,412	52,357	52,318	52,173	52,303	-55	-0.1	-94	-0.2	-239	-0.5	-110	-0.2
Indiana	25,555	25,495	25,479	25,428	25,471	-60	-0.2	-76	-0.3	-127	-0.5	-84	-0.3
Illinois	54,685	54,762	54,685	54,458	54,669	+77	+0.1	-	-	-227	-0.4	-16	-
Michigan	43,669	43,683	43,622	43,430	43,621	+14	-	-47	-0.1	-239	-0.5	-48	-0.1
Wisconsin	21,738	21,630	21,631	21,594	21,616	-108	-0.5	-107	-0.5	-144	-0.7	-122	-0.6
West North Central	80,323	79,993	80,028	80,039	79,936	-330	-0.4	-295	-0.4	-284	-0.4	-386	-0.5
Minnesota	18,722	18,608	18,614	18,586	18,592	-114	-0.6	-108	-0.6	-136	-0.7	-131	-0.7
Iowa	13,900	13,818	13,826	13,830	13,807	-82	-0.6	-74	-0.5	-71	-0.5	-93	-0.7
Missouri	23,015	23,003	23,009	23,005	22,995	-12	-0.1	-6	-	-10	-	-19	-0.1
North Dakota	3,040	3,019	3,023	3,031	3,020	-21	-0.7	-17	-0.6	-9	-0.3	-20	-0.6
South Dakota	3,278	3,255	3,259	3,269	3,253	-24	-0.7	-19	-0.6	-9	-0.3	-25	-0.8
Nebraska	7,301	7,265	7,269	7,278	7,257	-36	-0.5	-32	-0.4	-23	-0.3	-44	-0.6
Kansas	11,066	11,025	11,029	11,040	11,012	-41	-0.4	-37	-0.3	-26	-0.2	-55	-0.5
South	308,993	310,423	310,858	312,512	311,387	+1,430	+0.5	+1,865	+0.6	+3,519	+1.1	+2,393	+0.8
South Atlantic	150,915	151,823	151,850	152,305	152,219	+908	+0.6	+935	+0.6	+1,389	+0.9	+1,304	+0.9
Delaware	2,697	2,703	2,700	2,695	2,700	+6	+0.2	+3	+0.1	-2	-0.1	+3	+0.1
Maryland	19,300	19,393	19,345	19,260	19,366	+93	+0.5	+45	+0.2	-40	-0.2	+66	+0.3
District of Columbia	3,722	3,874	3,825	3,786	3,824	+152	-4.1	+103	+2.8	+64	+1.7	+102	+2.7
Virginia	22,872	22,985	22,972	22,989	23,025	+112	+0.5	+100	+0.4	+117	+0.5	+152	+0.7
West Virginia	8,582	8,537	8,565	8,597	8,566	-45	-0.5	-17	-0.2	+15	+0.2	-16	-0.2
North Carolina	25,006	25,167	25,198	25,349	25,278	+161	+0.6	+192	+0.8	+343	+1.4	+272	+1.1
South Carolina	12,746	12,891	12,921	13,041	13,003	+145	+1.1	+175	+1.4	+295	+2.3	+257	+2.0
Georgia	22,583	22,789	22,809	22,946	22,927	+207	+0.9	+226	+1.0	+363	+1.6	+344	+1.5
Florida	33,407	33,483	33,515	33,641	33,530	+76	+0.2	+108	+0.3	+234	+0.7	+123	+0.4
East South Central	63,004	63,293	63,524	64,204	63,683	+290	+0.5	+520	+0.8	+1,200	+1.9	+680	+1.1
Kentucky	15,840	15,800	15,838	15,898	15,864	-40	-0.3	-2	-	+57	+0.4	+24	+0.1
Tennessee	19,308	19,356	19,396	19,503	19,422	+48	+0.3	+88	+0.5	+195	+1.0	+113	+0.6
Alabama	16,947	17,083	17,148	17,348	17,200	+137	+0.8	+201	+1.2	+401	+2.4	+253	+1.5
Mississippi	10,908	11,054	11,142	11,455	11,198	+146	+1.3	+234	+2.1	+547	+5.0	+290	+2.7
West South Central	95,074	95,307	95,484	96,003	95,484	+232	+0.2	+410	+0.4	+929	+1.0	+410	+0.4
Arkansas	9,463	9,493	9,540	9,690	9,558	+29	+0.3	+77	+0.8	+227	+2.4	+95	+1.0
Louisiana	17,926	18,118	18,179	18,404	18,244	+192	+1.1	+253	+1.4	+478	+2.7	+319	+1.8
Oklahoma	12,593	12,553	12,569	12,620	12,543	-40	-0.3	-24	-0.2	+27	+0.2	-50	-0.4
Texas	55,092	55,144	55,196	55,290	55,139	+51	+0.1	+104	+0.2	+197	+0.4	+46	+0.1
West	171,276	170,591	170,517	170,128	170,235	-685	-0.4	-759	-0.4	-1,148	-0.7	-1,041	-0.6
Mountain	40,759	40,521	40,547	40,540	40,476	-237	-0.6	-212	-0.5	-219	-0.5	-282	-0.7
Montana	3,417	3,393	3,395	3,399	3,389	-24	-0.7	-22	-0.6	-18	-0.5	-27	-0.8
Idaho	3,508	3,484	3,488	3,494	3,482	-24	-0.7	-20	-0.6	-14	-0.4	-26	-0.7
Wyoming	1,636	1,625	1,626	1,627	1,624	-11	-0.7	-10	-0.6	-9	-0.5	-12	-0.7
Colorado	10,861	10,811	10,812	10,799	10,791	-50	-0.5	-49	-0.5	-61	-0.6	-69	-0.6
New Mexico	4,999	4,965	4,975	4,982	4,961	-34	-0.7	-24	-0.5	-18	-0.4	-38	-0.8
Arizona	8,721	8,668	8,676	8,671	8,664	-53	-0.6	-45	-0.5	-50	-0.6	-57	-0.7
Utah	5,212	5,177	5,181	5,179	5,172	-36	-0.7	-31	-0.6	-33	-0.6	-40	-0.8
Nevada	2,405	2,398	2,395	2,389	2,393	-6	-0.3	-10	-0.4	-16	-0.7	-12	-0.5
Pacific	130,518	130,069	129,970	129,588	129,759	-448	-0.3	-548	-0.4	-930	-0.7	-758	-0.6
Washington	16,774	16,683	16,680	16,640	16,657	-92	-0.5	-94	-0.6	-134	-0.8	-117	-0.7
Oregon	10,290	10,226	10,233	10,226	10,219	-64	-0.6	-57	-0.6	-64	-0.6	-72	-0.7
California	98,178	97,940	97,857	97,538	97,692	-237	-0.2	-321	-0.3	-640	-0.7	-486	-0.5
Alaska	1,487	1,479	1,474	1,466	1,472	-8	-0.5	-13	-0.9	-20	-1.4	-14	-1.0
Hawaii	3,788	3,740	3,725	3,717	3,719	-48	-1.3	-63	-1.7	-71	-1.9	-69	-1.8

- Rounds to less than 500,000 or to less than ± 0.05 percent.

[1] Based on population adjusted by national underenumeration rates for age, sex, and race groups.

Table 3. ALTERNATIVE ESTIMATES OF THE PERCENTS OF NET UNDERENUMERATION FOR THE TOTAL POPULATION, FOR REGIONS, DIVISIONS, AND STATES: 1970

(See text for explanation of alternative procedures. A minus sign denotes a net overcount)

Region, division, and State	SOR-3-1		SOR-3-2		SOR-3-1	Composite-1	Composite-2	Range			
	WCF-1		WCF-2		WCF-1			Low value	High value	Difference	Relative difference[1]
	BACF-1	BREF-1	BACF-2	BREF-2	BACF*-1						
United States, total	2.5	2.5	2.5	2.5	2.5	2.5	2.5	(X)	(X)	(X)	(X)
Regions:											
Northeast	1.3	1.1	1.3	1.1	1.3	1.7	2.0	1.1	2.0	0.9	29
North Central	1.6	1.4	1.4	1.2	1.6	1.4	1.4	1.2	1.6	0.4	14
South	4.0	4.2	3.8	4.0	4.0	4.0	3.9	3.8	4.2	0.4	5
West	3.2	3.2	3.9	4.1	3.2	3.0	2.7	2.7	4.1	1.4	21
Northeast:											
New England	0.9	0.9	1.0	0.9	0.9	1.2	1.4	0.9	1.4	0.5	22
Middle Atlantic	1.4	1.2	1.4	1.2	1.4	1.8	2.2	1.2	2.2	1.0	29
North Central:											
East North Central	1.5	1.3	1.5	1.2	1.5	1.5	1.5	1.2	1.5	0.3	11
West North Central	1.7	1.7	1.2	1.2	1.7	1.3	1.0	1.0	1.7	0.7	26
South:											
South Atlantic	4.1	4.3	4.1	4.3	4.2	4.5	4.4	4.1	4.5	0.4	5
East South Central	3.5	3.7	2.7	2.7	3.4	3.1	3.2	2.7	3.7	1.0	16
West South Central	4.2	4.6	4.1	4.4	4.2	3.6	3.5	3.5	4.6	1.1	14
West:											
Mountain	3.6	3.7	3.5	3.7	3.6	3.3	3.1	3.1	3.7	0.6	9
Pacific	3.1	3.1	4.0	4.2	3.1	2.9	2.6	2.6	4.2	1.6	24
New England:											
Maine	3.7	3.7	2.7	2.8	3.7	3.9	4.1	2.7	4.1	1.4	21
New Hampshire	1.9	1.9	2.0	2.0	1.8	2.1	2.3	1.8	2.3	0.5	12
Vermont	2.6	2.6	1.9	1.9	2.7	2.8	3.0	1.9	3.0	1.1	22
Massachusetts	0.6	0.5	0.6	0.6	0.6	0.9	1.0	0.5	1.0	0.5	(B)
Rhode Island	1.0	1.0	0.9	0.9	1.0	1.3	1.4	0.9	1.4	0.5	22
Connecticut	0.1	(Z)	0.7	0.5	0.1	0.4	0.6	(Z)	0.7	0.7	(B)
Middle Atlantic:											
New York	1.8	1.6	1.8	1.6	1.8	2.2	2.6	1.6	2.6	1.0	24
New Jersey	0.7	0.6	1.0	0.9	0.8	1.2	1.5	0.6	1.5	0.9	43
Pennsylvania	1.2	1.1	0.9	0.7	1.2	1.7	2.0	0.7	2.0	1.3	48
East North Central:											
Ohio	1.6	1.4	1.4	1.2	1.5	1.5	1.5	1.2	1.6	0.4	14
Indiana	1.7	1.6	1.3	1.2	1.6	1.6	1.7	1.2	1.7	0.5	17
Illinois	1.8	1.5	1.9	1.5	1.9	1.8	1.8	1.5	1.9	0.4	12
Michigan	2.0	1.7	2.1	1.8	1.9	2.0	2.0	1.7	2.1	0.4	11
Wisconsin	-0.5	-0.6	-0.6	-0.7	-0.5	-0.6	-0.5	-0.7	-0.5	0.2	(B)
West North Central:											
Minnesota	0.2	0.2	(Z)	-0.1	0.2	-0.1	-0.4	-0.4	0.2	0.6	(B)
Iowa	1.7	1.6	0.9	0.9	1.6	1.3	1.0	0.9	1.7	0.8	31
Missouri	2.7	2.7	2.6	2.6	2.7	2.3	2.0	2.0	2.7	0.7	15
North Dakota	2.5	2.5	0.8	0.8	2.5	2.1	1.8	0.8	2.5	1.7	52
South Dakota	3.5	3.5	2.3	2.2	3.7	3.2	2.9	2.2	3.7	1.5	25
Nebraska	1.5	1.4	0.8	0.7	1.5	1.1	0.8	0.7	1.5	0.8	36
Kansas	1.6	1.5	0.7	0.7	1.6	1.2	0.9	0.7	1.6	0.9	39
South Atlantic:											
Delaware	2.8	2.7	3.4	3.4	2.8	3.2	3.2	2.7	3.4	0.7	11
Maryland	1.5	1.2	1.9	1.5	1.7	1.9	1.9	1.2	1.9	0.7	23
District of Columbia	5.3	4.0	5.2	3.4	5.4	5.7	5.4	3.4	5.7	2.3	25
Virginia	3.3	3.1	2.9	2.6	3.2	3.7	3.6	2.6	3.7	1.1	17
West Virginia	6.3	6.7	4.6	4.9	6.2	6.7	6.7	4.6	6.7	2.1	17
North Carolina	3.4	3.3	3.1	3.0	3.4	3.8	3.7	3.0	3.8	0.8	12
South Carolina	5.9	6.8	5.5	6.4	6.1	6.3	6.2	5.5	6.8	1.3	11
Georgia	5.0	5.6	4.9	5.6	5.1	5.3	5.3	4.9	5.6	0.7	7
Florida	4.8	5.0	5.6	6.1	4.8	5.2	5.2	4.8	6.1	1.3	12
East South Central:											
Kentucky	3.6	3.8	2.7	2.8	3.4	3.2	3.2	2.7	3.8	1.1	17
Tennessee	4.0	4.4	3.7	4.0	3.9	3.6	3.7	3.6	4.4	0.8	10
Alabama	3.0	3.0	2.0	1.8	2.8	2.6	2.7	1.8	3.0	1.2	25
Mississippi	3.5	3.5	2.0	1.8	3.6	3.2	3.4	1.8	3.6	1.8	33
West South Central:											
Arkansas	6.2	7.2	4.7	5.1	6.6	5.6	5.6	4.7	7.2	2.5	21
Louisiana	3.1	3.1	2.8	2.8	3.1	2.5	2.5	2.5	3.1	0.6	11
Oklahoma	2.5	2.5	1.5	1.4	2.6	1.9	1.8	1.4	2.6	1.2	30
Texas	4.6	5.1	4.9	5.5	4.5	4.0	3.9	3.9	5.5	1.6	17
Mountain:											
Montana	1.8	1.8	0.9	0.9	1.9	1.5	1.4	0.9	1.9	1.0	36
Idaho	3.8	3.9	3.3	3.4	3.8	3.5	3.4	3.3	3.9	0.6	8
Wyoming	1.8	1.8	0.3	0.2	1.8	1.5	1.4	0.2	1.8	1.6	80
Colorado	2.5	2.6	2.3	2.3	2.5	2.2	2.1	2.1	2.6	0.5	11
New Mexico	8.3	9.1	8.3	9.2	8.2	8.0	7.8	7.8	9.2	1.4	8
Arizona	4.7	4.8	5.0	5.2	4.9	4.4	4.2	4.2	5.2	1.0	11
Utah	(Z)	-0.1	-0.1	-0.2	(Z)	-0.3	-0.5	-0.5	(Z)	0.5	(B)
Nevada	4.5	4.6	6.3	6.6	4.6	4.1	4.0	4.0	6.6	2.6	25
Pacific:											
Washington	2.0	1.9	2.1	2.0	2.1	1.8	1.5	1.5	2.1	0.6	17
Oregon	1.2	1.1	1.5	1.4	1.2	0.9	0.8	0.8	1.5	0.7	30
California	3.3	3.3	4.5	4.7	3.3	3.1	2.8	2.8	4.7	1.9	25
Alaska	7.5	6.9	5.6	5.0	8.1	7.3	6.9	5.0	8.1	3.1	24
Hawaii	5.9	6.0	5.5	6.3	5.2	5.6	5.0	5.0	6.3	1.3	12

B Base of percentage less than 1.0 percent.
X Not applicable.
Z Less than ± 0.05.
[1]Relative difference is defined as one-half of the difference of high and low values divided by the average of the high and low values.

Table 4. DISTRIBUTION OF ONE BILLION DOLLARS BY REGIONS, DIVISIONS, AND STATES ACCORDING TO THE 1970 CENSUS POPULATION AND THE 1970 CENSUS POPULATION CORRECTED FOR NET UNDERENUMERATION BY VARIOUS METHODS

(See text for explanation of the alternative procedures. Numbers in thousands of dollars)

Region, division, and State	Census	SOR-3-1	SOR-3-2	Composite-2	Difference from census distribution					
		WCF-1	WCF-2		SOR-3-1		SOR-3-2		Composite-	
		BACF-1	BACF-2		Amount	Percent	Amount	Percent	Amount	Percent
United States, total	1,000,000	1,000,000	1,000,000	1,000,000	(Z)	(Z)	(Z)	(Z)	(Z)	(Z)
Regions:										
Northeast	241,348	238,243	238,249	239,957	-3,105	-1.3	-3,099	-1.3	-1,391	-0.6
North Central	278,382	275,604	275,079	275,044	-2,778	-1.0	-3,303	-1.2	-3,338	-1.2
South	308,993	313,709	313,015	313,387	+4,716	+1.5	+4,022	+1.3	+4,394	+1.4
West	171,276	172,444	173,657	171,612	+1,168	+0.7	+2,381	+1.4	+336	+0.2
Northeast:										
New England	58,293	57,334	57,375	57,585	-959	-1.6	-918	-1.6	-708	-1.2
Middle Atlantic	183,056	180,908	180,874	182,373	-2,148	-1.2	-2,182	-1.2	-683	-0.4
North Central:										
East North Central	198,059	195,984	195,857	195,945	-2,075	-1.0	-2,202	-1.1	-2,114	-1.1
West North Central	80,323	79,619	79,222	79,100	-704	-0.9	-1,101	-1.4	-1,223	-1.5
South:										
South Atlantic	150,915	153,355	153,364	153,902	+2,440	+1.6	+2,449	+1.6	+2,987	+2.0
East South Central	63,004	63,642	63,088	63,451	+638	+1.0	+84	+0.1	+447	+0.7
West South Central	95,074	96,713	96,563	96,034	+1,639	+1.7	+1,489	+1.6	+960	+1.0
West:										
Mountain	40,759	41,189	41,161	40,992	+430	+1.1	+402	+1.0	+233	+0.6
Pacific	130,518	131,255	132,497	130,620	+737	+0.6	+1,979	+1.5	+102	+0.1
New England:										
Maine	4,889	4,946	4,899	4,967	+57	+1.2	+10	+0.2	+78	+1.6
New Hampshire	3,630	3,604	3,611	3,619	-26	-0.7	-19	-0.5	-11	-0.3
Vermont	2,188	2,189	2,173	2,198	+1	(Z)	-15	-0.7	+10	+0.5
Massachusetts	27,993	27,437	27,455	27,557	-556	-2.0	-538	-1.9	-436	-1.6
Rhode Island	4,673	4,599	4,596	4,619	-74	-1.6	-77	-1.6	-54	-1.2
Connecticut	14,920	14,559	14,641	14,626	-361	-2.4	-279	-1.9	-294	-2.0
Middle Atlantic:										
New York	89,754	89,037	89,078	89,771	-717	-0.8	-676	-0.8	+17	(Z)
New Jersey	35,270	34,614	34,733	34,897	-656	-1.9	-537	-1.5	-373	-1.1
Pennsylvania	58,031	57,257	57,062	57,705	-774	-1.3	-969	-1.7	-326	-0.6
East North Central:										
Ohio	52,412	51,880	51,799	51,875	-532	-1.0	-613	-1.2	-537	-1.0
Indiana	25,555	25,323	25,242	25,324	-232	-0.9	-313	-1.2	-231	-0.9
Illinois	54,685	54,285	54,302	54,256	-400	-0.7	-383	-0.7	-429	-0.8
Michigan	43,669	43,421	43,463	43,410	-248	-0.6	-206	-0.5	-259	-0.6
Wisconsin	21,738	21,075	21,051	21,080	-663	-3.0	-687	-3.2	-658	-3.0
West North Central:										
Minnesota	18,722	18,284	18,241	18,167	-438	-2.3	-481	-2.6	-555	-3.0
Iowa	13,900	13,773	13,666	13,687	-127	-0.9	-234	-1.7	-213	-1.5
Missouri	23,015	23,038	23,027	22,881	+23	+0.1	+12	+0.1	-134	-0.6
North Dakota	3,040	3,037	2,987	3,017	-3	-0.1	-53	-1.7	-23	-0.8
South Dakota	3,278	3,310	3,269	3,289	+32	+1.0	-9	-0.3	+11	+0.3
Nebraska	7,301	7,221	7,170	7,174	-80	-1.1	-131	-1.8	-127	-1.7
Kansas	11,066	10,955	10,862	10,884	-111	-1.0	-204	-1.8	-182	-1.6
South Atlantic:										
Delaware	2,697	2,704	2,720	2,715	+7	+0.3	+23	+0.9	+18	+0.7
Maryland	19,300	19,091	19,171	19,164	-209	-1.1	-129	-0.7	-136	-0.7
District of Columbia	3,722	3,832	3,825	3,832	+110	+3.0	+103	+2.8	+110	+3.0
Virginia	22,872	23,040	22,950	23,127	+168	+0.7	+78	+0.3	+255	+1.1
West Virginia	8,582	8,922	8,769	8,964	+340	+4.0	+187	+2.2	+382	+4.5
North Carolina	25,006	25,216	25,149	25,304	+210	+0.8	+143	+0.6	+298	+1.2
South Carolina	12,746	13,204	13,149	13,244	+458	+3.6	+403	+3.2	+498	+3.9
Georgia	22,583	23,153	23,131	23,229	+570	+2.5	+548	+2.4	+646	+2.9
Florida	33,407	34,193	34,500	34,322	+786	+2.4	+1,093	+3.3	+915	+2.7
East South Central:										
Kentucky	15,840	16,007	15,867	15,939	+167	+1.1	+27	+0.2	+99	+0.6
Tennessee	19,308	19,601	19,532	19,534	+293	+1.5	+224	+1.2	+226	+1.2
Alabama	16,947	17,016	16,846	16,974	+69	+0.4	-101	-0.6	+27	+0.2
Mississippi	10,908	11,017	10,843	11,004	+109	+1.0	-65	-0.6	+96	+0.9
West South Central:										
Arkansas	9,463	9,834	9,673	9,770	+371	+3.9	+210	+2.2	+307	+3.2
Louisiana	17,926	18,026	17,980	17,921	+100	+0.6	+54	+0.3	-5	(Z)
Oklahoma	12,593	12,583	12,453	12,491	-10	-0.1	-140	-1.1	-102	-0.8
Texas	55,092	56,270	56,457	55,852	+1,178	+2.1	+1,365	+2.5	+760	+1.4
Mountain:										
Montana	3,417	3,391	3,361	3,375	-26	-0.8	-56	-1.6	-42	-1.2
Idaho	3,508	3,555	3,537	3,540	+47	+1.3	+29	+0.8	+32	+0.9
Wyoming	1,636	1,623	1,598	1,616	-13	-0.8	-38	-2.3	-20	-1.2
Colorado	10,861	10,858	10,829	10,808	-3	(Z)	-32	-0.3	-53	-0.5
New Mexico	4,999	5,310	5,313	5,282	+311	+6.2	+314	+6.3	+283	+5.7
Arizona	8,721	8,921	8,950	8,875	+200	+2.3	+229	+2.6	+154	+1.8
Utah	5,212	5,078	5,072	5,055	-134	-2.6	-140	-2.7	-157	-3.0
Nevada	2,405	2,453	2,500	2,441	+48	+2.0	+95	+4.0	+36	+1.5
Pacific:										
Washington	16,774	16,674	16,704	16,603	-100	-0.6	-70	-0.4	-171	-1.0
Oregon	10,290	10,145	10,179	10,104	-145	-1.4	-111	-1.1	-186	-1.8
California	98,178	98,949	100,170	98,473	+771	+0.8	+1,992	+2.0	+295	+0.3
Alaska	1,487	1,565	1,535	1,556	+78	+5.2	+48	+3.2	+69	+4.6
Hawaii	3,788	3,922	3,908	3,884	+134	+3.5	+120	+3.2	+96	+2.5

Z Rounds to less than ± $500 or to less than ± 0.05 percent.

APPENDIX B

FACSIMILES OF QUESTIONNAIRES AND INSTRUCTION SHEETS FOR 1978 CENSUS OF THE RICHMOND, VIRGINIA, AREA

1. Long Form--Form D-2(x)
2. Instruction Sheet for Long Form--Form D-4(x)
3. Short Form--Form D-1(x)
4. Instruction Sheet for Short Form--Form D-3(x)

1978 Census of the Richmond, Virginia Area

(Richmond City, and Chesterfield and Henrico Counties)

Please fill out this Official Census Form and mail it back on Census Day, Tuesday, April 4, 1978

If the address shown below has the wrong apartment identification, please write the correct apartment number or location here:

D.O.	A1.	A2.	A4.	A5.	A6.	C.R.
				L		

- **Your answers are CONFIDENTIAL by law (title 13, United States Code).**

  This means that no one may see your answers except census workers who are sworn not to disclose your information, and who can be fined and/or imprisoned for any violation.

- **The law also requires that you answer the questions to the best of your knowledge.**

How to Fill This Form

1. **Use a black pencil to answer the questions.**
   This form is read by a computer. Black pencil is better to use than ballpoint or other pens.

   Fill circles "O" like this: ●
   The computer reads every circle you fill. If you fill the wrong circle, erase the mark completely, then fill the right circle.

   When you write in an answer, print or write clearly.

2. **See the filled-in example on the yellow instruction sheet.**
   This example shows how to fill circles and write in answers. If you are not sure of an answer, give the best answer you can.

   If you have a problem, look in the instruction sheet.
   All instructions are numbered the same as the questions on the census form.

   If you need more help, call the Census office.
   The telephone number of the local office is shown at the bottom of the address box to the left.

3. **Make sure that the information is shown for everyone here.**
   A boarder, roomer, or someone else in the household may sometimes not want to give you all the information for the form. Write in at least the person's name, relationship, and sex. A Census Taker will call to get the other information directly from the person.

4. **Answer the questions on pages 1 through 5, and fill a pair of pages for each person in the household. That is, pages 6 and 7 for the Person in column 1, and pages 8 and 9 for the Person in column 2, and so on. Check your answers. Then, write your name, the date, and telephone number on page 20.**

   Mail back this form on Tuesday, April 4 or as soon afterward as you can. Use the enclosed envelope; no stamp is needed.

PARA PERSONAS DE HABLA HISPANA (For Spanish-speaking persons):
SI USTED DESEA UN CUESTIONARIO DEL CENSO EN ESPAÑOL, llame a la oficina del censo. El número de teléfono se encuentra más arriba, en la casilla para la dirección al principio de la columna izquierda.
O marque este circulo "O" y devuelva este cuestionario por correo en el sobre color café que aquí se incluye.

U.S. DEPARTMENT OF COMMERCE
BUREAU OF THE CENSUS
FORM D-2(X) (12-19-77)

O.M.B. No. 41-S78006:
Approval Expires June 30, 1979

PLEASE CONTINUE →

Question 1:

What is the name of each person who was living here on Tuesday, April 4, 1978, or who was staying or visiting here and had no other home?

___

___

___

___

___

___

___

___

___

___

___

___

___

Instructions:

List in Question 1

- Family members living here, including babies still in the hospital.
- Relatives living here.
- Lodgers or boarders living here.
- Domestic employees or hired hands living here.
- Other persons living here.
- College students who stay here while attending college, even if their parents live elsewhere.
- Persons who usually live here but are temporarily away (including children in boarding school below the college level).
- Persons with a home elsewhere but who stay here most of the week while working.

Do Not List in Question 1

- Any person away from here in the Armed Forces.
- Any college student who stays somewhere else while attending college.
- Any person who usually stays somewhere else most of the week while working there.
- Any person away from here in an institution such as a home for the aged or mental hospital.
- Any person staying or visiting here who has a usual home elsewhere.

↓

NOTE

If everyone here is staying only temporarily and has a usual home elsewhere, please fill this circle O. Then please:

- answer the questions on pages 2 and 3, and
- enter the address of your usual home on page 4.

PLEASE CONTINUE →

Also answer the hous

Here are the QUESTIONS ↓ — These are the columns for ANSWERS → *Please fill one column for each person listed in Question 1.*	PERSON in column 1	PERSON in column 2
	Last name / First name / Middle initial	Last name / First name / Middle initial
2. How is this person related to the person in column 1? *Fill one circle.* *If "Other relative" of person in column 1, give exact relationship, such as mother-in-law, niece, grandson, etc.*	*START in this column with the household member (or one of the members) in whose name the home is owned or rented. If there is no such person, start in this column with any adult household member.*	If relative of person in column 1: ○ Husband/wife ○ Son/daughter ○ Brother/sister ○ Father/mother ○ Other relative → If not related to person in column 1: ○ Roomer, boarder ○ Partner, roommate ○ Paid employee ○ Other nonrelative →
3. Sex *Fill one circle.*	○ Male ○ Female	○ Male ○ Female
4. Race *Fill one circle.*	○ White ○ Black or Negro ○ Japanese ○ Chinese ○ Filipino ○ Korean ○ Vietnamese ○ Indian (Amer.) *Print tribe* → ○ Asian Indian ○ Hawaiian ○ Guamanian ○ Samoan ○ Eskimo ○ Aleut ○ Other — *Print race*	○ White ○ Black or Negro ○ Japanese ○ Chinese ○ Filipino ○ Korean ○ Vietnamese ○ Indian (Amer.) *Print tribe* → ○ Asian Indian ○ Hawaiian ○ Guamanian ○ Samoan ○ Eskimo ○ Aleut ○ Other — *Print race*
5. Age, and month and year of birth *a. Print age at last birthday.* *b. Print month and fill one circle.* *c. Print year in the spaces, and fill one circle below each number.*	a. Age at last birthday; b. Month of birth: ○ Jan.–Mar. ○ Apr.–June ○ July–Sept. ○ Oct.–Dec.; c. Year of birth: 1 ● 8 ○ 9 ○ Ø–9 ○ Ø–9 ○	a. Age at last birthday; b. Month of birth: ○ Jan.–Mar. ○ Apr.–June ○ July–Sept. ○ Oct.–Dec.; c. Year of birth: 1 ● 8 ○ 9 ○ Ø–9 ○ Ø–9 ○
6. Marital status *Fill one circle.*	○ Now married ○ Widowed ○ Divorced ○ Separated ○ Never married	○ Now married ○ Widowed ○ Divorced ○ Separated ○ Never married
7. Is this person's origin or descent — *Fill one circle.*	○ Mexican-Amer. ○ Mexican or Chicano ○ Puerto Rican ○ Cuban ○ Other Spanish ○ Not Spanish	○ Mexican-Amer. ○ Mexican or Chicano ○ Puerto Rican ○ Cuban ○ Other Spanish ○ Not Spanish
8. Since February 1, 1978, has this person attended regular school or college at any time? *Fill one circle. Count nursery school, kindergarten, elementary school and schooling which leads to a high school diploma or college degree.*	○ No, has not attended ○ Yes, public school, public college ○ Yes, private, church-related ○ Yes, private, not church-related	○ No, has not attended ○ Yes, public school, public college ○ Yes, private, church-related ○ Yes, private, not church-related
9. What is the highest grade (or year) of regular school this person has ever attended? *Fill one circle.* *If now attending school, mark grade person is in. If high school was finished by equivalency test (GED), mark "12".*	Highest grade attended: ○ Nursery school ○ Kindergarten; Elementary through high school *(grade or year)* 1 2 3 4 5 6 7 8 9 10 11 12; College *(academic year)* 1 2 3 4 5 6 7 8 or more; ○ Never attended school — *Skip question 10*	Highest grade attended: ○ Nursery school ○ Kindergarten; Elementary through high school *(grade or year)* 1 2 3 4 5 6 7 8 9 10 11 12; College *(academic year)* 1 2 3 4 5 6 7 8 or more; ○ Never attended school — *Skip question 10*
10. Did this person finish the highest grade (or year) attended? *Fill one circle.*	○ Now attending this grade *(or year)* ○ Finished this grade *(or year)* ○ Did not finish this grade *(or year)*	○ Now attending this grade *(or year)* ○ Finished this grade *(or year)* ○ Did not finish this grade *(or year)*
D-2(X) Fosdic 26.1:1	*CENSUS USE ONLY* A. ○ Inmate ○ Other ○ ○	*CENSUS USE ONLY* A. ○ Inmate ○ Other ○ ○

...sing questions on page 3. → Also answer the housing questions on page 3.

PERSON in column 3

Last name

First name — Middle initial

If relative of person in column 1:

○ Husband/wife ○ Son/daughter ○ Brother/sister ○ Father/mother ○ Other relative

If not related to person in column 1:

○ Roomer, boarder ○ Partner, roommate ○ Paid employee ○ Other nonrelative

○ Male ○ Female

○ White ○ Black or Negro ○ Japanese ○ Chinese ○ Filipino ○ Korean ○ Vietnamese ○ Indian (Amer.) *Print tribe* → ○ Asian Indian ○ Hawaiian ○ Guamanian ○ Samoan ○ Eskimo ○ Aleut ○ Other – *Print race*

a. Age at last birthday

b. Month of birth: ○ Jan.–Mar. ○ Apr.–June ○ July–Sept. ○ Oct.–Dec.

c. Year of birth: 1 — 1 ● — 8 ○ 9 ○ — Ø ○ 1 ○ 2 ○ 3 ○ 4 ○ 5 ○ 6 ○ 7 ○ 8 ○ 9 ○ — Ø ○ 1 ○ 2 ○ 3 ○ 4 ○ 5 ○ 6 ○ 7 ○ 8 ○ 9 ○

○ Now married ○ Widowed ○ Divorced ○ Separated ○ Never married

○ Mexican-Amer. ○ Mexican or Chicano ○ Puerto Rican ○ Cuban ○ Other Spanish ○ Not Spanish

○ No, has not attended ○ Yes, public school, public college ○ Yes, private, church-related ○ Yes, private, not church-related

Highest grade attended:

○ Nursery school ○ Kindergarten

Elementary through high school *(grade or year)*: 1 2 3 4 5 6 7 8 9 10 11 12

College *(academic year)*: 1 2 3 4 5 6 7 8 or more

○ Never attended school – *Skip question 10*

○ Now attending this grade *(or year)* ○ Finished this grade *(or year)*

CENSUS USE ONLY A. ○ Inmate ○ Other ○ ○

PERSON in column 4

Last name

First name — Middle initial

If relative of person in column 1:

○ Husband/wife ○ Son/daughter ○ Brother/sister ○ Father/mother ○ Other relative

If not related to person in column 1:

○ Roomer, boarder ○ Partner, roommate ○ Paid employee ○ Other nonrelative

○ Male ○ Female

○ White ○ Black or Negro ○ Japanese ○ Chinese ○ Filipino ○ Korean ○ Vietnamese ○ Indian (Amer.) *Print tribe* → ○ Asian Indian ○ Hawaiian ○ Guamanian ○ Samoan ○ Eskimo ○ Aleut ○ Other – *Print race*

a. Age at last birthday

b. Month of birth: ○ Jan.–Mar. ○ Apr.–June ○ July–Sept. ○ Oct.–Dec.

c. Year of birth: 1 — 1 ● — 8 ○ 9 ○ — Ø ○ 1 ○ 2 ○ 3 ○ 4 ○ 5 ○ 6 ○ 7 ○ 8 ○ 9 ○ — Ø ○ 1 ○ 2 ○ 3 ○ 4 ○ 5 ○ 6 ○ 7 ○ 8 ○ 9 ○

○ Now married ○ Widowed ○ Divorced ○ Separated ○ Never married

○ Mexican-Amer. ○ Mexican or Chicano ○ Puerto Rican ○ Cuban ○ Other Spanish ○ Not Spanish

○ No, has not attended ○ Yes, public school, public college ○ Yes, private, church-related ○ Yes, private, not church-related

Highest grade attended:

○ Nursery school ○ Kindergarten

Elementary through high school *(grade or year)*: 1 2 3 4 5 6 7 8 9 10 11 12

College *(academic year)*: 1 2 3 4 5 6 7 8 or more

○ Never attended school – *Skip question 10*

○ Now attending this grade *(or year)* ○ Finished this grade *(or year)* ○ Did not finish this grade *(or year)*

CENSUS USE ONLY A. ○ Inmate ○ Other ○ ○

PERSON in column 5

Last name

First name — Middle initial

If relative of person in column 1:

○ Husband/wife ○ Son/daughter ○ Brother/sister ○ Father/mother ○ Other relative

If not related to person in column 1:

○ Roomer, boarder ○ Partner, roommate ○ Paid employee ○ Other nonrelative

○ Male ○ Female

○ White ○ Black or Negro ○ Japanese ○ Chinese ○ Filipino ○ Korean ○ Vietnamese ○ Indian (Amer.) *Print tribe* → ○ Asian Indian ○ Hawaiian ○ Guamanian ○ Samoan ○ Eskimo ○ Aleut ○ Other – *Print race*

a. Age at last birthday

b. Month of birth: ○ Jan.–Mar. ○ Apr.–June ○ July–Sept. ○ Oct.–Dec.

c. Year of birth: 1 — 1 ● — 8 ○ 9 ○ — Ø ○ 1 ○ 2 ○ 3 ○ 4 ○ 5 ○ 6 ○ 7 ○ 8 ○ 9 ○ — Ø ○ 1 ○ 2 ○ 3 ○ 4 ○ 5 ○ 6 ○ 7 ○ 8 ○ 9 ○

○ Now married ○ Widowed ○ Divorced ○ Separated ○ Never married

○ Mexican-Amer. ○ Mexican or Chicano ○ Puerto Rican ○ Cuban ○ Other Spanish ○ Not Spanish

○ No, has not attended ○ Yes, public school, public college ○ Yes, private, church-related ○ Yes, private, not church-related

Highest grade attended:

○ Nursery school ○ Kindergarten

Elementary through high school *(grade or year)*: 1 2 3 4 5 6 7 8 9 10 11 12

College *(academic year)*: 1 2 3 4 5 6 7 8 or more

○ Never attended school – *Skip question 10*

○ Now attending this grade *(or year)* ○ Finished this grade *(or year)* ○ Did not finish this grade *(or year)*

CENSUS USE ONLY A. ○ Inmate ○ Other ○ ○

PERSON in column 6

Last name

First name — Middle initial

If relative of person in column 1:

○ Husband/wife ○ Son/daughter ○ Brother/sister ○ Father/mother ○ Other relative

If not related to person in column 1:

○ Roomer, boarder ○ Partner, roommate ○ Paid employee ○ Other nonrelative

○ Male ○ Female

○ White ○ Black or Negro ○ Japanese ○ Chinese ○ Filipino ○ Korean ○ Vietnamese ○ Indian (Amer.) *Print tribe* → ○ Asian Indian ○ Hawaiian ○ Guamanian ○ Samoan ○ Eskimo ○ Aleut ○ Other – *Print race*

a. Age at last birthday

b. Month of birth: ○ Jan.–Mar. ○ Apr.–June ○ July–Sept. ○ Oct.–Dec.

c. Year of birth: 1 — 1 ● — 8 ○ 9 ○ — Ø ○ 1 ○ 2 ○ 3 ○ 4 ○ 5 ○ 6 ○ 7 ○ 8 ○ 9 ○ — Ø ○ 1 ○ 2 ○ 3 ○ 4 ○ 5 ○ 6 ○ 7 ○ 8 ○ 9 ○

○ Now married ○ Widowed ○ Divorced ○ Separated ○ Never married

○ Mexican-Amer. ○ Mexican or Chicano ○ Puerto Rican ○ Cuban ○ Other Spanish ○ Not Spanish

○ No, has not attended ○ Yes, public school, public college ○ Yes, private, church-related ○ Yes, private, not church-related

Highest grade attended:

○ Nursery school ○ Kindergarten

Elementary through high school *(grade or year)*: 1 2 3 4 5 6 7 8 9 10 11 12

College *(academic year)*: 1 2 3 4 5 6 7 8 or more

○ Never attended school – *Skip question 10*

○ Now attending this grade *(or year)* ○ Finished this grade *(or year)* ○ Did not finish this grade *(or year)*

CENSUS USE ONLY A. ○ Inmate ○ Other ○ ○

NOW PLEASE ANSWER QUESTIONS H1-H12 FOR YOUR HOUSEHOLD

PERSON in column 7

Last name

First name — Middle initial

If relative of person in column 1:
- O Husband/wife
- O Son/daughter
- O Brother/sister
- O Father/mother
- O Other relative

If not related to person in column 1:
- O Roomer, boarder
- O Partner, roommate
- O Paid employee
- O Other nonrelative

- O Male
- O Female

- O White
- O Black or Negro
- O Japanese
- O Chinese
- O Filipino
- O Korean
- O Vietnamese
- O Indian (Amer.) Print tribe
- O Asian Indian
- O Hawaiian
- O Guamanian
- O Samoan
- O Eskimo
- O Aleut
- O Other – Print race

a. Age at last birthday

b. Month of birth
- O Jan.–Mar.
- O Apr.–June
- O July–Sept.
- O Oct.–Dec.

c. Year of birth: 1 ● | 8 O 9 O | 0 O 1 O 2 O 3 O 4 O 5 O 6 O 7 O 8 O 9 O | 0 O 1 O 2 O 3 O 4 O 5 O 6 O 7 O 8 O 9 O

- O Now married
- O Widowed
- O Divorced
- O Separated
- O Never married

- O Mexican-Amer.
- O Mexican or Chicano
- O Puerto Rican
- O Cuban
- O Other Spanish
- O Not Spanish

- O No, has not attended
- O Yes, public school, public college
- O Yes, private, church-related
- O Yes, private, not church-related

Highest grade attended:
- O Nursery school
- O Kindergarten

Elementary through high school *(grade or year)*
1 2 3 4 5 6 7 8 9 10 11 12

College *(academic year)*
1 2 3 4 5 6 7 8 or more

O Never attended school – *Skip question 10*

- O Now attending this grade *(or year)*
- O Finished this grade *(or year)*
- O Did not finish this grade *(or year)*

CENSUS USE ONLY — A. O Inmate O Other O O

If you listed more than 7 persons in Question 1, please see note on page 20.

H1. Did you leave anyone out of Question 1 because you were not sure if the person should be listed — *for example, a new baby still in the hospital, a lodger who also has another home, or a person who stays here once in a while and has no other home?*
- O Yes — *On page 20 give name(s) and reason left out.*
- O No

H2. Did you list anyone in Question 1 who is away from home now — *for example, on a vacation or in a hospital?*
- O Yes — *On page 20 give name(s) and reason person is away.*
- O No

H3. Is anyone visiting here who is not already listed?
- O Yes — *On page 20 give name of each visitor for whom there is no one at the home address to report the person to a census taker.*
- O No

H4. What best describes the building in which you live?
Fill one circle.
- O A mobile home or trailer
- O A one-family house detached from any other house
- O A one-family house attached to one or more houses
- O Boat, van, tent, etc.
- *or* An apartment house or building with the following number of living quarters:
  - O 1 O 2 O 3 O 4
  - O 5 O 6 O 7 O 8
  - O 9 O 10 to 19 O 20 to 49 O 50 or more

H5. Do you enter your living quarters —
- O Directly from the outside or through a common or public hall?
- O Through someone else's living quarters?

H6. Do you have complete plumbing facilities in your living quarters, that is, hot and cold piped water, a flush toilet, and a bathtub or shower?
- O Yes, for this household only
- O Yes, but also used by another household
- O No, have some but not all plumbing facilities
- O No plumbing facilities in living quarters

H7. How many rooms do you have in your living quarters?
Do not count bathrooms, porches, balconies, foyers, halls, or half-rooms.
- O 1 room O 2 rooms O 3 rooms
- O 4 rooms O 5 rooms O 6 rooms
- O 7 rooms O 8 rooms O 9 rooms or more

H8. Are your living quarters —
- O Owned or being bought by you or by someone else in this household?
- O Rented for cash rent?
- O Occupied without payment of cash rent?

H9. Is this apartment (house) part of a condominium or cooperative building or development?
- O No
- O Yes, a condominium building or development
- O Yes, a cooperatively-owned building or development

H10. If this is a one-family house —
a. Is the house on a property of 10 acres or more?
- O Yes O No

b. Is any part of the property used as a commercial establishment or medical office?
- O Yes O No

H11. *If you live in a one-family house or a condominium unit which you own or are buying —*
What is the value of this property, that is, how much do you think this property (house and lot or condominium unit) would sell for if it were for sale?
Do not answer this question if this is —
- A mobile home or trailer
- A house on 10 acres or more
- A house with a commercial establishment or medical office on the property

- O Less than $5,000
- O $5,000 to $9,999
- O $10,000 to $14,999
- O $15,000 to $17,499
- O $17,500 to $19,999
- O $20,000 to $22,499
- O $22,500 to $24,999
- O $25,000 to $27,499
- O $27,500 to $29,999
- O $30,000 to $32,499
- O $32,500 to $34,999
- O $35,000 to $37,499
- O $37,500 to $39,999
- O $40,000 to $44,999
- O $45,000 to $49,999
- O $50,000 to $54,999
- O $55,000 to $59,999
- O $60,000 to $69,999
- O $70,000 to $79,999
- O $80,000 to $89,999
- O $90,000 to $99,999
- O $100,000 to $149,999
- O $150,000 to $199,999
- O $200,000 or more

H12. *If you pay rent for your living quarters —*
What is the monthly rent?
If rent is not paid by the month, see the instruction sheet on how to figure a monthly rent.
- O Less than $40
- O $40 to $49
- O $50 to $59
- O $60 to $69
- O $70 to $79
- O $80 to $89
- O $90 to $99
- O $100 to $109
- O $110 to $119
- O $120 to $129
- O $130 to $139
- O $140 to $149
- O $150 to $159
- O $160 to $169
- O $170 to $179
- O $180 to $189
- O $190 to $199
- O $200 to $224
- O $225 to $249
- O $250 to $274
- O $275 to $299
- O $300 to $349
- O $350 to $399
- O $400 or more

FOR CENSUS USE ONLY

A4. Block number — 0 1 2 3 4 5 6 7 8 9 (three columns); O NC

A6. Serial number — 0 1 2 3 4 5 6 7 8 9 (four columns)

B. Type of unit or quarters
- Occupied: O First form O Continuation
- Vacant: O Regular O Usual home elsewhere
- Group quarters: O First form O Continuation

For Vacant Units
C1. Is this unit for —
- O Year round use — (Fill C2 and C3)
- O Seasonal/Mig.

C2. Vacancy status
- O For rent
- O For sale only
- O Rented or sold, not occupied
- O Held for occasional use
- O Other vacant

C3. Is this unit boarded up?
- O Yes O No

D. Months vacant
- O Less than 1 month
- O 1 up to 2 months
- O 2 up to 6 months
- O 6 up to 12 months
- O 1 year up to 2 years
- O 2 years or more

E. Quest're codes
1. O O Mail return
2. O O Pp. 2/3 Comp.
3. O O Pop./F

F. Total persons — 0 1 2 3 4 5 6 7 8 9 (three columns)

D-2(X)

ALSO ANSWER THESE QUESTIONS

H13a. How many stories (floors) are in this building?
- ○ 1 to 3 – *Skip to H14*
- ○ 4 to 6
- ○ 7 to 12
- ○ 13 stories or more

b. Is there a passenger elevator in this building?
- ○ Yes
- ○ No

H14. About when was this building originally built? *Mark when the building was first constructed, not when it was remodeled, added to, or converted.*
- ○ 1977 or 1978
- ○ 1973 to 1976
- ○ 1970 to 1972
- ○ 1960 to 1969
- ○ 1950 to 1959
- ○ 1940 to 1949
- ○ 1939 or earlier

H15a. Is this building –
- ○ On a city or suburban lot, or on a place of less than 1 acre? – *Skip to H16*
- ○ On a place of 1 to 9 acres?
- ○ On a place of 10 acres or more?

b. Last year, 1977, did sales of crops, livestock, and other farm products from this place amount to –
- ○ Less than $50 (or None)
- ○ $50 to $249
- ○ $250 to $599
- ○ $600 to $999
- ○ $1,000 to $2,499
- ○ $2,500 or more

H16. Do you get water from –
- ○ A public system *(city water department, etc.)* or private company?
- ○ An individual drilled well?
- ○ An individual dug well?
- ○ Some other source *(a spring, creek, river, cistern, etc.)*?

H17. Is this building connected to a public sewer?
- ○ Yes, connected to public sewer
- ○ No, connected to septic tank or cesspool
- ○ No, use other means

H18. How are your living quarters heated? *Fill one circle for the kind of heat used most.*
- ○ Steam or hot water system
- ○ Central warm-air furnace with ducts to the individual rooms *(Do not count electric heat pumps here.)*
- ○ Electric heat pump
- ○ Other built-in electric units *(permanently installed in wall, ceiling, or baseboard)*
- ○ Floor, wall, or pipeless furnace
- ○ Room heaters with flue or vent, burning gas, oil, or kerosene
- ○ Room heaters without flue or vent, burning gas, oil, or kerosene *(not portable)*
- ○ Fireplaces, stoves, or portable room heaters of any kind
- ○ No heating equipment

H19a. Which fuel is used most for house heating?
- ○ Gas: from underground pipes serving the neighborhood
- ○ Gas: bottled, tank, or LP
- ○ Electricity
- ○ Fuel oil, kerosene, etc.
- ○ Coal or coke
- ○ Wood
- ○ Other fuel
- ○ No fuel used

b. Which fuel is used most for water heating?
- ○ Gas: from underground pipes serving the neighborhood
- ○ Gas: bottled, tank, or LP
- ○ Electricity
- ○ Fuel oil, kerosene, etc.
- ○ Coal or coke
- ○ Wood
- ○ Other fuel
- ○ No fuel used

c. Which fuel is used most for cooking?
- ○ Gas: from underground pipes serving the neighborhood
- ○ Gas: bottled, tank, or LP
- ○ Electricity
- ○ Fuel oil, kerosene, etc.
- ○ Coal or coke
- ○ Wood
- ○ Other fuel
- ○ No fuel used

H20. What are the costs of utilities and fuels for your living quarters?

a. Electricity

$ ______ .00 OR ○ Included in rent or no charge ○ Electricity not used

Average monthly cost

b. Gas

$ ______ .00 OR ○ Included in rent or no charge ○ Gas not used

Average monthly cost

c. Water

$ ______ .00 OR ○ Included in rent or no charge

Yearly cost

d. Oil, coal, kerosene, wood, etc.

$ ______ .00 OR ○ Included in rent or no charge ○ These fuels not used

Yearly cost

H21. Do you have complete kitchen facilities? *Complete kitchen facilities are a sink with piped water, a range or cookstove, and refrigerator.*
- ○ Yes
- ○ No

H22. How many bedrooms do you have?
Count rooms used mainly for sleeping even if used also for other purposes.
- ○ No bedroom
- ○ 1 bedroom
- ○ 2 bedrooms
- ○ 3 bedrooms
- ○ 4 bedrooms
- ○ 5 bedrooms or more

H23. How many bathrooms do you have?
A complete bathroom is a room with flush toilet, bathtub or shower, and wash basin with piped water.

A half bathroom has at least a flush toilet or bathtub or shower, but does not have all the facilities for a complete bathroom.
- ○ No bathroom, or only a half bathroom
- ○ 1 complete bathroom
- ○ 1 complete bathroom, plus half bath(s)
- ○ 2 or more complete bathrooms

H24a. Does this house (apartment) have open cracks or holes in the interior walls or ceiling?
Do not include hairline cracks.
- ○ Yes
- ○ No

b. Does this house (apartment) have holes in the floors?
- ○ Yes
- ○ No

H25. Is there any area of broken plaster on the ceiling or inside walls which is larger than the size of this page?
- ○ Yes
- ○ No

H26. Is there any area of peeling paint on the ceiling or inside walls which is larger than the size of this page?
- ○ Yes
- ○ No

H27. Do you have a telephone in your living quarters?
- ○ Yes
- ○ No

H28. Do you have air-conditioning?
- ○ Yes, a central air-conditioning system
- ○ Yes, 1 individual room unit
- ○ Yes, 2 or more individual room units
- ○ No

H29. How many automobiles are kept at home for use by members of your household?
- ○ None
- ○ 1 automobile
- ○ 2 automobiles
- ○ 3 or more automobiles

H30. How many vans or trucks of one-ton capacity or less are kept at home for use by members of your household?
- ○ None
- ○ 1 van or truck
- ○ 2 vans or trucks
- ○ 3 or more vans or trucks

CENSUS USE

H20a. 0 0 0 / 1 1 1 / 2 2 2 / 3 3 3 / 4 4 4 / 5 5 5 / 6 6 6 / 7 7 7 / 8 8 8 / 9 9 9

H20b. 0 0 0 / 1 1 1 / 2 2 2 / 3 3 3 / 4 4 4 / 5 5 5 / 6 6 6 / 7 7 7 / 8 8 8 / 9 9 9

H20c. 0 0 0 / 1 1 1 / 2 2 2 / 3 3 3 / 4 4 4 / 5 5 5 / 6 6 6 / 7 7 7 / 8 8 8 / 9 9 9

H20d. 0 0 0 0 / 1 1 1 1 / 2 2 2 2 / 3 3 3 3 / 4 4 4 4 / 5 5 5 5 / 6 6 6 6 / 7 7 7 7 / 8 8 8 8 / 9 9 9 9

PH ○ ○

0 0 0 0 / 1 1 1 1 / 2 2 2 2 / 3 3 3 3 / 4 4 4 4 / 5 5 5 5 / 6 6 6 6 / 7 7 7 7 / 8 8 8 8 / 9 9 9 9

0 0 0 0 / 1 1 1 1 / 2 2 2 2 / 3 3 3 3 / 4 4 4 4 / 5 5 5 5 / 6 6 6 6 / 7 7 7 7 / 8 8 8 8 / 9 9 9 9

D-2(X)

Please answer H31–H34 if you live in a one-family house which you own or are buying, unless this is –

- A mobile home or trailer
- A house on 10 acres or more
- A cooperative or condominium unit
- A house with a commercial establishment or medical office on the property

If any of these, or if you rent your unit or this is a multi-family structure, skip H31 to H34 and turn to page 6.

H31. What were the real estate taxes on this property last year?

$ ______________ .00 OR ○ None

H32. What is the annual premium for fire and hazard insurance on this property?

$ ______________ .00 OR ○ None

H33a. Do you have a mortgage, deed of trust, contract to purchase or similar debt on this property?

○ Yes, mortgage, deed of trust, or similar debt

○ Yes, contract to purchase

○ No – *Skip to H34*

b. Do you have a second or junior mortgage on this property?

○ Yes ○ No

c. How much is your total regular monthly payment to the lender?
Also include payments on a contract to purchase and to lenders holding second or junior mortgages on this property.

$ ______________ .00 OR ○ No regular payment required – *Skip to H34*

d. Does your regular monthly payment (amount entered in H33c) include payments for real estate taxes on this property?

○ Yes, taxes included in payment

○ No, taxes paid separately or taxes not required

e. Does your regular monthly payment (amount entered in H33c) include payments for fire and hazard insurance on this property?

○ Yes, insurance included in payment

○ No, insurance paid separately or no insurance

H34. Do you have a property improvement loan for repair, rehabilitation, or improvement of this property?

○ Yes ○ No

Please turn to page 6 →

FOR CENSUS USE ONLY

①	2.	4.	②	2.	4.	③	2.	4.
S.S.	0 0	0 0 0	S.S.	0 0	0 0 0	S.S.	0 0	0 0 0
	1 1	1 1 1		1 1	1 1 1		1 1	1 1 1
	2 2	2 2 2		2 2	2 2 2		2 2	2 2 2
Yes ○	3 3	3 3 3	Yes ○	3 3	3 3 3	Yes ○	3 3	3 3 3
	4 4	4 4 4		4 4	4 4 4		4 4	4 4 4
	5 5	5 5 5		5 5	5 5 5		5 5	5 5 5
	6 6	6 6 6		6 6	6 6 6		6 6	6 6 6
No ○	7 7	7 7 7	No ○	7 7	7 7 7	No ○	7 7	7 7 7
	8 8	8 8 8		8 8	8 8 8		8 8	8 8 8
	9 9	9 9 9		9 9	9 9 9		9 9	9 9 9

④	2.	4.	⑤	2.	4.	⑥	2.	4.
S.S.	0 0	0 0 0	S.S.	0 0	0 0 0	S.S.	0 0	0 0 0
	1 1	1 1 1		1 1	1 1 1		1 1	1 1 1
	2 2	2 2 2		2 2	2 2 2		2 2	2 2 2
Yes ○	3 3	3 3 3	Yes ○	3 3	3 3 3	Yes ○	3 3	3 3 3
	4 4	4 4 4		4 4	4 4 4		4 4	4 4 4
	5 5	5 5 5		5 5	5 5 5		5 5	5 5 5
	6 6	6 6 6		6 6	6 6 6		6 6	6 6 6
No ○	7 7	7 7 7	No ○	7 7	7 7 7	No ○	7 7	7 7 7
	8 8	8 8 8		8 8	8 8 8		8 8	8 8 8
	9 9	9 9 9		9 9	9 9 9		9 9	9 9 9

⑦	2.	4.	GQ.	H31.	H32.	H33c.
S.S.	0 0	0 0 0	0 0	0 0 0 0	0 0 0	0 0 0 0
	1 1	1 1 1	1 1	1 1 1 1	1 1 1	1 1 1 1
	2 2	2 2 2	2 2	2 2 2 2	2 2 2	2 2 2 2
Yes ○	3 3	3 3 3	3 3	3 3 3 3	3 3 3	3 3 3 3
	4 4	4 4 4	4 4	4 4 4 4	4 4 4	4 4 4 4
	5 5	5 5 5	5 5	5 5 5 5	5 5 5	5 5 5 5
	6 6	6 6 6	6 6	6 6 6 6	6 6 6	6 6 6 6
No ○	7 7	7 7 7	7 7	7 7 7 7	7 7 7	7 7 7 7
	8 8	8 8 8	8 8	8 8 8 8	8 8 8	8 8 8 8
	9 9	9 9 9	9 9	9 9 9 9	9 9 9	9 9 9 9

D-2(X)

Pages 6-7 of the form (shown on pages 150-151) are for person 1. Pages 8-9 of the form are for person 2; pages 10-11, person 3; pages 12-13, person 4; pages 14-15, person 5; pages 16-17, person 6; and pages 18-19, person 7. To conserve space, pages 8-19 are not reproduced here.

ANSWER THESE QUESTIONS FOR

Name of Person 1 on page 2
Last name First name Middle initial

11. In what State or foreign country was this person born?
Print the State where this person's mother was living when this person was born. Do not give the location of the hospital unless the mother's home and the hospital were in the same State.
Be sure to name the State of birth, even if this person no longer lives in that State.
Name of State or foreign country; or Puerto Rico, Guam, etc.

12. *If this person was born in a foreign country –*
a. Is this person a naturalized citizen of the United States?
○ Yes, a naturalized citizen
○ No, not a citizen
○ Born abroad of American parents

b. When did this person come to the United States to stay?
○ 1975 to 1978 ○ 1965 to 1969 ○ 1950 to 1959
○ 1970 to 1974 ○ 1960 to 1964 ○ Before 1950

13. What is this person's ancestry?
If uncertain about how to report ancestry, see instruction sheet.
(For example – Afro-Amer., English, French, German, Honduran, Hungarian, Italian, Jamaican, Korean, Lebanese, Mexican, Nigerian, Polish, Ukrainian, Venezuelan, etc.)

14a. Does this person speak a language other than English at home?
○ Yes ○ No, only speaks English – *Skip to 15*

b. What is this language?
(For example – Chinese, Italian, Spanish, etc.)

c. Does this person speak this language at home more often than English?
○ Yes, more often than English
○ No, less often than English
○ Doesn't speak English

15. When did this person move into this house (or apartment)?
○ 1973 to 1978 ○ 1960 to 1969 ○ 1949 or earlier
○ 1970 to 1972 ○ 1950 to 1959 ○ Always lived here

16a. Did this person live in this house five years ago (April 1, 1973)? *If in college or Armed Forces in April 1973, report place of residence there.*
○ Born April 1973 or later – *Turn to next page for next person*
○ Yes, this house – *Skip to 17*
○ No, different house

b. Where did this person live five years ago (April 1, 1973)?
(1) State, foreign country, Puerto Rico, Guam, etc.: ______
(2) County: ______
(3) City, town, village, etc.: ______
(4) Inside the incorporated (legal) limits of that city, town, village, etc.?
○ Yes ○ No, in unincorporated area

17. When was this person born?
○ Born before April 1964 – *Please go on with questions 18–34*
○ Born April 1964 or later – *Turn to next page for next person.*

18. In April 1973 *(five years ago)* was this person –
a. On active duty in the Armed Forces?
○ Yes ○ No
b. Attending college?
○ Yes ○ No
c. Working at a job or business?
○ Yes, full time ○ No
○ Yes, part time

19a. Is this person a veteran of active-duty military service in the Armed Forces of the United States?
If service was in National Guard or Reserves only, see instruction sheet.
○ Yes ○ No – *Skip to 20*

b. Was active duty military service during –
(Fill a circle for each period in which this person served.)
○ May 1975 or later
○ Vietnam era *(August 1964–April 1975)*
○ February 1955–July 1964
○ Korean conflict *(June 1950–January 1955)*
○ World War II *(September 1940–July 1947)*
○ World War I *(April 1917–November 1918)*
○ Any other time

20. Does this person have a physical, mental, or other health condition which . . .
See instruction sheet for definition of health condition.

	Yes	No
a. Limits the kind or amount of work this person can do at a job?	○	○
b. Prevents this person from working at a job?	○	○
c. Limits or prevents this person from using public transportation?	○	○

21. *If this person is a female –*
How many babies has she ever had, not counting stillbirths?
Do not count her stepchildren or children she has adopted.
None 1 2 3 4 5 6
7 8 9 10 11 12 or more

22. *If this person has ever been married –*
a. Has this person been married more than once?
○ Once ○ More than once
b. Month and year of marriage? *(Month) (Year)*
Month and year of first marriage? *(Month) (Year)*
c. *If married more than once –* Did the first marriage end because of the death of the husband (or wife)?
○ Yes ○ No

23a. Did this person work at any time last week?
○ Yes – *Fill this circle if this person worked full time or part time. (Count part-time work such as delivering papers, or helping without pay in a family business or farm. Also count active duty in the Armed Forces.)*
○ No – *Fill this circle if this person did not work, or did only own housework, school work, or volunteer work.* *Skip to 26*

b. How many hours did this person work last week (at all jobs)?
Subtract any time off; add overtime or extra hours worked.
Hours

24. At what location did this person work last week?
If this person worked at more than one location, print where he or she worked most last week.
If one location cannot be specified, see instruction sheet.
a. Address *(Number and street)* ______
If street address is not known, enter the building name, shopping center, or other physical location description.
b. Name of city, town, village, borough, etc.
c. Is the place of work inside the incorporated (legal) limits of that city, town, village, borough, etc.?
○ Yes ○ No, in unincorporated area
d. County ______
e. State ______ f. ZIP Code ______

25a. Last week, how long did it usually take this person to get from home to work (one way)?
Minutes

b. How did this person usually get to work last week?
If this person used more than one method, give the one usually used for most of the distance.
○ Car ○ Subway or elevated
○ Truck ○ Taxicab
○ Van ○ Walked only
○ Bus or streetcar ○ Worked at home
○ Railroad ○ Other – *Specify*

If car, truck, or van in 25b, go to 25c. Otherwise, skip to 29.

FOR CENSUS USE ONLY

11.	13.	W.	14b.	16b.	22b.	23b.	24.	○ VL
0 0 0	0 0 0	0	0 0 0	0 0 0 0 0 0	0 0	0 0	0 0 0 0 0 0	0 0 0
1 1 1	1 1 1	1	1 1 1	1 1 1 1 1 1	1 1	1 1	1 1 1 1 1 1	1 1 1
2 2 2	2 2 2	2	2 2 2	2 2 2 2 2 2	1 2 2	2 2	2 2 2 2 2 2	2 2 2
3 3 3	3 3 3	3	3 3 3	3 3 3 3 3 3	3 3	3 3	3 3 3 3 3 3	3 3 3
4 4 4	4 4 4	4	4 4 4	4 4 4 4 4 4	2 4 4	4 4	4 4 4 4 4 4	4 4 4
5 5 5	5 5 5	5	5 5 5	5 5 5 5 5 5	5 5	5 5	5 5 5 5 5 5	5 5 5
6 6 6	6 6 6	6	6 6 6	6 6 6 6 6 6	3 6 6	6 6	6 6 6 6 6 6	6 6 6
7 7 7	7 7 7	7	7 7 7	7 7 7 7 7 7	7 7	7 7	7 7 7 7 7 7	7 7 7
8 8 8	8 8 8	8	8 8 8	8 8 8 8 8 8	4 8 8	8 8	8 8 8 8 8 8	8 8 8
9 9 9	9 9 9	9	9 9 9	9 9 9 9 9 9	9 9	9 9	9 9 9 9 9 9	9 9 9

D-2(X)

c. When going to work last week, did this person usually –
- ○ Drive alone – *Skip to 29*
- ○ Drive others only
- ○ Share driving
- ○ Ride as passenger only

d. How many people, including this person, usually rode to work in the car, truck, or van last week?

After answering 25d, skip to 29.

26. Was this person temporarily absent or on layoff from a job or business last week?
- ○ Yes, on layoff
- ○ Yes, on vacation, temporary illness, labor dispute, etc.
- ○ No

27a. Has this person been looking for work during the past 4 weeks?
- ○ Yes
- ○ No – *Skip to 28*

b. Could this person have taken a job last week?
- ○ No, already has a job
- ○ No, temporarily ill
- ○ No, other reasons *(in school, etc.)*
- ○ Yes, could have taken a job

28. When did this person last work, even for a few days?
- ○ 1978
- ○ 1977
- ○ 1976
- ○ 1972 to 1975
- ○ 1968 to 1971
- ○ 1967 or earlier } *Skip to 33*
- ○ Never worked } *Skip to 33*

29–31. Current or most recent job activity

Describe clearly this person's chief job activity or business last week. If this person had more than one job, describe the one at which this person worked the most hours. If this person had no job or business last week, give information for last job or business since 1968.

29. Industry

a. For whom did this person work? *If now on active duty in the Armed Forces, print "AF" and skip to question 32.*

(Name of company, business, organization, or other employer)

b. What kind of business or industry was this? *Describe activity at location where employed.*

(For example: Junior high school, retail supermarket, dairy farm, TV and radio service, auto assembly plant, road construction)

c. Is this mainly – *(Fill one circle)*
- ○ Manufacturing
- ○ Retail trade
- ○ Wholesale trade
- ○ Other – *(agriculture, construction, service, government, etc.)*

30. Occupation

a. What kind of work was this person doing?

(For example: TV repair, sewing machine operator, spray painter, civil engineer, farm operator, farm work, junior high English teacher)

b. What were this person's most important activities or duties?

(For example: Types, keeps account books, files, sells cars, operates printing press, cleans buildings, finishes concrete)

31. Was this person *(Fill one circle)*
- Employee of private company, business, or individual, for wages, salary, or commissions ... ○
- Federal government employee ... ○
- State government employee ... ○
- Local government employee *(city, county, etc.)* ... ○
- Self-employed in own business, professional practice, or farm –
  - Own business not incorporated ... ○
  - Own business incorporated ... ○
- Working without pay in family business or farm ... ○

CENSUS USE

25a. 0–9 0–9

25d. 0–9 0–9

29. A B C / D E F / G H J / K L M; 0–9 0–9 0–9; AF ○ NW ○

30. N P Q / R S T / U V W / X Y Z; 0–9 0–9 0–9

32a. Last year (1977), did this person work, even for a few days, at a paid job or in a business or farm?
- ○ Yes
- ○ No – *Skip to 33*

b. How many weeks did this person work in 1977? *Count paid vacation, paid sick leave, and military service.*

Weeks

c. During the weeks worked in 1977, how many hours did this person usually work each week?

Hours

33. Income in 1977 –

Fill circles and print dollar amounts. If net income was a loss, write "Loss" above the dollar amount. If exact amount is not known, give best estimate. For income received jointly by household members, see instruction sheet.

During 1977 did this person receive any income from the following sources?

If "Yes" to any of the sources below – How much did this person receive for the entire year?

a. Wages, salary, commissions, bonuses, or tips from all jobs ... *Report amount before deductions for taxes, bonds, dues, or other items.*
○ Yes → $ .00 *(Dollars only)*
○ No

b. Own nonfarm business, partnership, or professional practice ... *Report net income after business expenses.*
○ Yes → $ .00 *(Dollars only)*
○ No

c. Own farm ... *Report net income after operating expenses. Include earnings as a tenant farmer or sharecropper.*
○ Yes → $ .00 *(Dollars only)*
○ No

d. Interest, dividends, royalties, or net rental income ... *Report even small amounts credited to an account.*
○ Yes → $ .00 *(Dollars only)*
○ No

e. Social Security or Railroad Retirement ...
○ Yes → $ .00 *(Dollars only)*
○ No

f. Supplemental Security (SSI), Aid to Families with Dependent Children (AFDC), or other public assistance or public welfare payments ...
○ Yes → $ .00 *(Dollars only)*
○ No

g. Unemployment compensation, veterans' payments, pensions, alimony or child support, or any other sources of income received regularly ... *Exclude lump-sum payments such as money from an inheritance or the sale of a home.*
○ Yes → $ .00 *(Dollars only)*
○ No

34. What was this person's total income in 1977?

$ .00 *(Dollars only)*

OR ○ None

Add entries in questions 33a through g; subtract any losses. If total amount was a loss, write "Loss" above amount.

CENSUS USE ONLY

32b. 32c. Person number

33a. 33b. 33c. 33d. 33e. 33f. 33g. 34.

X. Y. Z.

D-2(X)

➔ **Please turn to the next page and answer the questions for Person 2 on page 2.**

Page 20

Please Make Sure You Have Filled This Form Completely

For persons who answered in Question 1 that they are staying here only temporarily and have a usual home elsewhere, enter the address of usual home here:

House number ______ Street or road ______ Apartment number or location ______

City ______ County ______

State ______ ZIP Code ______

For Answers to Questions H1, H2, and H3:

H1. Name of person(s) left out and reason:

H2. Name of person(s) away from home and reason away:

H3. Name of visitor(s) for whom there is no one at the home address to report the person to a Census Taker:

NOTE

If you have listed more than 7 persons in Question 1, please make sure that you have filled the form for the first 7 people. Then mail back this form. A Census Taker will call to obtain the information for the other people.

1 Check to be certain you have:

- Answered Question 1 on page 1.
- Answered Questions 2 through 10 for each person you listed at the top of pages 2 and 3.
- Answered Questions H1 through H34 on pages 3, 4, and 5.
- Filled a pair of pages for each person listed on pages 2 and 3. That is, pages 6 and 7 should be filled for the Person in column 1; pages 8 and 9 for the Person in column 2, etc.

Please notice we need answers to questions 18 through 34 for every person born before April 1964 even though they may not seem to apply to the particular person.

For example, you may have forgotten to fill all the necessary circles on work or on income for a housewife, a teenager going to school, or an older retired person. To avoid our having to check with you to make sure of the answer, please be certain you have given all the necessary answers.

2 Write here the name of the person who filled the form, the date, and the telephone number on which the people in this household can be called.

Name ______

Date ______

Telephone Number ______

3 Then fold the form the way it was sent to you. Mail it back in the enclosed envelope. The address of the U.S. Census Office appears on the front cover of this questionnaire. Please be sure that before you seal the envelope the address shows through the window. No stamp is required.

Thank you very much .

FORM D-2(X) (12-19-77)

☆ GPO : 1978 O - 252-692

1978 Census of the Richmond, Virginia Area

(Richmond City, and Chesterfield and Henrico Counties)

○ Need help?

○ Use this

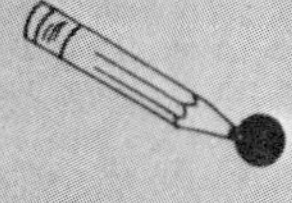

● **Instruction Sheet**

This sheet gives helpful information on filling out your census form. If you need more help, call the local U.S. Census office. The telephone number is given in the address box on the cover of the census form.

Form D-4(X)
(1-20-78)

U.S. DEPARTMENT OF COMMERCE
BUREAU OF THE CENSUS

- There may be a question you cannot answer exactly. For example, you might not know the age of an elderly person or the price for which your house would sell. See if someone else in your household knows; if no one does, give your best estimate.
- If you are not sure if you should list a person, see the rules on page 1 of the census form.
- If there are more than seven people in your household, please list **all** the persons in question 1, complete the form for seven people, and mail it back in the enclosed envelope. A census taker will call to obtain the additional information.

INSTRUCTIONS FOR QUESTIONS 1 THROUGH 10

1. List in question 1 (on page 1), the names of all the people who usually live here. Then turn to pages 2 and 3 where there are columns to list up to seven persons. In the first column print the name of one of the household members in whose name this home is owned or rented. If no household member owns or rents the living quarters, list in the first column any adult household member who is not a roomer, boarder, or paid employee. Print the names of the other household members, if any, in the columns which follow, using question 1 as a checklist.

2. Fill a circle to show how each person is related to the person in column 1.

   A stepchild or legally adopted child of the person in column 1 should be marked **Son/daughter.** Foster children or wards living in the household should be marked **Roomer, boarder.**

3. Be sure to fill a circle for the sex of each person.

4. Fill the circle for the category with which the person most closely identifies. Print the specific race if so instructed; if **Indian (American)**, print specific tribe.

5. Enter age at last birthday in the space provided ("0" for babies less than one year old). Also enter month and year of birth, and fill the appropriate circles. For an illustration of how to complete question 5, see the example. If age or month or year of birth is not known, give your best estimate.

6. If the person's only marriage was annulled, mark **Never married.**

7. *Origin or descent* refers to a person's nationality group, lineage, or the country in which the person, or the person's parents or ancestors were born.

8. Do not count enrollment in a trade or business school, company training, or tutoring unless the course would be accepted for credit at a regular high school or college. A *public* school is any school or college which is controlled and supported primarily by a local, county, State, or Federal government.

9. Fill only one circle. Mark the highest grade *ever* attended even if the person did not finish it. If the person is still in school, mark the grade in which now enrolled. Schooling received in foreign or ungraded schools should be reported as the equivalent grade or year in the regular American school system. If uncertain whether Head Start is for nursery school or kindergarten, mark the circle for **Nursery school.**

   If the person skipped or repeated grades, mark the highest grade ever attended regardless of how long it took to get there. Persons who did not attend any college but who completed high school by finishing the 12th grade or by passing an equivalency test, such as the General Educational Development (GED) examination, should fill the circle for the 12th grade.

10. Mark **Finished this grade (or year)** only if the person finished the *entire* grade or year marked in question 9 or if the highest grade was completed by passing a high school equivalency test.

EXAMPLE

Page 2

Also answer the housing questions on page 3.

Here are the QUESTIONS ↓ These are the columns for ANSWERS → *Please fill one column for each person listed in Question 1.*	PERSON in column 1	PERSON in column 2	PERSON in column 3	PERSON in column 4
	Last name: Doe First name: Arthur Middle initial: T.	Last name: Doe First name: Frances Middle initial:	Last name: Doe First name: Patricia Middle initial: J.	Last name: Smith First name: Mary Middle initial: J.
2. How is this person related to the person in column 1? *Fill one circle* *If "Other relative" of person in column 1, give exact relationship, such as mother-in-law, niece, grandson, etc.*	*START in this column with the household member (or one of the members) in whose name the home is owned or rented. If there is no such person, start in this column with any adult household member.*	If relative of person in column 1 ● Husband/wife ○ Father/mother ○ Son/daughter ○ Other relative ○ Brother/sister If not related to person in column 1 ○ Roomer, boarder ○ Other nonrelative ○ Partner, roommate ○ Paid employee	If relative of person in column 1 ○ Husband/wife ○ Father/mother ● Son/daughter ○ Other relative ○ Brother/sister If not related to person in column 1 ○ Roomer, boarder ○ Other nonrelative ○ Partner, roommate ○ Paid employee	If relative of person in column 1 ○ Husband/wife ○ Father/mother ○ Son/daughter ● Other relative Grandmother ○ Brother/sister If not related to person in column 1 ○ Roomer, boarder ○ Other nonrelative ○ Partner, roommate ○ Paid employee
3. Sex *Fill one circle.*	● Male ○ Female	○ Male ● Female	○ Male ● Female	○ Male ● Female
4. Race *Fill one circle.*	● White ○ Asian Indian ○ Black or Negro ○ Hawaiian ○ Japanese ○ Guamanian ○ Chinese ○ Samoan ○ Filipino ○ Eskimo ○ Korean ○ Aleut ○ Vietnamese ○ Other – *Print race* ○ Indian (Amer.) *Print tribe* →	● White ○ Asian Indian ○ Black or Negro ○ Hawaiian ○ Japanese ○ Guamanian ○ Chinese ○ Samoan ○ Filipino ○ Eskimo ○ Korean ○ Aleut ○ Vietnamese ○ Other – *Print race* ○ Indian (Amer.) *Print tribe* →	● White ○ Asian Indian ○ Black or Negro ○ Hawaiian ○ Japanese ○ Guamanian ○ Chinese ○ Samoan ○ Filipino ○ Eskimo ○ Korean ○ Aleut ○ Vietnamese ○ Other – *Print race* ○ Indian (Amer.) *Print tribe* →	● White ○ Asian Indian ○ Black or Negro ○ Hawaiian ○ Japanese ○ Guamanian ○ Chinese ○ Samoan ○ Filipino ○ Eskimo ○ Korean ○ Aleut ○ Vietnamese ○ Other – *Print race* ○ Indian (Amer.) *Print tribe* →
5. Age, and month and year of birth *a. Print age at last birthday.* *b. Print month and fill one circle.* *c. Print year in the spaces, and fill one circle below each number.*	a. Age at last birthday: 28 b. Month of birth: June ○ Jan.–Mar. ● Apr.–June ○ July–Sept. ○ Oct.–Dec. c. Year of birth: 1 9 4 9	a. Age at last birthday: 28 b. Month of birth: January ● Jan.–Mar. ○ Apr.–June ○ July–Sept. ○ Oct.–Dec. c. Year of birth: 1 9 5 0	a. Age at last birthday: 0 b. Month of birth: December ○ Jan.–Mar. ○ Apr.–June ○ July–Sept. ● Oct.–Dec. c. Year of birth: 1 9 7 7	a. Age at last birthday: 78 b. Month of birth: August ○ Jan.–Mar. ○ Apr.–June ● July–Sept. ○ Oct.–Dec. c. Year of birth: 1 8 9 9
6. Marital status *Fill one circle.*	● Now married ○ Separated ○ Widowed ○ Never married ○ Divorced	● Now married ○ Separated ○ Widowed ○ Never married ○ Divorced	○ Now married ○ Separated ○ Widowed ● Never married ○ Divorced	○ Now married ○ Separated ● Widowed ○ Never married ○ Divorced
7. Is this person's origin or descent – *Fill one circle.*	○ Mexican-Amer. ○ Cuban ○ Mexican or Chicano ○ Other Spanish ○ Puerto Rican ● Not Spanish	○ Mexican-Amer. ○ Cuban ○ Mexican or Chicano ○ Other Spanish ○ Puerto Rican ● Not Spanish	○ Mexican-Amer. ○ Cuban ○ Mexican or Chicano ○ Other Spanish ○ Puerto Rican	○ Mexican-Amer. ○ Cuban ○ Mexican or Chicano ○ Other Spanish ○ Puerto Rican ● Not Spanish

HOUSING QUESTIONS
INSTRUCTIONS FOR QUESTIONS H4 THROUGH H33

H4. *Detached* means there is open space on all sides, or the house is joined only to a shed or garage. *Attached* means that the house is joined to another house or building by at least one wall which goes from ground to roof.

Mark **A one-family house: Detached from any other house** if one or more rooms have been added to or built onto a mobile home or trailer. A porch or shed is not considered a room.

Count all occupied and vacant living quarters in the house or building, but not stores or office space.

H5. Mark the second circle only if you *must* go through someone else's living quarters to get to your own.

H6. Consider that you have hot water even if you have it only part of the time.

Mark **Yes, but also used by another household** if someone else who lives in the same building, but is not a member of your household, also uses the facilities. Mark this circle also if the occupants of living quarters now vacant would also use the facilities in your living quarters.

H7. Count only whole rooms used for living purposes, such as living rooms, dining rooms, kitchens, bedrooms, finished recreation rooms, family rooms, etc. Do not count bathrooms, kitchenettes, strip or pullman kitchens, utility rooms, or unfinished attics, basements, or other space used for storage.

H8. Mark **Owned or being bought** if the living quarters are owned outright or are mortgaged. Also mark **Owned or being bought** if the living quarters are owned but the land is rented.

Mark **Rented for cash rent** if any money rent is paid. Rent may be paid by persons who are not members of your household.

Occupied without payment of cash rent includes, for example, a parsonage, a house or apartment provided free of rent by the owner, or a house or apartment occupied by a janitor or caretaker in exchange for services.

H9. A *condominium* is a type of ownership that enables a person to own an apartment or house in a development of similar units. The owner holds the deed and, very likely, has a mortgage on the unit. A *cooperative* is housing which is owned by a corporation of member-owners.

H10b. A *commercial establishment* is easily recognized from the outside: for example, a grocery store or barber shop. A *medical office* is a doctor's or dentist's office regularly visited by patients.

H11. Include the value of the house, the land it is on, and any other structures on the same property. If the house is owned but the land is rented, estimate the combined value of the house and the land. If this is a condominium unit, enter the estimated value for your living quarters and your share of the common elements.

H12. Report the rent agreed to or contracted for, even if the rent is unpaid or paid by someone else.

If rent is not paid by the month, change the rent to a monthly amount; and then fill the appropriate circle in question H12.

If rent is paid:	Multiply rent by:
By the day	30
By the week	4
Every other week	2

If rent is paid:	Divide rent by:
4 times a year	3
2 times a year	6
Once a year	12

H13a. Do not count unfinished basements or attics. However, a basement or attic with finished room(s) for living purposes should be counted as a story.

b. Mark **Yes** if there is a stairway elevator or wheelchair lift installed in your home. Do not count elevators used only for freight.

H15a. A *city or suburban* lot is usually located in a city, a community, or any built-up area outside a city or community, and is not larger than the house and yard. All living quarters in apartment buildings, including garden-type apartments in the city or suburbs, are considered on a city or suburban lot.

A *place* is a farm, ranch, or any other property, other than a city or suburban lot, on which this *residence* is located.

H16. If a well provides water for six or more houses or apartments, mark **A public system.** If a well provides water for five or fewer houses or apartments, mark one of the categories for *individual well.*

Drilled wells, or small diameter wells, are usually less than 1½ feet in diameter. *Dug wells* are generally hand dug and are wider.

H17. A *public sewer* is operated by a government body or a private organization. A *septic tank or cesspool* is an underground tank or pit used for disposal of sewage.

H18. This question refers to the type of *heating equipment* and not to the fuel used.

An *electric heat pump* is sometimes known as a reverse cycle system. It may be centrally installed with ducts to the rooms or individual heat pumps in the rooms.

A *floor, wall, or pipeless furnace* delivers warm air to the room right above the furnace or to the room(s) on one or both sides of the wall in which the furnace is installed and does not have ducts leading to other rooms.

Any heater that you plug into an electric outlet should be counted as a *portable room heater.*

H19. *Gas from underground pipes* is piped in from a central system such as a public utility company or a municipal government. *Bottled, tank, or LP gas* is stored in tanks which are refilled or exchanged when empty. *Other fuel* includes any fuel not separately listed, for example, purchased steam, fuel briquettes, waste material, etc.

H20. If your living quarters are rented, enter the costs for utilities and fuels only if you pay for them in addition to the rent entered in H12. If already included in rent, fill the appropriate circle.

The amounts to be reported should be for the past 12 months, i.e., for electricity and gas, the monthly *average* for the past 12 months; for water and other fuels, the *total* amount for the past 12 months.

Estimate as closely as possible when exact costs are not known.

Report amounts even if your bills are unpaid or paid by someone else. If the bills include utilities or fuel used also by another apartment or a business establishment, estimate the amounts for your own living quarters. If gas and electricity are billed together, enter the combined amount on the electricity line and bracket ({) the two utilities.

H21. The kitchen sink, stove, and refrigerator must be located in the building but do *not* have to be in the same room. Portable cooking equipment is not considered as a range or cook stove.

H24. Do *not* include very small holes caused by nails or other similar objects. Also, do not include *hairline cracks* or openings or traps leading to the attic. Do *not* consider ventilation or heating ducts or similar throughways as *holes.*

H25. The area of broken plaster must be on the *inside* walls or ceilings.

H26. The area of peeling paint must be on the *inside* walls or ceilings.

H27. Answer **Yes** *only* if the telephone is located *in* your living quarters.

H28. Count only equipment used to cool the air by means of a refrigeration unit.

H29 – H30. Count company cars (including police cars and taxicabs) and company trucks that are regularly kept at home and used by household members. Do *not* count cars or trucks permanently out of working order.

H31. Report taxes for all taxing jurisdictions even if they are included in mortgage payment, not paid yet, paid by someone else, or are delinquent.

H32. When premiums are paid on other than a yearly basis, convert to a yearly basis and enter the yearly amount, even if no payment was made during the past 12 months.

H33a. The word "mortgage" is used as a general term to indicate all types of loans which are secured by real estate.

b. A junior mortgage is also secured by real estate but its lender's claim to the property is second or junior to that of the first mortgage lender.

c. Enter a monthly amount even if it is unpaid or paid by someone else. If the amount is paid on some other periodic basis, see instructions for H12 to change it to a monthly amount.

INSTRUCTIONS FOR QUESTIONS 11 THROUGH 34

11. *For persons born in the United States:*
Print the name of the State in which this person's mother was living when this person was born. For persons born in a hospital, do not give the State in which the hospital was located unless the hospital and the mother's home were in the same State or the location of the mother's home is not known. For example, if a person was born in a hospital in Washington, D.C., but the mother's home was in Virginia at the time of the person's birth, enter "Virginia."

For persons born outside the United States:
Print the full name of the foreign country or Puerto Rico, Guam, etc., where the person was born. Use international boundaries as now recognized by the United States. Specify whether Northern Ireland or Ireland (Eire); East or West Germany; England, Scotland or Wales (*not* Great Britain or United Kingdom). Specify the particular island in the Caribbean, *not,* for example, West Indies.

12. This question is only for persons born in a foreign country. Fill the **Yes, a naturalized citizen** circle only if the person has *completed* the naturalization process and is now a citizen.

If the person has entered the U.S. more than once, fill the circle for the year he or she came to stay permanently.

13. Ancestry (or origin) refers to the nationality group, the lineage, or the country in which the person or the person's parents or ancestors were born before their arrival in the United States. Ancestry may be based on the origin of the person, near relatives, or some far-removed ancestor. Print the ancestry group with which the person most identifies. Do not report a religious group. If specific ancestry is "Indian," specify whether American Indian, Asian, or East Indian.

For persons who are of more than one origin, and who cannot identify with a single origin group, print the multiple origin (for example, Scotch-Irish).

14. Mark **Yes** if the person speaks a language other than English *at home.* Do not report a language if it is only being studied as a course in school or is limited to a few expressions or slang. Print the non-English language in 14b and fill a circle in 14c to show how often the language is spoken compared with English. If this person speaks two or more non-English languages at home and cannot determine which is spoken most often, report the first language the person learned to speak.

Mark **No, only speaks English** if the person speaks only English *at home* and skip to question 15.

15. Mark when this person last moved into *this* house or apartment.

16a. Mark **Yes, this house** if this person lived in this same house or apartment on April 1, 1973, but moved away and came back between then and now. Mark **No, different house** if this person lived in the same building but in a different apartment (or in the same mobile home or trailer but on a different trailer site).

b. If this person lived in a different house or apartment on April 1, 1973, give the location of this person's usual home at that time.

Part (2) If in Louisiana, print the parish name. If in Alaska, print the borough name. If in New York city – print the borough name if the county name is not known.

If an *independent city,* print the name of the city and the word "city," for example, "Baltimore city."

Part (3) If in Connecticut, Maine, Massachusetts, New Hampshire, Rhode Island or Vermont, print the name of the town rather than the name of the village or city, unless the name of the town is unknown.

Part (4) Mark **Yes** if you know that the location is *now* inside the limits of a city, town, village or other incorporated place, even if it was not inside the limits on April 1973.

18a. Mark **Yes** only if this person was on *active* duty in the U.S. Army, Navy, Air Force, Marine Corps, or Coast Guard. Mark **No** if the person was in the National Guard, the reserves, or the merchant marine.

b. Mark **Yes** if the person was attending a college or university either full or part time and was enrolled for credit toward a degree. Mark **No** if the person was taking only non-credit courses or was attending a vocational or trade school, such as secretarial, beauty, or auto mechanic school.

c. Mark **Yes, full time** if the person worked full time (35 hours or more per week). Mark **Yes, part time** if the person worked part time (less than 35 hours per week). Mark **No** if the person only did unpaid volunteer work, housework or yard work at own home, or if the only work done was as an inmate of an institution.

19a. Mark **Yes** if this person was ever on active duty in the U.S. Army, Navy, Air Force, Marine Corps, or Coast Guard, even if the time served was short. For persons in the National Guard or military reserve units, mark **Yes** *only* if the person was ever called to active duty; mark **No** if the only service was active duty for training.

b. If this person served during more than one period, fill all circles which apply, even if service was for a short time.

20. The term "health condition" refers to any physical or mental problem which has lasted or is expected to last for 6 *or more* months. A serious problem with seeing, hearing, or speech should be considered a health condition. Pregnancy or temporary health problem such as a broken bone that is expected to heal normally should *not* be considered a health condition.

21. Count all children born alive, including any who have died (even shortly after birth) or who no longer live with her.

22. If exact date of first marriage is not known, give your best estimate.

23a. Mark **Yes** if the person worked, either full or part time, on any day of last week (Sunday through Saturday).

Count as work:	**Do not count as work:**
Work for someone else for wages, salary, piece rate, commission, tips, or payments "in kind."	Housework or yard work at home.
Work in own business, professional practice, or farm.	Unpaid volunteer work.
Any work in a family business or farm, paid or not.	Work done as an inmate of an institution.
Any part-time work including babysitting, paper routes, etc.	
Active duty in Armed Forces.	

b. Give the *actual* number of hours worked at *all jobs last week,* even if that was more or fewer hours than usually worked.

24. If the person worked at several locations, but reported to the same location each day to begin work, print where he or she reported. If the person did not report to the same location each day to begin work, print the words "various locations" for 24a, and give as much information as possible in the remainder of 24 to identify the area in which he or she worked most last week.

If the person's employer operates in more than one location (such as a grocery store chain or public school system), give the *exact address* of the location or branch where the *person* worked.

If the person worked in a foreign country or Puerto Rico, Guam, etc., print the name of the country in 24e and leave the other parts of 24 blank.

25a. Travel time is from door to door. Include time taken waiting for public transportation, picking up passengers in carpools, etc.

b. Mark **Worked at home** for a person who works on a farm where he or she lives, or in an office or shop in the person's home.

c. Mark **Drive alone** for persons who were driven to work by someone who then drove back home or to a non-work destination.

d. Do not include riders who rode to school or some other non-work destination.

26. Mark **No** if the person works only during certain seasons or on a day-to-day basis when work is available.

27a. Mark **Yes** if the person tried to get a job or to start a business or profession at any time in the past *four* weeks; for example, registered at an employment office, went to a job interview, placed or answered ads, or did anything toward starting a business or profession.

b. Mark **No, already has a job** if the person was on layoff or was expecting to report to a job within 30 days.

Mark **No, temporarily ill** if the person expects to be able to work within 30 days.

Mark **No, other reasons** if the person could not have taken a job because he or she was going to school, taking care of children, etc.

28. Look at the instructions for 23a to see what to count as work. Mark **Never worked** if the person: (1) never worked at any kind of job or business, either full or part time, (2) never did any work, with or without pay, in a family business or farm *and* (3) never served in the Armed Forces.

29a. If the person worked for a company, business, or government agency, print the name of the company, not the name of the person's supervisor. If the person worked for an individual or a business that has no company name, print the name of the individual worked for. If the person worked in his or her own business, print "self-employed."

b. Print two or more words to tell what the business, industry, or individual named in 29a does. If there is more than one activity, describe only the major activity *at the place where the person works.* Enter what is made, what is sold, or what service is given.

Some examples of what is needed to make an answer acceptable are shown on the census form and here.

Unacceptable	**Acceptable**
Furniture company	Metal furniture manufacturing
Grocery store	Wholesale grocery store
Oil company	Retail gas station
Ranch	Cattle ranch

c. Mark **Manufacturing** if the factory, plant, mill, etc., mostly makes things, even if it also sells them.

Mark **Wholesale trade** if the business primarily sells things to stores or other companies.

Mark **Retail trade** if the business mostly sells things (not services) to individuals.

Mark **Other** if the main activity of the employer is not making or selling things. Some examples of **Other** are farming, construction, and services such as those provided by hotels, dry cleaners, repair shops, schools, and banks.

30a. Print two or more words to describe the kind of work the person does. If the person is a trainee, apprentice, or helper, include that in the description.

Some examples of what is needed to make an answer acceptable are shown on the census form and here.

Unacceptable	**Acceptable**
Clerk	Production clerk
Helper	Carpenter's helper
Mechanic	Auto engine mechanic
Nurse	Registered nurse

b. Print the most important things that the person does on the job. Some examples are shown on the census form.

31. If the person was an employee of a *private* nonprofit organization, such as a church, fill the first circle.

Mark **Local government employee** for a teacher working in an elementary or secondary public school.

32a. Look at the instruction for question 23a to see what to count as work.

b. Count every week in which the person did any work at all, even if for an hour.

33. Fill the **Yes** or **No** circle for each part and enter the appropriate amount. If income from any source was received jointly by household members, report if possible, the appropriate share for each person; otherwise, report the whole amount for only one person and mark **No** for the other person, unless the other person has additional income of the same type.

a. Include sick leave pay. Exclude reimbursement for business expenses and pay "in kind."

b. Include net earnings (gross earnings minus business expenses) from a nonfarm business.

c. Include net earnings (gross receipts minus operating expenses) from a farm.

d. Include interest and dividends credited to the person's account (e.g., from savings accounts and stock shares), net royalties, and net income from rental property.

e. Include Social Security Administration or Railroad Retirement payments to retired persons, to dependents of deceased insured workers, or to disabled workers.

f. Include payments received from Federal, State, or local public programs. Exclude private (nongovernment) welfare payments.

g. Include all other *regular* payments, such as government employee retirement, union or private pensions and annuities; unemployment benefits; workmen's compensation; Armed Forces allotments; regular contributions; etc.

Exclude lump-sum payments received from the sale of property (capital gains), insurance policies, inheritances, etc.

34. If no income was received in 1977, fill the **None** circle. If total income was a loss, write "Loss" above the amount.

1978 Census of the Richmond, Virginia Area

(Richmond City, and Chesterfield and Henrico Counties)

Please fill out this Official Census Form and mail it back on Census Day, Tuesday, April 4, 1978

If the address shown below has the wrong apartment identification, please write the correct apartment number or location here:

D.O.	A1.	A2.	A4.	A5. S	A6.	C.R.

- **Your answers are CONFIDENTIAL by law (title 13, United States Code).**

  This means that no one may see your answers except census workers who are sworn not to disclose your information, and who can be fined and/or imprisoned for any violation.

- **The law also requires that you answer the questions to the best of your knowledge.**

How to Fill This Form

1. **Use a black pencil to answer the questions.**
   This form is read by a computer. Black pencil is better to use than ballpoint or other pens.

   Fill circles "O" like this: ●
   The computer reads every circle you fill. If you fill the wrong circle, erase the mark completely, then fill the right circle.

   When you write in an answer, print or write clearly.

2. **See the filled-in example on the yellow instruction sheet.**
   This example shows how to fill circles and write in answers. If you are not sure of an answer, give the best answer you can.

   If you have a problem, look in the instruction sheet.
   All instructions are numbered the same as the questions on the census form.

   If you need more help, call the Census office.
   The telephone number of the local office is shown at the bottom of the address box to the left.

3. **Make sure that the information is shown for everyone here.**
   A boarder, roomer, or someone else in the household may sometimes not want to give you all the information for the form. Write in at least the person's name, relationship, and sex. A Census Taker will call to get the other information directly from the person.

4. **Answer the questions on pages 1, 2, and 3. Check your answers. Then, write your name, the date, and telephone number on page 4. Mail back this form on Tuesday, April 4, or as soon afterward as you can. Use the enclosed envelope; no stamp is needed.**
   Your cooperation in carefully filling out the form and mailing it back will help make the census successful. It will save the government the expense of calling on you for the information.

PARA PERSONAS DE HABLA HISPANA (For Spanish-speaking persons):

SI USTED DESEA UN CUESTIONARIO DEL CENSO EN ESPAÑOL, llame a la oficina del censo. El número de teléfono se encuentra más arriba, en la casilla para la dirección al principio de la columna izquierda.

O marque este círculo "O" y devuelva este cuestionario por correo en el sobre color café que aquí se incluye.

U.S. DEPARTMENT OF COMMERCE
BUREAU OF THE CENSUS
FORM D-1 (X) (12/19/77)

O.M.B. No. 41-S78006:
Approval Expires June 30, 1979

PLEASE CONTINUE →

Question 1:

What is the name of each person who was living here on Tuesday, April 4, 1978, or who was staying or visiting here and had no other home?

↓

NOTE

If everyone here is staying only temporarily and has a usual home elsewhere, please fill this circle O. Then please:

- answer the questions on pages 2 and 3, and
- enter the address of your usual home on page 4.

Instructions:

List in Question 1

- Family members living here, including babies still in the hospital.
- Relatives living here.
- Lodgers or boarders living here.
- Domestic employees or hired hands living here.
- Other persons living here.
- College students who stay here while attending college, even if their parents live elsewhere.
- Persons who usually live here but are temporarily away (including children in boarding school below the college level).
- Persons with a home elsewhere but who stay here most of the week while working.

Do Not List in Question 1

- Any person away from here in the Armed Forces.
- Any college student who stays somewhere else while attending college.
- Any person who usually stays somewhere else most of the week while working there.
- Any person away from here in an institution such as a home for the aged or mental hospital.
- Any person staying or visiting here who has a usual home elsewhere.

PLEASE CONTINUE →

Also answer the hou[...]

Here are the QUESTIONS ↓ / These are the columns for ANSWERS → *Please fill one column for each person listed in Question 1.*	PERSON in column 1 Last name First name / Middle initial	PERSON in column 2 Last name First name / Middle initial
2. How is this person related to the person in column 1? *Fill one circle.* *If "Other relative" of person in column 1, give exact relationship, such as mother-in-law, niece, grandson, etc.*	*START in this column with the household member (or one of the members) in whose name the home is owned or rented. If there is no such person, start in this column with any adult household member.*	If relative of person in column 1: ○ Husband/wife ○ Father/mother ○ Son/daughter ○ Other relative ○ Brother/sister If not related to person in column 1: ○ Roomer, boarder ○ Other nonrelative ○ Partner, roommate ○ Paid employee
3. Sex *Fill one circle.*	○ Male ○ Female	○ Male ○ Female
4. Race *Fill one circle.*	○ White ○ Asian Indian ○ Black or Negro ○ Hawaiian ○ Japanese ○ Guamanian ○ Chinese ○ Samoan ○ Filipino ○ Eskimo ○ Korean ○ Aleut ○ Vietnamese ○ Other – *Print race* ○ Indian (Amer.) *Print tribe*	○ White ○ Asian Indian ○ Black or Negro ○ Hawaiian ○ Japanese ○ Guamanian ○ Chinese ○ Samoan ○ Filipino ○ Eskimo ○ Korean ○ Aleut ○ Vietnamese ○ Other – *Print race* ○ Indian (Amer.) *Print tribe*
5. Age, and month and year of birth *a. Print age at last birthday.* *b. Print month and fill one circle.* *c. Print year in the spaces, and fill one circle below each number.*	a. Age at last birthday b. Month of birth ○ Jan.–Mar. ○ Apr.–June ○ July–Sept. ○ Oct.–Dec. c. Year of birth 1 1 ● / 8 ○ 9 ○ / Ø ○ 1 ○ 2 ○ 3 ○ 4 ○ 5 ○ 6 ○ 7 ○ 8 ○ 9 ○ / Ø ○ 1 ○ 2 ○ 3 ○ 4 ○ 5 ○ 6 ○ 7 ○ 8 ○ 9 ○	a. Age at last birthday b. Month of birth ○ Jan.–Mar. ○ Apr.–June ○ July–Sept. ○ Oct.–Dec. c. Year of birth 1 1 ● / 8 ○ 9 ○ / Ø ○ 1 ○ 2 ○ 3 ○ 4 ○ 5 ○ 6 ○ 7 ○ 8 ○ 9 ○ / Ø ○ 1 ○ 2 ○ 3 ○ 4 ○ 5 ○ 6 ○ 7 ○ 8 ○ 9 ○
6. Marital status *Fill one circle.*	○ Now married ○ Separated ○ Widowed ○ Never married ○ Divorced	○ Now married ○ Separated ○ Widowed ○ Never married ○ Divorced
7. Is this person's origin or descent – *Fill one circle.*	○ Mexican-Amer. ○ Cuban ○ Mexican or Chicano ○ Other Spanish ○ Puerto Rican ○ Not Spanish	○ Mexican-Amer. ○ Cuban ○ Mexican or Chicano ○ Other Spanish ○ Puerto Rican ○ Not Spanish
D-1(X) Fosdic 26.1:1	*CENSUS USE ONLY* A. ○ Inmate ○ Other ○ ○	*CENSUS USE ONLY* A. ○ Inmate ○ Other ○ ○

sing questions on page 3. → *Also answer the housing questions on page 3.*

PERSON in column 3

Last name

First name | Middle initial

If relative of person in column 1:
- ○ Husband/wife
- ○ Son/daughter
- ○ Brother/sister
- ○ Father/mother
- ○ Other relative

If not related to person in column 1:
- ○ Roomer, boarder
- ○ Partner, roommate
- ○ Paid employee
- ○ Other nonrelative

○ Male ○ Female

- ○ White
- ○ Black or Negro
- ○ Japanese
- ○ Chinese
- ○ Filipino
- ○ Korean
- ○ Vietnamese
- ○ Indian (Amer.) *Print tribe*
- ○ Asian Indian
- ○ Hawaiian
- ○ Guamanian
- ○ Samoan
- ○ Eskimo
- ○ Aleut
- ○ Other – *Print race*

a. Age at last birthday

b. Month of birth
- ○ Jan.–Mar.
- ○ Apr.–June
- ○ July–Sept.
- ○ Oct.–Dec.

c. Year of birth 1

1 ●	8 ○	Ø ○	Ø ○
	9 ○	1 ○	1 ○
		2 ○	2 ○
		3 ○	3 ○
		4 ○	4 ○
		5 ○	5 ○
		6 ○	6 ○
		7 ○	7 ○
		8 ○	8 ○
		9 ○	9 ○

- ○ Now married
- ○ Widowed
- ○ Divorced
- ○ Separated
- ○ Never married

- ○ Mexican-Amer.
- ○ Mexican or Chicano
- ○ Puerto Rican
- ○ Cuban
- ○ Other Spanish
- ○ Not Spanish

CENSUS USE ONLY A. ○ Inmate ○ Other ○ ○

PERSON in column 4

Last name

First name | Middle initial

If relative of person in column 1:
- ○ Husband/wife
- ○ Son/daughter
- ○ Brother/sister
- ○ Father/mother
- ○ Other relative

If not related to person in column 1:
- ○ Roomer, boarder
- ○ Partner, roommate
- ○ Paid employee
- ○ Other nonrelative

○ Male ○ Female

- ○ White
- ○ Black or Negro
- ○ Japanese
- ○ Chinese
- ○ Filipino
- ○ Korean
- ○ Vietnamese
- ○ Indian (Amer.) *Print tribe*
- ○ Asian Indian
- ○ Hawaiian
- ○ Guamanian
- ○ Samoan
- ○ Eskimo
- ○ Aleut
- ○ Other – *Print race*

a. Age at last birthday

b. Month of birth
- ○ Jan.–Mar.
- ○ Apr.–June
- ○ July–Sept.
- ○ Oct.–Dec.

c. Year of birth 1

1 ●	8 ○	Ø ○	Ø ○
	9 ○	1 ○	1 ○
		2 ○	2 ○
		3 ○	3 ○
		4 ○	4 ○
		5 ○	5 ○
		6 ○	6 ○
		7 ○	7 ○
		8 ○	8 ○
		9 ○	9 ○

- ○ Now married
- ○ Widowed
- ○ Divorced
- ○ Separated
- ○ Never married

- ○ Mexican-Amer.
- ○ Mexican or Chicano
- ○ Puerto Rican
- ○ Cuban
- ○ Other Spanish
- ○ Not Spanish

CENSUS USE ONLY A. ○ Inmate ○ Other ○ ○

PERSON in column 5

Last name

First name | Middle initial

If relative of person in column 1:
- ○ Husband/wife
- ○ Son/daughter
- ○ Brother/sister
- ○ Father/mother
- ○ Other relative

If not related to person in column 1:
- ○ Roomer, boarder
- ○ Partner, roommate
- ○ Paid employee
- ○ Other nonrelative

○ Male ○ Female

- ○ White
- ○ Black or Negro
- ○ Japanese
- ○ Chinese
- ○ Filipino
- ○ Korean
- ○ Vietnamese
- ○ Indian (Amer.) *Print tribe*
- ○ Asian Indian
- ○ Hawaiian
- ○ Guamanian
- ○ Samoan
- ○ Eskimo
- ○ Aleut
- ○ Other – *Print race*

a. Age at last birthday

b. Month of birth
- ○ Jan.–Mar.
- ○ Apr.–June
- ○ July–Sept.
- ○ Oct.–Dec.

c. Year of birth 1

1 ●	8 ○	Ø ○	Ø ○
	9 ○	1 ○	1 ○
		2 ○	2 ○
		3 ○	3 ○
		4 ○	4 ○
		5 ○	5 ○
		6 ○	6 ○
		7 ○	7 ○
		8 ○	8 ○
		9 ○	9 ○

- ○ Now married
- ○ Widowed
- ○ Divorced
- ○ Separated
- ○ Never married

- ○ Mexican-Amer.
- ○ Mexican or Chicano
- ○ Puerto Rican
- ○ Cuban
- ○ Other Spanish
- ○ Not Spanish

CENSUS USE ONLY A. ○ Inmate ○ Other ○ ○

PERSON in column 6

Last name

First name | Middle initial

If relative of person in column 1:
- ○ Husband/wife
- ○ Son/daughter
- ○ Brother/sister
- ○ Father/mother
- ○ Other relative

If not related to person in column 1:
- ○ Roomer, boarder
- ○ Partner, roommate
- ○ Paid employee
- ○ Other nonrelative

○ Male ○ Female

- ○ White
- ○ Black or Negro
- ○ Japanese
- ○ Chinese
- ○ Filipino
- ○ Korean
- ○ Vietnamese
- ○ Indian (Amer.) *Print tribe*
- ○ Asian Indian
- ○ Hawaiian
- ○ Guamanian
- ○ Samoan
- ○ Eskimo
- ○ Aleut
- ○ Other – *Print race*

a. Age at last birthday

b. Month of birth
- ○ Jan.–Mar.
- ○ Apr.–June
- ○ July–Sept.
- ○ Oct.–Dec.

c. Year of birth 1

1 ●	8 ○	Ø ○	Ø ○
	9 ○	1 ○	1 ○
		2 ○	2 ○
		3 ○	3 ○
		4 ○	4 ○
		5 ○	5 ○
		6 ○	6 ○
		7 ○	7 ○
		8 ○	8 ○
		9 ○	9 ○

- ○ Now married
- ○ Widowed
- ○ Divorced
- ○ Separated
- ○ Never married

- ○ Mexican-Amer.
- ○ Mexican or Chicano
- ○ Puerto Rican
- ○ Cuban
- ○ Other Spanish
- ○ Not Spanish

CENSUS USE ONLY A. ○ Inmate ○ Other ○ ○

PERSON in column 7

Last name

First name — Middle initial

If relative of person in column 1:
- ○ Husband/wife
- ○ Father/mother
- ○ Son/daughter
- ○ Other relative
- ○ Brother/sister

If not related to person in column 1:
- ○ Roomer, boarder
- ○ Other nonrelative
- ○ Partner, roommate
- ○ Paid employee

○ Male ○ Female

- ○ White
- ○ Asian Indian
- ○ Black or Negro
- ○ Hawaiian
- ○ Japanese
- ○ Guamanian
- ○ Chinese
- ○ Samoan
- ○ Filipino
- ○ Eskimo
- ○ Korean
- ○ Aleut
- ○ Vietnamese
- ○ Other — *Print race*
- ○ Indian (Amer.) *Print tribe*

a. Age at last birthday

c. Year of birth

1 ● 8 ○ 9 ○ | Ø ○ 1 ○ 2 ○ 3 ○ 4 ○ 5 ○ 6 ○ 7 ○ 8 ○ 9 ○ | Ø ○ 1 ○ 2 ○ 3 ○ 4 ○ 5 ○ 6 ○ 7 ○ 8 ○ 9 ○

b. Month of birth
- ○ Jan.–Mar.
- ○ Apr.–June
- ○ July–Sept.
- ○ Oct.–Dec.

- ○ Now married
- ○ Separated
- ○ Widowed
- ○ Never married
- ○ Divorced

- ○ Mexican-Amer.
- ○ Cuban
- ○ Mexican or Chicano
- ○ Other Spanish
- ○ Puerto Rican
- ○ Not Spanish

CENSUS USE ONLY — A. ○ Inmate ○ Other ○ ○

NOW PLEASE ANSWER QUESTIONS H1-H12 FOR YOUR HOUSEHOLD

If you listed more than 7 persons in Question 1, please see note on page 4.

H1. Did you leave anyone out of Question 1 because you were not sure if the person should be listed — *for example, a new baby still in the hospital, a lodger who also has another home, or a person who stays here once in a while and has no other home?*
- ○ Yes — *On page 4 give name(s) and reason left out.*
- ○ No

H2. Did you list anyone in Question 1 who is away from home now — *for example, on a vacation or in a hospital?*
- ○ Yes — *On page 4 give name(s) and reason person is away.*
- ○ No

H3. Is anyone visiting here who is not already listed?
- ○ Yes — *On page 4 give name of each visitor for whom there is no one at the home address to report the person to a census taker.*
- ○ No

H4. What best describes the building in which you live?
Fill one circle.
- ○ A mobile home or trailer
- ○ A one-family house detached from any other house
- ○ A one-family house attached to one or more houses
- ○ Boat, van, tent, etc.
- or ○ An apartment house or building with the following number of living quarters:

○ 1 ○ 2 ○ 3 ○ 4 ○ 5 ○ 6 ○ 7 ○ 8 ○ 9 ○ 10 to 19 ○ 20 to 49 ○ 50 or more

H5. Do you enter your living quarters —
- ○ Directly from the outside or through a common or public hall?
- ○ Through someone else's living quarters?

H6. Do you have complete plumbing facilities in your living quarters, that is, hot and cold piped water, a flush toilet, and a bathtub or shower?
- ○ Yes, for this household only
- ○ Yes, but also used by another household
- ○ No, have some but not all plumbing facilities
- ○ No plumbing facilities in living quarters

H7. How many rooms do you have in your living quarters?
Do not count bathrooms, porches, balconies, foyers, halls, or half-rooms.

○ 1 room ○ 2 rooms ○ 3 rooms ○ 4 rooms ○ 5 rooms ○ 6 rooms ○ 7 rooms ○ 8 rooms ○ 9 rooms or more

H8. Are your living quarters —
- ○ Owned or being bought by you or by someone else in this household?
- ○ Rented for cash rent?
- ○ Occupied without payment of cash rent?

H9. Is this apartment (house) part of a condominium or cooperative building or development?
- ○ No
- ○ Yes, a condominium building or development
- ○ Yes, a cooperatively-owned building or development

H10. If this is a one-family house —

a. Is the house on a property of 10 acres or more?
○ Yes ○ No

b. Is any part of the property used as a commercial establishment or medical office?
○ Yes ○ No

H11. *If you live in a one-family house or a condominium unit which you own or are buying —*

What is the value of this property, that is, how much do you think this property (house and lot or condominium unit) would sell for if it were for sale?

Do not answer this question if this is —
- A mobile home or trailer
- A house on 10 acres or more
- A house with a commercial establishment or medical office on the property

○ Less than $5,000	○ $37,500 to $39,999
○ $5,000 to $9,999	○ $40,000 to $44,999
○ $10,000 to $14,999	○ $45,000 to $49,999
○ $15,000 to $17,499	○ $50,000 to $54,999
○ $17,500 to $19,999	○ $55,000 to $59,999
○ $20,000 to $22,499	○ $60,000 to $69,999
○ $22,500 to $24,999	○ $70,000 to $79,999
○ $25,000 to $27,499	○ $80,000 to $89,999
○ $27,500 to $29,999	○ $90,000 to $99,999
○ $30,000 to $32,499	○ $100,000 to $149,999
○ $32,500 to $34,999	○ $150,000 to $199,999
○ $35,000 to $37,499	○ $200,000 or more

H12. *If you pay rent for your living quarters —*
What is the monthly rent?
If rent is not paid by the month, see the instruction sheet on how to figure a monthly rent.

○ Less than $40	○ $150 to $159
○ $40 to $49	○ $160 to $169
○ $50 to $59	○ $170 to $179
○ $60 to $69	○ $180 to $189
○ $70 to $79	○ $190 to $199
○ $80 to $89	○ $200 to $224
○ $90 to $99	○ $225 to $249
○ $100 to $109	○ $250 to $274
○ $110 to $119	○ $275 to $299
○ $120 to $129	○ $300 to $349
○ $130 to $139	○ $350 to $399
○ $140 to $149	○ $400 or more

FOR CENSUS USE ONLY

A4. Block number — Ø Ø Ø / 1 1 1 / 2 2 2 / 3 3 3 / 4 4 4 / 5 5 5 / 6 6 6 / 7 7 7 / 8 8 8 / 9 9 9 — ○ NC

A6. Serial number — Ø Ø Ø Ø / 1 1 1 1 / 2 2 2 2 / 3 3 3 3 / 4 4 4 4 / 5 5 5 5 / 6 6 6 6 / 7 7 7 7 / 8 8 8 8 / 9 9 9 9

B. Type of unit or quarters
- Occupied: ○ First form ○ Continuation
- Vacant: ○ Regular ○ Usual home elsewhere
- Group quarters: ○ First form ○ Continuation

For Vacant Units

C1. Is this unit for —
- ○ Year round use — (Fill C2 and C3)
- ○ Seasonal/Mig

C2. Vacancy status
- ○ For rent
- ○ For sale only
- ○ Rented or sold, not occupied
- ○ Held for occasional use
- ○ Other vacant

C3. Is this unit boarded up? ○ Yes ○ No

D. Months vacant
- ○ Less than 1 month
- ○ 1 up to 2 months
- ○ 2 up to 6 months
- ○ 6 up to 12 months
- ○ 1 year up to 2 years
- ○ 2 years or more

E. Quest're codes
1. ○ ○ Mail return
2. ○ ○ Pp. 2/3 Comp.
3. ○ ○ Pop./F

F. Total persons — Ø Ø Ø / 1 1 1 / 2 2 2 / 3 3 3 / 4 4 4 / 5 5 5 / 6 6 6 / 7 7 7 / 8 8 8 / 9 9 9

D-1(X)

Please Make Sure You Have Filled This Form Completely

For persons who answered in Question 1 that they are staying here only temporarily and have a usual home elsewhere, enter the address of usual home here:

House number | Street or road | Apartment number or location

City | County

State | ZIP Code

For Answers to Questions H1, H2, and H3:

H1. Name of person(s) left out and reason:

H2. Name of person(s) away from home and reason away:

H3. Name of visitor(s) for whom there is no one at the home address to report the person to a Census Taker:

NOTE

If you have listed more than 7 persons in Question 1, please make sure that you have filled the form for the first 7 people. Then mail back this form. A Census Taker will call to obtain the information for the other people.

1 Check to be certain you have:

- Answered Question 1 on page 1.
- Answered Questions 2 through 7 for each person you listed at the top of pages 2 and 3.
- Answered Questions H1 through H12 on page 3.

2 Write here the name of the person who filled the form, the date, and the telephone number on which the people in this household can be called.

Name

Date

Telephone Number

3 Then fold the form the way it was sent to you. Mail it back in the enclosed envelope. The address of the U.S. Census Office appears on the front cover of this questionnaire. Please be sure that before you seal the envelope the address shows through the window. No stamp is required.

Thank you very much .

FORM D-1 (X)

☆ GPO : 1978 O - 252-690

1978 Census of the Richmond, Virginia Area

(Richmond City, and Chesterfield and Henrico Counties)

○ Need help?

○ Use this

● **Instruction Sheet**

This sheet gives helpful information on filling out your census form. If you need more help, call the local U.S. Census office. The telephone number is given in the address box on the cover of the census form.

FORM D-3(X)
(1-16-78)

U.S. DEPARTMENT OF COMMERCE
BUREAU OF THE CENSUS

- There may be a question you cannot answer exactly. For example, you might not know the age of an elderly person or the price for which your house would sell. See if someone else in your household knows; if no one does, give your best estimate.
- If you are not sure if you should list a person, see the rules on page 1 of the census form.
- If there are more than seven people in your household, please list *all* the persons in question 1, complete the form for seven people, and mail it back in the enclosed envelope. A census taker will call to obtain the additional information.

EXAMPLE

Also answer the housing questions on page 3.

Here are the QUESTIONS ↓ — These are the columns for ANSWERS → *Please fill one column for each person listed in Question 1.*	PERSON in column 1	PERSON in column 2	PERSON in column 3	PERSON in column 4
	Last name: Doe First name: Arthur Middle initial: T.	Last name: Doe First name: Frances Middle initial:	Last name: Doe First name: Patricia Middle initial: J.	Last name: Smith First name: Mary Middle initial: J.
2. How is this person related to the person in column 1? *Fill one circle.* *If "Other relative" of person in column 1, give exact relationship, such as mother-in-law, niece, grandson, etc.*	*START in this column with the household member (or one of the members) in whose name the home is owned or rented. If there is no such person, start in this column with any adult household member.*	If relative of person in column 1: ● Husband/wife ○ Father/mother ○ Son/daughter ○ Other relative ○ Brother/sister If not related to person in column 1: ○ Roomer, boarder ○ Other nonrelative ○ Partner, roommate ○ Paid employee	If relative of person in column 1: ○ Husband/wife ○ Father/mother ● Son/daughter ○ Other relative ○ Brother/sister If not related to person in column 1: ○ Roomer, boarder ○ Other nonrelative ○ Partner, roommate ○ Paid employee	If relative of person in column 1: ○ Husband/wife ○ Father/mother ○ Son/daughter ● Other relative — Grandmother ○ Brother/sister If not related to person in column 1: ○ Roomer, boarder ○ Other nonrelative ○ Partner, roommate ○ Paid employee
3. Sex *Fill one circle.*	● Male ○ Female	○ Male ● Female	○ Male ● Female	○ Male ● Female
4. Race *Fill one circle.*	● White ○ Asian Indian ○ Black or Negro ○ Hawaiian ○ Japanese ○ Guamanian ○ Chinese ○ Samoan ○ Filipino ○ Eskimo ○ Korean ○ Aleut ○ Vietnamese ○ Other – *Print race* ○ Indian (Amer.) *Print tribe*	● White ○ Asian Indian ○ Black or Negro ○ Hawaiian ○ Japanese ○ Guamanian ○ Chinese ○ Samoan ○ Filipino ○ Eskimo ○ Korean ○ Aleut ○ Vietnamese ○ Other – *Print race* ○ Indian (Amer.) *Print tribe*	● White ○ Asian Indian ○ Black or Negro ○ Hawaiian ○ Japanese ○ Guamanian ○ Chinese ○ Samoan ○ Filipino ○ Eskimo ○ Korean ○ Aleut ○ Vietnamese ○ Other – *Print race* ○ Indian (Amer.) *Print tribe*	● White ○ Asian Indian ○ Black or Negro ○ Hawaiian ○ Japanese ○ Guamanian ○ Chinese ○ Samoan ○ Filipino ○ Eskimo ○ Korean ○ Aleut ○ Vietnamese ○ Other – *Print race* ○ Indian (Amer.) *Print tribe*
5. Age, and month and year of birth *a. Print age at last birthday.* *b. Print month and fill one circle.* *c. Print year in the spaces, and fill one circle below each number.*	a. Age at last birthday: 28 b. Month of birth: June ○ Jan.–Mar. ● Apr.–June ○ July–Sept. ○ Oct.–Dec. c. Year of birth: 1 9 4 9	a. Age at last birthday: 28 b. Month of birth: January ● Jan.–Mar. ○ Apr.–June ○ July–Sept. ○ Oct.–Dec. c. Year of birth: 1 9 5 0	a. Age at last birthday: 0 b. Month of birth: December ○ Jan.–Mar. ○ Apr.–June ○ July–Sept. ● Oct.–Dec. c. Year of birth: 1 9 7 7	a. Age at last birthday: 78 b. Month of birth: August ○ Jan.–Mar. ○ Apr.–June ● July–Sept. ○ Oct.–Dec. c. Year of birth: 1 8 9 9
6. Marital status *Fill one circle.*	● Now married ○ Separated ○ Widowed ○ Never married ○ Divorced	● Now married ○ Separated ○ Widowed ○ Never married ○ Divorced	○ Now married ○ Separated ○ Widowed ● Never married ○ Divorced	○ Now married ○ Separated ● Widowed ○ Never married ○ Divorced
7. Is this person's origin or descent – *Fill one circle.*	○ Mexican-Amer. ○ Cuban ○ Mexican or Chicano ○ Other Spanish ○ Puerto Rican ● Not Spanish	○ Mexican-Amer. ○ Cuban ○ Mexican or Chicano ○ Other Spanish ○ Puerto Rican ● Not Spanish	○ Mexican-Amer. ○ Cuban ○ Mexican or Chicano ○ Other Spanish ○ Puerto Rican ● Not Spanish	○ Mexican-Amer. ○ Cuban ○ Mexican or Chicano ○ Other Spanish ○ Puerto Rican ● Not Spanish
D-1(X) Fosdic 26.1:1	*CENSUS USE ONLY* A. ○ Inmate ○ Other ○ ○	*CENSUS USE ONLY* A. ○ Inmate ○ Other ○ ○	*CENSUS USE ONLY* A. ○ Inmate ○ Other ○ ○	*CENSUS USE ONLY* A. ○ Inmate ○ Other ○ ○

FORM D-3(X) (1-16-78)

INSTRUCTIONS FOR QUESTIONS 1 THROUGH 7

1. List in question 1 (on page 1), the names of all the people who usually live here. Then turn to pages 2 and 3 where there are columns to list up to seven persons. In the first column print the name of one of the household members in whose name this home is owned or rented. If no household member owns or rents the living quarters, list in the first column any adult household member who is not a roomer, boarder, or paid employee. Print the names of the other household members, if any, in the columns which follow, using question 1 as a checklist.

2. Fill a circle to show how each person is related to the person in column 1.

   A stepchild or legally adopted child of the person in column 1 should be marked **Son/daughter.** Foster children or wards living in the household should be marked **Roomer, boarder.**

3. Be sure to fill a circle for the sex of each person.

4. Fill the circle for the category with which the person most closely identifies. Print the specific race if so instructed; if **Indian (American),** print specific tribe.

5. Enter age at last birthday in the space provided ("0" for babies less than one year old). Also enter month and year of birth, and fill the appropriate circles. For an illustration of how to complete question 5, see the example. If age or month or year of birth is not known, give your best estimate.

6. If the person's only marriage was annulled, mark **Never married.**

7. *Origin or descent* refers to a person's nationality group, lineage, or the country in which the person, or the person's parents or ancestors were born.

INSTRUCTIONS FOR QUESTIONS H4 THROUGH H12

H4. *Detached* means there is open space on all sides, or the house is joined only to a shed or garage. *Attached* means that the house is joined to another house or building by at least one wall which goes from ground to roof.

Mark **A one-family house: Detached from any other house** if one or more rooms have been added to or built onto a mobile home or trailer. A porch or shed is not considered a room.

Count all occupied and vacant living quarters in the house or building, but not stores or office space.

H5. Mark the second circle only if you *must* go through someone else's living quarters to get to your own.

H6. Consider that you have hot water even if you have it only part of the time.

Mark **Yes, but also used by another household** if someone else who lives in the same building, but is not a member of your household, also uses the facilities. Mark this circle also if the occupants of living quarters now vacant would also use the facilities in your living quarters.

H7. Count only whole rooms used for living purposes, such as living rooms, dining rooms, kitchens, bedrooms, finished recreation rooms, family rooms, etc. Do not count bathrooms, kitchenettes, strip or pullman kitchens, utility rooms, or unfinished attics, basements, or other space used for storage.

H8. Mark **Owned or being bought** if the living quarters are owned outright or are mortgaged. Also mark **Owned or being bought** if the living quarters are owned but the land is rented.

Mark **Rented for cash rent** if any money rent is paid. Rent may be paid by persons who are not members of your household.

Occupied without payment of cash rent includes, for example, a parsonage, a house or apartment provided free of rent by the owner, or a house or apartment occupied by a janitor or caretaker in exchange for services.

H9. A *condominium* is a type of ownership that enables a person to own an apartment or house in a development of similar units. The owner holds the deed and, very likely, has a mortgage on the unit. A *cooperative* is housing which is owned by a corporation of member-owners.

H10. A *commercial establishment* is easily recognized from the outside: for example, a grocery store or barber shop. A *medical office* is a doctor's or dentist's office regularly visited by patients.

H11. Include the value of the house, the land it is on, and any other structures on the same property. If the house is owned but the land is rented, estimate the combined value of the house and the land. If this is a condominium unit, enter the estimated value for your living quarters and your share of the common elements.

H12. Report the rent agreed to or contracted for, even if the rent is unpaid or paid by someone else.

If rent is not paid by the month, change the rent to a monthly amount; and then fill the appropriate circle in question H12:

If rent is paid:	Multiply rent by:
By the day	30
By the week	4
Every other week	2

If rent is paid:	Divide rent by:
4 times a year	3
2 times a year	6
Once a year	12

APPENDIX C

TABLE OF RESIDENCE RULES FOR ENUMERATORS AND EDITORS

This table is divided into two columns. The type of person (student, member of the Armed Forces, etc.) is described in the left-hand column. The right-hand column tells you whether the person is a resident of this household or some other place.

	Type of Person	Resident of--
1.	Lives in this household but is temporarily absent on a visit, business trip, vacation, in connection with job (bus driver, traveling salesperson, boat operator, etc.).	This household
2.	Lives in this household on weekends only. Works most of the week in another place and maintains a room or apartment there.	The other place
3.	Lives in this household but is in a general or VA hospital, including new babies in the hospital who have not yet been brought home.	This household (unless in a psychiatric, TB, chronic ward, etc.; if so, count in the hospital).
4.	Member of the Armed Forces:	
	a. Living on military installation	The military installation
	b. Stationed on nearby installation but living off base in this household,	This household
	c. Assigned to a military vessel which is "deployed" to the 6th or 7th fleet. OR The home port of the vessel is 50 miles or more away from this household.	The vessel
	d. Assigned to a military vessel which is not deployed to the 6th or 7th fleet <u>and</u> the household is within 50 miles of the home port of this vessel.	This household

TABLE OF RESIDENCE (continued)

	Type of Person	Resident of--
5.	Officer or crew member of a merchant vessel, vessel engaged in coastwide, intercoastal, or foreign transportation (including Great Lakes).	The vessel
6.	Officer or crew member of a merchant vessel engaged in inland waterway transportation.	This household
7.	College student:	
	a. Away at college on Census Day -- here only on vacation.	The college
	b. Attending college but living in this household.	This household
8.	Student away attending school below college level (other than students at institutional-type schools).	This household
9.	Nurse living in hospital, nurses' home, etc.	Hospital, nurses' home
10.	Family members working and living away from home.	Place where they live while working away from home
11.	Person who has more than one home and divides time between them.	List at place where he or she spends largest part of the calendar year.
12.	Person who lives in this household most of the time because he or she works nearby but has a home elsewhere where the person stays less frequently or on weekends.	This household

TABLE OF RESIDENCE RULES (continued)

Type of Person	Resident of--
13. American citizen abroad:	
a. Temporarily on vacation or away in connection with his or her work.	This household
b. Employed by U.S. Government with place of duty abroad or member of the family of such person living with him or her.	This is a special case. DO NOT LIST.
c. Any other American working or living abroad for extended period of time.	DO NOT LIST
14. Person in institution where people usually stay for long periods of time such as correctional or penal institutions, penitentiaries, jails, workhouses, reformatories, convict camps, schools for delinquents (regardless of length of sentence or stay), mental institutions, homes for needy or aged, hospitals and asylums for the chronically ill and handicapped, homes or schools for the deaf, blind, or mentally retarded.	This institution
15. Members of religious orders living in a monastery, convent, etc.	The monastery or convent
16. Persons in places which have shifting populations composed mainly of persons with no fixed residence, such as convict camps, railroad camps, and highway and other construction camps.	The camp
17. Citizens of a foreign country:	
a. Studying or working in the United States or the members of the family of such person living with him or her.	This household
b. Temporarily traveling or visiting in the U.S.	Not to be counted
c. Living on the premises of an Embassy, Ministry, Legation, Chancellery, or Consulate.	Not to be counted

TABLE OF RESIDENCE RULES (continued)

Type of Person	Resident of--
18. Domestic servants who "live-in."	Determine if the servant occupies a housing unit separate from the main household. If YES, list on a separate census questionnaire. If NO, list on the household census questionnaire.
19. Visitors.	Ask if there is someone at home to report the person to a census taker. If NO, list the person in H3 on page 5 (page 20 on the long form). If YES, do not list name of visitor on this form.

Source: U.S. Bureau of the Census, 1980 Census Dress Rehearsal: Questionnaire Reference Book, Form D-56a(x). Washington, D.C.: U.S. Department of Commerce. Appendix A, pp. 181-184.

APPENDIX D

SELECTED BIBLIOGRAPHY

Azores, Tania. "Participation in the Pretest of Camden, New Jersey," memorandum to the acting director, U.S. Bureau of the Census, January 25, 1977.

Brooks, Camilla A., and Barbara A. Bailar. "An Error Profile: Employment as Measured by the Current Population Survey," in Proceedings of the Social Statistics Section, American Statistical Association, Part IV, pp. 26-34. Washington, D.C.: American Statistical Association, 1978.

Budd, E., D. Radner, and J. Hinrichs. "Size Distribution of Family Personal Income: Methodology and Estimates for 1964," Bureau of Economic Analysis Staff Paper, No. 21, 1978.

Ellett, Charles A. "A Study of Data Requirements of Population-Based Formula Grants." Statistical Reporter, pp. 48-66, November 1976.

Goldfield, Edwin D. "Patching Up the Census." Committee on National Statistics, National Research Council. January 1976.

__________, Anthony Turner, Charles D. Cowan, and John C. Scott. "Privacy and Confidentiality as Factors in Survey Reponse," in Proceedings of the Social Statistics Section, American Statistical Association, Part I, pp. 219-231. Washington, D.C.: American Statistical Association, 1978.

Hagan, Robert L. Statement before the Subcommittee on Census and Population of the House Committee on Post Cffice and Civil Service. April 20, 1977.

Hill, Robert B. "Estimating the 1970 Census Undercount for States and Local Areas." The Urban League Review, pp. 36-45, January 1975.

Johnston, Denis F., and James R. Wetzel. "Effect of the Census Undercount on Labor Force Estimates." Monthly Labor Review, Vol. 92, pp. 3-13, March 1969.

Kaplan, David L. "Some Current Thoughts on the 1980 Census." Statistical Reporter, pp. 25-30, August 1975.

Klein, Deborah. "Status of Men Missed in the Census." Monthly Labor Review, March 1970.

Lancaster, Clarise, and Frederick J. Scheuren. "Counting the Uncountable Illegals: Some Intial Statistical Speculations Employing Capture-Recapture Techniques," in Proceedings of the Social Statistics Section, American Statistical Association, Part I, pp. 530-535. Washington, D.C.: American Statistical Association, 1978.

__________. The Use of Population Data in Federal Assistance Programs, prepared by Barbara O. Maffei, Congressional Research Service, for use of the Subcommittee on Census and Population of the House Committee on Post Office and Civil Service, 95th Congress, 2nd session. Committee Print No. 95-16. Washington, D.C.: U.S. Government Printing Office, 1978.

National Research Council. America's Uncounted People, Report of the Advisory Committee on Problems of Census Enumeration. Washington, D.C.: National Academy of Sciences, 1972.

National Science Foundation, Research Applied to National Needs. Synthesis of Formula Research (Volume 3). General Revenue Sharing, Research Utilization Project, NSF-RA-S-75-048. Washington, D.C.: U.S. Government Printing Office, 1975.

Office of Management and Budget. Speical Analyses, Budget of the United States GOvernment, Fiscal Year 1977. Washington, D.C.: U.S. Government Printing Office.

Savage, I. Richard, and Bernard M. Windham. The Importance of Bias Removal in Official Use of United States Census Counts. FSU Statistics Report M. 265. Tallahassee, Florida: Florida State University, July 1973.

Scott, Christopher. "Research on Mail Surveys." Journal of the Royal Statistical Society, Vol. 124, No. 2, 1961, pp. 143-205.

Slater, Courtenay M. Statement before the Subcommittee on Census and Population of the House Committee on Post Office and Civil Service, March 21, 1978.

Stack, Carol A., and John Lombardi. "Conclusion" in All Our Kin, ed. Carol A. Stack. New York: Harper & Rowy, 1974.

Strauss, Robert P., and Peter B. Harkins. The 1970 Census Undercount and Revenue Sharing: Effect on Allocations in New Jersey and Virginia. Washington, D.C.: Joint Center for Political Studies, June 1974.

Sudman, Seymour, and Norman Bradburn. Response Effects in Surveys: A Review and Synthesis. Chicago: Aldine, 1974.

United Nations Economic and Social Council, Statistical Commission and Economic Commission for Europe. "Design of Questionnaires." Papers prepared by Canada, Romania, and Switzerland for the meeting on Population and Housing Censuses, November 21-25, 1977.

U.S. Commission on Civil Rights. Counting the Forgotten: The 1970 Census Count of Persons of Spanish Speaking Background in the United States. Washington, D.C.: U.S. Government Printing Office, 1974.

U.S. Congress, House. The Census Reform Act, Hearings before the Subcommittee on Census and Population of the Committee on Post Office and Civil Service on H.R. 8871. 95th Congress, 1st session, September 12 & 23, 1977. Serial No. 95-46. Washington, D.C.: U.S. Government Printing Office, 1977.

__________. Federal Formula Grant-in-Aid Programs that Use Population as a Factor in Allocating Funds, compiled by the Congressional Research Service for the use of the Subcommittee on Census and Population of the Committee on Post Office and Civil Service. Committee Print No. 94-6 (October 24). Washington, D.C.: U.S. Government Printing Office, 1975.

__________. H.R. 10386, A Bill to Amend Title 13 of the United States Code to Establish a Decennial Census Procedure, and for Other Purposes. 95th Congress, 1st session, December 15, 1977.

__________. The 1980 Census, Hearings before the Subcommittee on Census and Population of the Committee on POst Office and Civil Service. 95th Congress, 1st session, June 9, 10, & 24, 1977. Serial No. 95-41. Washington, D.C.: U.S. Government Printing Office.

__________. Pretest Census in Oakland, California and Camden, New Jersey, Hearings before the Subcommittee on Census and Population of the Committee on Post Office and Civil Service. 95th Congress,

1st session, March 25 & May 16, 1977. Serial No. 95-42. Washington, D.C.: U.S. Government Printing Cffice, 1977.

U.S. Congress, Senate. Title 13, United States Code, Census. Prepared by the Committee on Post Office and Civil Service. Committee Print No. 2. 94th Congress, 2nd session, December 31, 1976. Washington, D.C.: U.S. Government Printing Office, 1977.

U.S. Department of Commerce, Bureau of the Census.

Current Population Reports:

Characteristics of the Population by Ethnic Crigin: March 1972 and 1971. Population Characteristics, Series P-20, No. 249. Washington, D.C.: U.S. Government Printing Office, 1973.

Persons of Spanish Origin in the United States: March 1972 and 1971. Population Characteristics, Series P-20, No. 250. Washington, D.C.: U.S. Government Printing Office, 1973.

Coverage of Population in the 1970 Census and Some Implications for Public Programs. Series P-23, No. 56. Washington, D.C.: U.S. Government Printing Office, 1975.

"Language Usage in the United States: July 1975" (Advance Report). Special Studies, Series P-23, No. 60 (Revised). Washington, D.C.: U.S. Government Printing Office, 1976.

Developmental Estimates of the Coverage of the Population of States in the 1970 Census: Demographic Analysis. Series P-23, No. 65. Washington, D.C.: U.S. Government Printing Office, 1977.

"Households and Families by Type: March 1977" (Advance Report). Population Characteristics, Series P-20, No. 313. Washington, D.C.: U.S. Government Printing Office, 1977.

"Persons of Spanish Origin in the United States: March 1977" (Advance Report). Population Characteristics, Series P-20, No. 317. Washington, D.C.: U.S. Government Printing Office, 1977.

"Population Estimates by Race, for States: July 1, 1973 and 1975." Special Studies, Series P-23, No. 67. Washington, D.C.: U.S. Government Printing Office, 1978.

Evaluation and Research Program Reports, PHC(E):

(1) The Quality of Residential Geographic Coding. January 1973.

(2) Test of Birth Registration Completeness: 1964 to 1968. March 1973.

(3) Results and Analysis of the Experimental Mail Extension Test. June 1973.

(4) Estimates of Coverage of Population by Sex, Race, and Age: Demographic Analysis. February 1974.

(5) The Coverage of Housing in the 1970 Census. October 1973.

(6) Effect of Special Procedures to Improve Coverage in the 1970 Census. November 1974.

(7) The Medicare Record Check: An Evaluation of Persons 65 Years of Age and Over in the 1970 Census. December 1973.

(8) Coding Performance in the 1970 Census. April 1974.

(9) Accuracy of Data for Selected Population Characteristics as Measured by Reinterviews. August 1974.

(10) Accuracy of Data for the Selected Housing Characteristics as Measured by Reinterviews. March 1975.

(11) Accuracy of Data for Selected Population Characteristics as Measured by the CPS-Census Match. January 1975.

General:

General Population Characteristics. 1970 Census of Population, PC(1)-B1, U.S. Summary. Washington, D.C.: U.S. Government Printing Office, 1972.

Investigation of the Census Bureau Interviewer Characteristics, Performance and Attitude: A Summary, prepared by Gail Poe Inderfurth, Working Paper No. 34. Washington, D.C.: U.S. Government Printing Office, 1972.

"Participation of the American Indian Community in the Planning of the 1980 Census." November 1, 1975.

Procedural History. 1970 Census of Population and Housing, PHC(R)-1. Washington, D.C.: U.S. Government Printing Office, 1976.

"Summary of Census Bureau Review of Federal Agency Council Recommendations on Subject Content for the 1980 Census of Population and Housing." December 3, 1976.

"Minority Statistics Program of the Bureau of the Census." March 9, 1977.

"Summary Notes on Population Coverage Elements in the 1970 Census." November 1977.

"Validating 1980 Census Selection Procedures: A Report to Census Advisory Committees," prepared by Barbara Lacey, Larry Love, and Maria Urrutia. November 1977.

"Summary Descriptions of Data Use for Subjects" and "Questions Planned for Inclusion in the 1980 Census." April 1978.

"1980 Census Update." Issues: No. 1 (January 1977), No. 2 (April 1977), No. 3 (July 1977), No. 4 (October 1977), and No. 5 (January 1978). [Quarterly reports on the planning and preparatory activities for the Twentieth Decennial Census.]

Meetings:

"Coverage Evaluation Plans for the 1980 Census." Background material for the March 1977 meeting of the Census Advisory Committee of the American Statistical Association.

"Coverage Improvements for the 1980 Census" (Agenda Topic D). Prepared for the September 1977 meeting of the Census Advisory Committee of the American Statistical Association. [Includes "Status of Coverage Improvement Procedures in the 1980 Census," "Plans for Improvement of Coverage in the 1980 Census," and twelve attachments.]

"Alternatives and Issues Concerning 1980 Census Products and Services." Prepared for the 1977 Summary Tape Processing Center Conferences, November 1977.

Minutes of Meetings of the Census Advisory Committees.

1. Of the American Marketing Association, May 10, 1977.

2. Of the American Statistical Association, March 3-4, 1977.

3. On Asian and Pacific Americans Population for the 1980 Census, August 12-13, 1976; January 27-28, 1977; and February 24, 1978.

4. On the Black Population for the 1980 Census, September 24, 1976 and March 11, 1977.

5. On the Black and Spanish-Origin Populations for the 1980 Census (combined meeting), September 23, 1976.

6. On the Black, Spanish-Origin, and Asian and Pacific Americans Populations for the 1980 Census (combined meeting), September 8, 1977.

7. On Housing for the 1980 Census, January 24, 1977 and April 15, 1977.

8. On Population Statistics, April 1, 1977.

9. On the Spanish Origin Population for the 1980 Census, February 17-18, 1977; June 3, 1977; and September 9, 1977.

"Evaluation Plans for the 1980 Census" (Agenda Topic B). Prepared for the March 1978 meeting of the Census Advisory Committee of the American Statistical Association. [Includes background statement, "An Overview of Population and Housing Census Evaluation Programs Conducted at the U.S. Bureau of the Census," "Proposals for Coverage Evaluation of the 1980 Census," "Proposals for 1980 Census Evaluation and Research Studies (Excluding Coverage Evaluation and Experiments)," and "Preliminary Report from Task Group on Experimental Projects for the 1980 Evaluation Program."]

Technical Papers:

(31) Consistency of Reporting of Ethnic Origin in the Current Population Survey, prepared by Edward W. Fernandez, Jr., Washington, D.C.: U.S. Government Printing Office, 1974.

(38) Comparison of Persons of Spanish Surname and Persons of Spanish Origin in the United States, prepared by Edward W. Fernandez. Washington, D.C.: U.S. Government Printing Office, 1975.

(39) Guide for Local Area Population Projections, prepared by Richard Irwin. Washington, D.C.: U.S. Government Printing Office, 1977.

(40) The Current Population Survey: Design and Methodology. Washington, D.C.: U.S. Government Printing Office, 1978.

U.S. Department of Commerce, Office of Federal Statistical Policy and Standards. "Report on Statistics for Allocation of Funds," Statistical Working Paper 1. Washington, D.C.: U.S. Department of Commerce, 1978.

__________. Statistical Policy Handbook. Washington, D.C.: U.S. Department of Commerce, 1978.

U.S. General Accounting Office. Programs to Reduce the Decennial Census Undercount. Report to the House Committee on Post Office and Civil Service by the Comptroller General of the United States. Washington, D.C.: U.S. Government Printing Cffice, 1976.

U.S. Social Security Administration, Studies from Interagency Data Linkages (especially Report No. 4). Washington, D.C.: U.S. Department of Health, Education, and Welfare.

Yuskavage, Robert, David Hirschberg, and Frederick J. Scheuren. "The Impact on Personal and Family Income of Adjusting the Current Population Survey for Undercoverage," in Proceedings of the Social Statistics Section, American Statistical Association, Part I, pp. 70-80. Washington, D.C.: American Statistical Association, 1978.

APPENDIX E

BIOGRAPHICAL SKETCHES OF PANEL MEMBERS AND STAFF

NATHAN KEYFITZ (Chairman) is Andelot Professor of sociology and demography and chairman of the sociology department at Harvard University. He received a B.Sc. in mathematics from McGill University in 1934 and a Ph.D. in sociology from the University of Chicago in 1952. Dr. Keyfitz spent more than 20 years as statistician with the Dominion Bureau of Statistics in Ottawa. He has lectured and advised on population concerns around the world, including Argentina, Ceylon, Chile, Germany, India, Indonesia, Italy, and the Soviet Union. His current research interests are the mathematics of population, urbanization, and the sociology of fertility. He is a fellow of the Royal Statistical Society and the American Statistical Association and has served as vice president and president of the Population Association of America. Dr. Keyfitz is a member of the National Academy of Sciences.

PATRICIA C. BECKER is head of the data coordination division in the planning department for the city of Detroit. She received a B.A. in political science in 1961 from the University of Michigan and an M.S. in sociology from the University of Wisconsin in 1964. Ms. Becker has been with the city of Detroit for ten years, following several years' experience with academic survey research centers. Her professional interests are data development for use of the information in planning and decision making at the local level. Ms. Becker is chair of the Detroit regional census advisory committee and has served on the boards of the Urban and Regional Informations Systems Association and the Association for Public Data Users.

CHARLES F. CANNELL is program director at the Institute for Social Research and professor of psychology in journalism at the University of Michigan. He received a B.A. from the University of New Hampshire (1936) and an M.A. (1940) and a Ph.D. (1952) in psychology from Ohio State University. With colleagues from the division of program surveys of the U.S. Department of Agriculture, he established the Survey Research Center on the Michigan campus in 1946. His concern with issues of quality and validity in survey data has led him to the investigation, development, and testing of new techniques for improving data quality. Dr. Cannell has been a frequent consultant to the U.S. Public Health Service and the World Health Organization.

WAYNE A. DANIELSON is dean of the School of Communication and professor of journalism and computer science at the University of Texas (Austin). A graduate of the University of Iowa (B.A. in journalism) and Stanford University (M.A. in journalism and Ph.D. in mass communication research), he has taught at Stanford, the University of Wisconsin (Madison), and the University of North Carolina (Chapel Hill). His general field is mass communication research, and most of his work has been in computer applications in communication. Dr. Danielson was a member of the earlier National Research Council advisory committee that produced the 1972 report, America's Uncounted People. He is especially concerned with the public information efforts of the U.S. Bureau of the Census and communicative aspects of the census process itself.

WALTER E. DUFFETT was vice president of the Conference Board in Canada until his retirement in February 1978. He graduated in economics from the University of Toronto in 1933 and obtained an M.Sc. from the London School of Economics in 1935. Mr. Duffett's area of expertise is statistical administration. He was chief statistician of Canada from 1957 to 1972, in charge of Statistics Canada. Mr. Duffett is a member of the International Statistical Institute, a fellow of the American Statistical Association, and has served as Canadian delegate to the United Nations Statistical Commission and numerous other international statistical associations. He is vice president of the Inter-American Statistical Institute.

LEOBARDO F. ESTRADA is a visiting assistant professor in the School of Architecture and Urban Planning at the University of California at Los Angeles. He is a former employee of the population division, U.S. Bureau of the Census. He received a B.A. from Baylor University in 1966 and an M.S. and a Ph.D. from Florida State University in 1968 and 1970. His principal research interests are racial and ethnic statistics, particularly in regard to the Spanish-origin population of the United States. He is a member of the Spanish-origin population census advisory committee, and he has committee responsibilities in the Population Association of America, the American Sociological Association, and the American Statistical Association.

LESTER R. FRANKEL is executive vice president of Audits & Surveys, Inc., in New York City. He received a B.A. from New York University in 1934 and an M.A. from Columbia in 1936. At the Work Projects Administration in 1939, he designed the first national sample survey of the United States for the monthly report on the labor force, the forerunner of the current population survey. In his career, Mr. Frankel has been involved with large-scale sample surveys in government and in studies of consumer behavior and attitudes in connection with marketing and advertising for business. Formerly, he was adjunct professor of statistics, New York University. He has published papers on the application of statistical techniques for sample selection and for control of response variation and biases in sample surveys. Mr. Frankel is past president of the American Statistical Association, a former director of the American Marketing Association, and a regular member of the International Statistical Institute.

CHARLES B. KEELY is associate at the Center for Policy Studies of the Population Council. He was formerly associate professor of sociology at Fordham University and at Western Michigan University. He received a B.A. in 1965 and a Ph.D. in 1970 from Fordham University. His principal research and publication activities have centered on United States immigration policy, its demographic effects, and the quality of data collected by United States agencies on immigration and the foreign population. He is on the editorial board of the International Migration Review.

HYLAN LEWIS is professor of sociology at the Graduate Center, City University of New York, and professor emeritus of sociology at Brooklyn College, City University of New York. He received a B.A. from Virginia Union University in 1932 and an M.A. and a Ph.D. in sociology from the University of Chicago in 1936 and 1951, respectively. He has taught at Howard University, Atlanta University, and Talladega College. Dr. Lewis has worked for several federal agencies, including the Department of Labor, the Office of War Information, and the Department of Health, Education, and Welfare. His principal research has focused on urban and small-town communities, United States minorities, and the effects of poverty.

DWAINE MARVICK is professor of political science at the University of California at Los Angeles. He received a B.A. in government and history from Iowa State University (1947) and both an M.A. (1949) and a Ph.D. (1952) in public law and government from Columbia University. Much of his work has focused on political elites. He has taught at City College of New York, Rutgers University, and the University of Michigan. He has also taught or conducted research in France, Austria, Germany, India, and Sierra Leone. Dr. Marvick has been president of the Pacific Association for the Advancement of Public Opinion Research, chairman of the Executive Council of the Interuniversity Consortium, and active in the Council of Social Science Data Archives, the American Political Science Association, and the International Political Science Association.

JAMES N. MORGAN is professor of economics and research scientist for the Institute for Social Research at the University of Michigan. He received a B.A. from Northwestern University in 1939 and an M.A. and a Ph.D. from Harvard University in 1941 and 1947. Dr. Morgan has published widely on income and welfare and on the economic behavior of different population subgroups. He has been associated with the University of Michigan since 1951 and received the University's distinguished faculty award in 1977. He is a member of the National Academy of Sciences and of advisory committees to the U.S. Bureau of the Census, the Social Security Administration, and the Urban Institute. Dr. Morgan has served on the boards of directors of the Social Science Research Council and of Consumers Union.

PRISCILLA C. REINING is project director for the Office of International Science at the American Association for the Advancement of Science and research associate in the department of anthropology at the Catholic University of America, both in Washington, D.C. She studied anthropology at the University of Chicago, receiving a B.A. in 1946, an M.A. in 1949, and a Ph.D. in 1967. One of Dr. Reining's interests is population and land tenure and use; in this connection, she has done research on the use of remote sensing data sources, particularly to identify and design pilot studies to aid in the reversal of desertification. She has also studied kinship in sub-Saharan Africa and has worked as a consultant for the U.S. Department of Justice, the World Bank, and the Agency for International Development, among others.

T. JAMES TRUSSELL is assistant professor of economics and faculty associate for the Office of Population Research at Princeton University. He received a B.A. in mathematics from Davidson College in 1971, a B. Phil. in economics from Oxford University in 1973, and a Ph.D. in economics from Princeton University in 1974. Dr. Trussell's expertise is demography, and he has written extensively in that field. He is a member of the Population Association of America and the International Union for the Scientific Study of Population.

EDDIE N. WILLIAMS has been president of the Joint Center for Political Studies in Washington, D.C., since 1972. Prior to that time, he was associated with the University of Chicago as vice president for public affairs and as director of the Center for Policy Study. He received a degree in journalism from the University of Illinois in 1954 and has taken graduate courses in political science at Atlanta University and Howard University. Mr. Williams also served in the Department of State for 7 years, as director of the Office of Equal Employment Opportunity, as special assistant to the assistant secretary for Near Eastern and South Asian Affairs, and as protocol officer. He is on the governing boards of several organizations, including the Drug Abuse Council and the Children's Television Workshop, and is former chairman of the Census Bureau's advisory committee on the black population for the 1980 census.

LENORE EPSTEIN BIXBY held various positions in the Office of Research and Statistics of the Social Security Administration, including 9 years as deputy assistant commissioner for research and statistics and 7 years as director of the Division of Retirement and Survivor Studies, until her retirement in late 1977. She graduated in economics from Wellesley College in 1935 and received an M.A. from Columbia in 1937. Before joining the Social Security Administration in 1954, Mrs. Bixby worked for the Marshall Plan, first in Washington and then as reports officer for the special mission to France. Earlier she was responsible for sample studies of family income and expenditures at the Bureau of Labor Statistics of the Department of Labor and contributed to Gunnar Myrdal's study of the Negro in America. She has written extensively on retirement issues, resources of the aged, and family expenditures. She is a fellow of the American Statistical Association and the Gerontological Society.

HAROLD GOLDSTEIN is an economic consultant in Washington, D.C. He received a B.A. from the University of Illinois and an M.A. from the University of Chicago. He was an economist in the U.S. Department of Labor for 34 years, most recently in the Bureau of Labor Statistics as assistant commissioner for manpower and employment statistics. Mr. Goldstein has lectured and published on employment, unemployment, manpower projections, and the relationship between education and work; he has worked on these subjects in Western European countries, Japan, Israel, Venezuela, and Jamaica. He is a fellow of the American Statistical Association and the American Association for the Advancement of Science and a member of the American Economic Association, the Industrial Relations Research Association, and the American Personnel and Guidance Association.

JESSICA A. KAPLAN was research assistant with the Committee on National Statistics. Before her work with this Panel, she was involved for two and a half years with another Committee project, the Study Group on Environmental Monitoring; the Study Group's report, Environmental Monitoring, was published as Volume IV of the National Research Council's Analytical Studies for the U.S. Environmental Protection Agency in March 1977. Ms. Kaplan graduated from the University of Michigan in 1974 and received an M.A. in planning and administration from Antioch College in 1977. Currently, she is working at Rand Corporation and studying at the Rand Graduate Institute for a Ph.D. in policy analysis.